Law and Regulation of
Public Offering of Corporate Securities

Law and Regulation of Public Offering of Corporate Securities

Raghvendra K. Singh
Shailendera K. Singh

OXFORD
UNIVERSITY PRESS

OXFORD
UNIVERSITY PRESS

Oxford University Press is a department of the University of Oxford.
It furthers the University's objective of excellence in research, scholarship,
and education by publishing worldwide. Oxford is a registered trademark of
Oxford University Press in the UK and in certain other countries

Published in India by
Oxford University Press
YMCA Library Building, 1 Jai Singh Road, New Delhi 110001, India

ISBN-13: 978-0-19-946668-9
ISBN-10: 0-19-946668-8

Typeset in Adobe Jenson Pro 10.7/13.3
by The Graphics Solution, New Delhi 110092
Printed in India by Replika Press Pvt. Ltd

Contents

Foreword

The authors' declared purpose for the book is to present, at the same time, the laws and norms applicable to regulation of public offering of corporate securities, and to state the principles logically and coherently.

Securities law and practice occupies a niche area in the legal firmament. Its relative lack of visibility should not, however, be confused with its impact and importance in the corporate legal sector. The close intersection between the securities regulatory regime and the rapid changes in legal principles governing corporate behaviour generally and securities as well as public offerings particularly, poses challenges to practitioners and securities regulators alike. Add to this technological advancements and the difficulty in capturing all elements in a broad sweep. Attempting a scholarly work on this topic is thus magnified. It is here that the authors have managed to put together, sequentially and clearly, all the elements into the work on law and regulation of public offering of corporate securities: concepts, historical perspective, regulatory agencies, general principles relating to public offerings of corporate securities, liabilities, and regulatory actions. The work is lucid, based on painstaking research and legal analysis. It dispels the mists that shroud law and principles, which have eluded clarity so desperately needed for the subject. The work is a timely and pioneering one; hopefully more compositions by the authors in other fields will follow it.

This work is more commendable because the authors have come out with it at a relatively early stage of their professional careers. Lawyers, academics, and those interested in securities law on public offerings will read this book for its analysis, coverage, and scholarship.

Justice S. Ravindra Bhat
Judge, Delhi High Court

Preface

Public offering of corporate securities is an important source of corporate finance in India. The number of companies making public offerings and the amount of capital being raised continues to grow, thereby supplementing bank finance—the traditional source of external finance for companies. Like any other economic activity, law and regulation of this activity has a direct nexus with its growth. The present state of the law and regulation of the public offering of corporate securities is, however, somewhat discouraging. It is dispersed over several sources and a number of authorities administer and enforce it. It has received little or no attention from legal scholars. It is rarely rigorously analysed and exposited by the higher judiciary as very few cases reach up to the high courts and the Supreme Court of India. These limitations pose two major challenges for students and practitioners in this area of law and for officials of companies intending to raise capital from the public. First, they find it time consuming and, at times, confusing to study the law and regulation of the public offering of corporate securities in a singular and coherent fashion. Second, even if they manage to put the bare laws together, they are quite often unable to understand them properly due to the absence of legal writing on the principles and policies underlying these laws. Another offshoot of the limitations pointed earlier is that it is still customary in India to regard the law and regulation of public offering of corporate securities as a subset of company law, which is far from the truth.

This book provides a solution to these problems. Its origin lies in our belief that the law and regulation of public offering of corporate securities can and must be studied as a whole with an emphasis on the conceptual underpinnings of its constituents. This exercise will also facilitate an enquiry into and a study of this subject as an independent branch of law—a much-needed exercise for its proper development. Though not intended to be a treatise, the goal of the book is to provide a comprehensive legal exposition of the public offering of corporate securities in the backdrop of corporate finance and Indian securities law. It also analyses certain areas of law that are uncertain and conceptually tenuous. However, the book has been written with a focus on India and it is not a work of comparative law. To maintain authenticity, we have been careful not to refer to the statutes and judgments of other common law countries, unless they are very similar to the Indian law on the point being discussed and their reference is not just of limited value. Further, securities transactions after completion of the public offering are not within the scope of this book. This book, therefore, does not examine the law and regulation of trading in securities and its settlement.

With these objectives, we first examine and study the terms and concepts that are its cardinal features and foundation, and add coherence to this field of law. We then trace the evolution of regulation of public offerings, as the law and regulation of this activity cannot be properly understood without reference to its history. Next, we look at public offer and prospectus, and their legal contexts. We also study the regulatory agencies that administer and enforce securities laws on public offerings. We then consider the legal setting in and mechanics by which the public offering of corporate securities is undertaken. Lastly, we analyse the range of liabilities and regulatory actions in relation to the public offering of corporate securities. Stylistically, we have written this book not as a static commentary of the statutory provisions, rules, and regulations governing the public offering of corporate securities. Instead, we have written it in a linear fashion. The book begins with the basic concepts; each subsequent topic, section, and chapter logically builds on the earlier analysis, leading to a coherent study of the law and regulation of public offering of corporate securities. However, care has been taken to write them in a manner that the sections and chapters can also be read independently by those who may wish to refer to a specific topic. This book can therefore be read from cover-to-cover as well as by referring to its separate parts. It will thus be of interest to students, academics, practitioners, and officials of companies and securities market intermediaries involved in raising capital from the public, as well as the investors.

Some explanation is in order for the choice of title for this book, as the usage of 'corporate' as opposed to 'company' is not accidental. 'Corporate' and its equivalent 'corporation' are distinctly American in origin and usage. In terms of legal origins, 'company' is the more appropriate term for India. However, in terms of usage, 'corporate securities' is more popular and a familiar expression instead of 'company securities'. We lean towards usage and familiarity in our choice of title for the book without compromising in any way on the conceptual analysis.

Authoring this book would not have been possible without the support and patience of Antra Singh (wife of Raghvendra K. Singh) who had her own doctoral study to attend to otherwise. We are grateful to her. We are also grateful to Satish Sharma for his encouragement and to Gargi Bohra and Pragya Vats for their comments on the manuscript. Several individuals have assisted us in locating and sharing primary research materials. We are extremely grateful to all of them, and in particular to Abhimanyu George Jain. Of course, we are alone responsible for any errors. Finally, we would like to thank our publisher for the support during the production of the book.

We dedicate this book to our parents, Shri Awadh Kishore Singh and Smt. Minti Singh, who despite humble beginnings ensured that we pursue education and excellence to our fullest potential.

Table of Cases

Table of Legislation, Bills, and Provisions of the Constitution of India

Table of Delegated Legislation

Notifications Issued by SEBI

Notifications Issued by the Central Government

Schemes Framed and Orders Passed by the Central Government

Directions Issued by the RBI

Circulars Issued by SEBI

Abbreviations and Acronyms

AIF	Alternative Investment Fund
AMC	Asset Management Company
Art.	Article
ASBA	Application Supported by Blocked Amount
BSE	Bombay Stock Exchange
CBDT	Central Board of Direct Taxes
CCI	Controller of Capital Issues
CIS	Collective Investment Scheme
CPSE	Central Public Sector Enterprise
Debenture Trustees Regulations	Securities and Exchange Board of India (Debenture Trustees) Regulations, 1993
Debt Securities Regulations	Securities and Exchange Board of India (Issue and Listing of Debt Securities) Regulations, 2008
ESOP	Employee Stock Option Plan
FCCB	Foreign Currency Convertible Bond
FCRA	Forward Contracts (Regulation) Act, 1952

FEMA	Foreign Exchange Management Act, 1999
FIBV	World Federation of Stock Exchanges
FPI	Foreign Portfolio Investor
FPO	Further Public Offering
FVCI	Foreign Venture Capital Investor
GDR	Global Depository Receipt
HUF	Hindu Undivided Family
ICDR Regulations	Securities and Exchange Board of India (Issue of Capital and Disclosure Requirements) Regulations, 2009
IDR	Indian Depository Receipt
InvIT	Infrastructure Investment Trust
IPC	Indian Penal Code, 1860
IPO	Initial Public Offering
IRDA	Insurance Regulatory and Development Authority
ITAT	Income Tax Appellate Tribunal
ITP	Institutional Trading Platform
LODR Regulations	Securities and Exchange Board of India (Listing Obligations and Disclosure Requirements) Regulations, 2015
LLP	Limited Liability Partnership
MBS	Mortgage Backed Security
MCA	Ministry of Corporate Affairs
MD&A	Management's Discussion and Analysis
MoF	Ministry of Finance
NHB	National Housing Bank
NSE	National Stock Exchange of India Limited
OTC	Over the Counter
PFUTP Regulations	Securities and Exchange Board of India (Prohibition of Fraudulent and Unfair Trade Practices Relating to Securities Market) Regulations, 2003
PIT Regulations, 1992	Securities and Exchange Board of India (Prohibition of Insider Trading) Regulations, 1992
PIT Regulations	Securities and Exchange Board of India (Prohibition of Insider Trading) Regulations, 2015

Preference Shares Regulations	Securities and Exchange Board of India (Issue and Listing of Non-Convertible Redeemable Preference Shares) Regulations, 2013
PSE	Public Sector Enterprise
QIP	Qualified Institutions Placement
RBI	Reserve Bank of India
REIT	Real Estate Investment Trust
SARFAESI Act	Securitisation and Reconstruction of Financial Assets and Enforcement of Security Interest Act, 2002
SAT	Securities Appellate Tribunal
SCB	Scheduled Commercial Bank
SCRA	Securities Contracts (Regulation) Act, 1956
SCRR	Securities Contracts (Regulation) Rules, 1957
SCSB	Self Certified Syndicate Bank
SEBI	Securities and Exchange Board of India
SEBI Act	Securities and Exchange Board of India Act, 1992
SEBI (AIF) Regulations	Securities and Exchange Board of India (Alternative Investment Funds) Regulations, 2012
SEBI (CIS) Regulations	Securities and Exchange Board of India (Collective Investment Schemes) Regulations, 1999
Securitised Debt Instruments Regulations	Securities and Exchange Board of India (Public Offer and Listing of Securitised Debt Instruments) Regulations, 2008
SEBI (FPI) Regulations	Securities and Exchange Board of India (Foreign Portfolio Investors) Regulations, 2014
SEBI (MF) Regulations	Securities and Exchange Board of India (Mutual Funds) Regulations, 1996
SEBI Underwriters Regulations	Securities and Exchange Board of India (Underwriters) Regulations, 1993
SME	Small and Medium Enterprise
ULIP	Unit Linked Insurance Policy
VCF	Venture Capital Fund

1. Foundational Terms and Concepts*

Newspaper advertisements and public hoardings announcing a proposed offering of corporate securities or an initial public offering (IPO) are familiar to us all. They contain standardized commercial and legal information, and the form is banal and factual, without any forecasts or promises. One never sees celebrities endorsing them. Such advertisements are the most visible part, albeit a minor one, of the law governing the public offering of corporate securities. The rest of it is characterized by its enormity and relative flux, and there is a danger of being overwhelmed. Thus, we start by examining the terms and concepts that are its cardinal features and foundation, and add coherence to this field of law. We examine the company as a business organization and its need for capital, since companies are the most common form of business entities today and dominate the field of public offerings. Then we view the concept and form of securities in detail, as securities are

* Unless otherwise specified, all references to the Companies Act are to the Companies Act, 2013.

the subject matter of public offerings. The chapter then examines the methods of raising capital by issue of securities, the securities market, and securities law.

The Company as a Business Organization

The Indian legal system provides and recognizes a range of organizational forms for carrying out non-profit activities and activities for earning profit.[1] In the former category fall entities such as society, trust, and company; the latter category includes entities such as proprietorship, Hindu Undivided Family (HUF), association of persons, general partnership, limited liability partnership (LLP), cooperative society, business trust, and company. An enquiry into their origin and evolution and why one form is preferred over the other is beyond the scope of this book. Suffice to say that most of these organizational forms cannot practically be formed by an act of parties through contract alone.[2] The law governing the different organizations play an important role in their utility for the stakeholders and in enhancing the welfare of society. Quite often, the choice of an organizational form is dictated by a legislative fiat.

Among for-profit or business organizations, the most common entity today is a company having the liability of its members limited by shares.[3] There are two primary reasons for this. First, this type of company offers significant advantages over other forms of business organizations due to its defining characteristics—legal personality, limited liability of its

---

[1] 'Non-profit activities' is used here to include activities that may generate profits, but such profits would be applied to further the object of the organization and not be distributed among its members or other persons who control the organization.

[2] Henry Hansmann and Reinier Kraakman, 'The Essential Role of Organizational Law' (2000) 110 The Yale Law Journal 387.

[3] Other kinds of companies are a company limited by guarantee and a company with unlimited liability. Among the three, a company limited by shares is the most popular. Its popularity can be understood by the fact that as on 31 March 2014 there were 946,651 companies limited by shares as against 5,407 companies limited by guarantee, and 375 companies with unlimited liability. See Ministry of Corporate Affairs, Government of India, *58th Annual Report on the Working & Administration of the Companies Act, 1956* (31 March 2014).

members, transferable shared ownership, and specialized management that is separate from its members. This is not to say that these attributes are exclusive to limited liability companies. Other business organizations like cooperative societies and business trusts do exhibit some of these traits. However, it is in the corporate form that each of these elements is distinct and well developed, thereby making it unique and attractive. Second, law prohibits the formation of associations or partnerships consisting of more than 50 persons for the purpose of carrying on any business that has for its object the acquisition of gain, unless it is registered or formed as a company.[4] Its prevalence is also due to the ease with which it can be formed. One or more persons can form a company limited by shares by following a simple administrative process under the Companies Act.[5] The Companies Act provides the legal framework for the corporate form of business management in which organization, capital, and labour are brought together in a particular form of relationship, which constitutes the essence of private enterprise.[6] Thus, it deals with the organization and creation of the company, raising of capital by issue of securities such as shares, relationship with members and creditors, management and administration, and winding up.

Under the Companies Act, a company limited by shares can be either a private company or a public company. A private company refers to a company having a minimum paid-up share capital, as prescribed by law. This company, by its articles of association, restricts the right to transfer its shares, limits the number of its members to 200 (excluding certain kinds of employees), and prohibits any invitation to the public to subscribe for any securities of the company.[7] A public company, on the other hand, means a company that is not a private company and

---

[4] Section 464 of the Companies Act read with rule 10 of the Companies (Miscellaneous) Rules, 2014.

[5] Many government companies have been incorporated not under the Companies Act but under other legislation, for example, the Life Insurance Corporation of India was formed under the Life Insurance Corporation Act, 1956.

[6] Department of Economic Affairs, Ministry of Finance, Government of India, *Report of the Company Law Committee* (1952), at p. 11.

[7] Clause (68) of section 2 of the Companies Act.

has a minimum paid-up share capital, as prescribed by law.[8] A public company has the choice of inviting the public to subscribe for its securities and get them listed on a stock exchange—a choice that only a small percentage of public companies make. As a result, 'public company' is not synonymous with a 'listed company', which is a company that has any of its securities listed on any recognized stock exchange.

Previously we referred to the fact that a company has a separate legal personality. Being an artificial person it can only exercise its powers in accordance with its memorandum of association and the Companies Act through some other person. Though the issue of through whom a company exercises its powers caused significant debate in the past, it is now well settled that a company exercises its powers through its two primary organs—board of directors and shareholders in general meeting.[9] In this regard, sub-section (1) of section 179 of the Companies Act states that 'the board of directors of a company shall be entitled to exercise all such powers, and to do all such acts and things, as the company is authorised to exercise and do'. This wide power of the board of directors is subject to two limitations. First, in exercising such power or doing such act or thing, the board of directors is subject to the provisions contained in that behalf in the Companies Act, or in the memorandum of association or articles of association, or in any regulations not inconsistent therewith and duly made thereunder, including regulations made by the company in general meeting. Secondly, the board must not exercise any power or

---

[8] Additionally, a company which is a subsidiary of a company, not being a private company, is deemed to be a public company for the purposes of the Companies Act even where such subsidiary company continues to be a private company in its articles of association. Clause (71) of section 2 of the Companies Act.

[9] *Baldevdas Raheja v. Union of India*, 1977 (79) BomLR 581; *Bennet Coleman and Co. v. Union of India*, [1977] 47 Comp Cas 92 (Bom); *Murarka Paint and Varnish Works Limited v. Mohanlal Murarka*, AIR 1961 Cal 251. The powers of the board of directors can be further divided into powers exercisable by certain whole-time key managerial individuals such as the managing director or manager, and the residual powers exercisable by the board of directors. In such a situation, there is a threefold division of the powers of the company. See clauses (53) and (54) of section 2, read with section 203 of the Companies Act. See also *In Re: Shri Ambica Mills Limited*, [1986] 59 Comp Cas 368 (Guj).

do any act or thing which is directed or required, whether under the Companies Act or by the memorandum or articles of association of the company or otherwise, to be exercised or done by the company in general meeting. Despite the division of powers between the board of directors and the company (or shareholders) in general meeting, the Companies Act preserves the right of the shareholders 'in general meeting to impose restrictions and conditions on the exercise by the board of any of the powers.'[10] Shareholders in general meeting also retain ultimate control through their power to amend the articles of association and to change the composition of the board of directors. A consequence of the division of powers of the company between its organs is that lack of authority to exercise power may affect the validity of acts and things done. Thus, the act of the board of directors in selling a business undertaking without the consent of the shareholders in general meeting is invalid.[11]

Capital Requirement of Companies

A company, like any other business organization, must have capital to establish itself and carry on its business as a going concern. The word 'capital' must be distinguished from money earned upon carrying on the business (with the help of the capital), which is typically referred to as 'revenue.'[12] The initial capital of a company limited by shares is the amount of share capital with which it is registered. Share capital must be divided into 'shares' of a fixed amount called the nominal or par value and is contributed by the prospective members of the company—the subscribers to the memorandum of association being the first of the lot.[13] The Companies Act defines 'share(s)' to mean 'a share in the share capital of a company and includes stock.'[14] This definition is misleading because

[10] Sub-section (4) of section 179 of the Companies Act.

[11] *CDS Financial Services (Mauritius) Ltd.* v. *BPL Communications Ltd.*, (2004) 121 Comp Cas 374 (Bom).

[12] *Tuticorin Alkali Chemicals and Fertilizers Limited* v. *Commissioner of Income Tax*, [1997] 227 ITR 172 (SC).

[13] Clause (e) of sub-section (1) of section 4 of the Companies Act.

[14] Clause (84) of section 2 of the Companies Act defines share to mean 'a share in the share capital of a company and includes stock'.

share capital is corporate property and, as a company is a separate legal entity, no other person including its members or creditors has a share in the corporate property. The definition then perhaps means the extent of the contribution made to the share capital. However, such a meaning can help in determining *whether* something is a share or not, and not *what* a share is.

The legal nature of a share is perhaps best explained by an old English case:

> A share is the interest of a shareholder in the company measured by a sum of money, for the purpose of liability in the first place, and of interest in the second, but also consisting of a series of mutual covenants entered into by all the shareholders inter se in accordance with [section 10 of the Companies Act]. The contract contained in the articles of association is one of the original incidents of the share.[15]

L.C.B. Gower has further explained this meaning of 'share':[16]

> It will be observed that this definition, though it lays considerable and perhaps disproportionate stress on the contractual nature of the shareholder's rights, also emphasises the fact that he has an interest in the company. The theory seems to be that the contract constituted by the articles of association defines the nature of the rights, which, however, are not purely personal rights but instead confer some sort of proprietary interest in the company though not in its property. The company itself is treated not merely as a person, the subject of rights and duties, but also as a *res*, the object of rights and duties. In an attempt to distinguish the *persona* from the *res* the latter is often described as 'capital stock' or 'share capital'.

The rights of a shareholder generally consist of declared dividend, attendance and voting at general meetings, and return of capital on winding up.

---

[15] *Borland's Trustee v. Steel Brothers & Co., Limited*, [1901] 1 Ch. 279. See also *Morgan Stanley Mutual Fund v. Kartick Das*, [1994] 74 Taxman 409 (SC); *Life Insurance Corporation of India v. Escorts Limited and Ors*, AIR 1986 SC 1370; *Commissioner of Wealth Tax v. Mahadeo Jalan*, [1972] 86 ITR 621 (SC); *Commissioner of Income Tax v. Standard Vacuum Oil Co.*, [1966] 59 ITR 685 (SC); *Charanjit Lal Chaudhury v. Union of India*, AIR 1951 SC 41.

[16] L.C.B. Gower and others, *Gowers' Principles of Modern Company Law* (4th edn, Stevens & Sons 1979), at p. 399.

With this initial share capital as its asset, a company commences its business and earns money. Generally speaking, persons are free to deal with their assets in any manner in pursuit of their business. However, this is not entirely true in the case of companies. A company's share capital occupies a unique place among its assets and the company law has special rules restricting dealings in it. Why these rules exist will serve as an appropriate backdrop to what they are. Recall that the principal legal attributes of a company are legal personality, limited liability of its members, and transferable shared ownership. These features lead to specific kinds of problems that perhaps do not arise in other business organizations. Thus, though a company is a separate legal entity, it has no personal character that can be trusted unlike say an individual trader or a partnership.[17] Further, the liability of its members is limited to the amount unpaid, if any, on the shares they hold, which are transferable. Due to these reasons, there is a risk that controlling members may manipulate the company to the detriment of one of the key participants in a company, namely creditors—a risk that cannot be mitigated entirely through a contract.[18] Hence, rules have been developed to make share capital the permanent capital to back the credit of the company.[19] Additionally, there is an assurance to the creditors that the persons utilizing the corporate form will at the very least always have a certain amount of their own money at stake.[20]

The rules restricting dealings in share capital can be broken down into four categories: raising capital, minimum capital requirements, capital maintenance, and financial assistance.[21] The rule on raising

[17] Gower (n. 16), at p. 216.

[18] 'Creditors' has been used in the wider sense to include any other person whose dues are unpaid such as employees and governmental authorities.

[19] The rules owe their origin to English common law and English legislation. For an excellent overview of the historical development of the concept of share capital as a permanent fund to be kept intact, see Irving J. Levy, 'Purchase by an English Company of its Own Shares' (1930) 79 University of Pennsylvania Law Review 45.

[20] John Armour, 'Legal Capital: An outdated concept?' (2006) 1 European Business Organization Law Review 5, at p. 15.

[21] For obvious reasons, these rules have no application to a company limited by guarantee and an unlimited company. John Armour, 'Share Capital and Creditor Protection: Efficient Rules for a Modern Company Law' (2000) 63 The Modern Law Review 355, at p. 363.

capital, contained in section 53 of the Companies Act, is that a company will not issue shares at a discount, and shares issued by a company at a discounted price would be void.[22] Discount means a discount to the nominal value of the shares, which is generally of small denominations such as Re 1 or Rs 10 to enhance liquidity. However, the nominal value need not be the market value of the shares. Neither is there a requirement under the Companies Act that shares must be issued at their best price or their market value nor does the Companies Act provide for a method of determining such a value. But there is nothing to stop the company from issuing its shares at a price exceeding their nominal value, that is, at a premium. This is indeed the common practice.[23] The next rule on minimum capital is that a company must have a minimum paid-up share capital, which means a minimum aggregate amount of money received as paid-up in respect of shares issued.[24] Formerly, an extension of the minimum capital rule was that a company having share capital must not commence any business or exercise any borrowing powers unless every subscriber to the memorandum of association has paid the value of the shares agreed to be taken by them.[25] This rule has now been done away with.[26]

The capital maintenance rule restricts returning of the issued share capital (total of the nominal value of the shares that the company has so far issued for subscription) and the share premium back to the shareholders, so long as the company is a going concern. Key statutory provisions

[22] The only exception to this rule is the issue of sweat equity shares, which we discuss in the section 'Raising Capital by Issue of Securities' later in the chapter. The Companies (Amendment) Bill, 2016, introduced in the lower house of Parliament on 16 March 2016, has proposed another exception to this rule. The exception is a situation when a company issues 'shares at a discount to its creditors when its debt is converted into shares in pursuance of any statutory resolution plan or debt restructuring scheme in accordance with any guidelines or directions or regulations specified by the Reserve Bank of India under the Reserve Bank of India Act, 1934 or the Banking (Regulation) Act, 1949'.

[23] Gower (n. 16), at p. 221.

[24] Clauses (64), (68) and (71) of section 2 of the Companies Act.

[25] Section 11 of the Companies Act omitted by the Companies (Amendment) Act, 2015 with effect from 29 May 2015.

[26] Section 4 of the Companies (Amendment) Act, 2015.

embodying this rule are section 66 and sections 68–70 (reduction of share capital), section 52 (application of share premium), and section 63 (issue of bonus shares) of the Companies Act.

Section 66 permits reduction of share capital upon complying with prescribed requirements and subject to confirmation by the National Company Law Tribunal. An exception to this method is sections 68–70 of the Companies Act that provide for reduction of share capital by way of the company purchasing its own shares (referred to as a buyback). Access to both methods is subject to their respective set of conditions, the most important being creditor protection. Under the former route, the tribunal gives notice of every application for reduction of share capital to the creditors of the company. Then it may, 'if it is satisfied that debt or claim of every creditor of the company has been discharged or determined or has been secured or his consent obtained, make an order confirming the reduction of share capital on such terms and conditions as it deems fit'.[27] A pre-condition for the latter route is that, among others, 'the ratio of aggregate of secured and unsecured debts owed by the company after buyback is not more than twice the paid-up capital and its free reserves'.[28] In certain cases, few of the directors must make a declaration of solvency and the company must not have defaulted in repayment of deposits and interest payments thereon, redemption of debentures or preference shares or payment of dividend to any shareholder, or repayment of any term loan or interest payable thereon to any financial institution or banking company.[29]

Next, section 52 creates a statutory fiction and treats share premium as if it were issued and paid-up share capital of the company. Thus, 'where a company issues shares at a premium...a sum equal to the aggregate amount of the premium received on those shares shall be transferred to a "securities premium account"'.[30] Thereafter the provisions of the Companies Act relating to reduction of share capital of a company

---

[27] See sub-sections (2) and (3) of section 66 of the Companies Act.

[28] Clause (d) of sub-section (2) of section 68 of the Companies Act.

[29] Provided that the buy-back is not prohibited, if the default is remedied and a period of three years has lapsed after such default ceased to subsist. Clause (c) of sub-section (1) of section 70 of the Companies Act.

[30] Sub-section (1) of section 52 of the Companies Act.

(except as provided in section 52) apply as if the securities premium account were the paid-up share capital of the company.

Finally, section 63 permits a company to issue fully paid-up bonus shares to its members only out of specified reserves other than the share capital. One of the pre-conditions to issuing bonus shares is that the company must not have 'defaulted in payment of interest or principal in respect of fixed deposits or debt securities issued by it.'[31]

The last is the financial assistance rule. This rule is applicable only to public companies and is embodied in section 67 of the Companies Act. Thus, 'no public company shall give, whether directly or indirectly and whether by means of a loan, guarantee, the provision of security, or otherwise, any financial assistance for the purpose of, or in connection with, a purchase or subscription made or to be made, by any person of or for any shares in the company or in its holding company.'[32] This rule owes its origin to the recommendation of the (UK) Greene Committee, 1925–6 that found its way into the Indian Companies Act, 1913.[33] The committee recommended the rule to curb the practice of using debt to purchase sufficient shares to control the company from the shareholders, and thereafter, obtaining a loan from the company to repay the first debt. This amounted to an indirect return of capital, whereby 'the "old" shareholders are cashed out at the expense of the creditors.'[34] However, as is evident, the text of the rule imposes very broad prohibitions whose effect extends far beyond actions that infringe capital maintenance rules. This aspect is analysed in detail in Chapter 5 of this volume.

In addition to share capital, a company can access capital by way of loan capital, retained earnings, and sale of assets in order to generate money. Loan capital comprises term loans from financial institutions or issuance of debt securities such as debentures. Retained earnings are the accumulated profits of the company that have not been distributed

---

[31] Clause (c) of sub-section (2) of section 63 of the Companies Act.

[32] Sub-section (2) of section 67 of the Companies Act. Sub-section (3) of section 67 lays down three exceptions to this rule for the benefit of employees of the company, and to exempt banking companies.

[33] See paragraph 30 of the *Report of the U.K. Company Law Amendment Committee* (1925–26) chaired by Mr Wilfield Greene and section 54A of the Indian Companies Act, 1913.

[34] Armour (n. 21), at p. 368.

to its shareholders as dividends. The decision to adopt one of the methods or a combination thereof is more of a subject matter of financial management, and less of a legal issue. Important factors that influence the decision of a company to choose one source over the other include the type of business the company is engaged in and the size of the company, the cost of raising the finance (debt capital is cheaper than equity capital from the point of view of its cost and interest being deductible for income tax purposes, whereas no such deduction is allowed for dividends), the consequential risk (excessive debt leads to higher interest payout by the company and also exposes the company to viability risk since the company could be wound up if it is unable to pay its debt), dilution of control (additional equity shares to new investors will dilute the control being exercised by the existing controlling shareholders), and the existing condition of the securities markets. The last factor is quite significant for access to share capital and we examine this in detail in Chapter 3 of this volume.

Concept of Securities

Share capital and loan capital of certain types, are securities issued by a company to raise finance. Securities should generally be understood as financial instruments that are issued or sold as investments and are freely transferable.[35] The term 'securities' is used differently in different jurisdictions. Among common law countries, while New Zealand, South Africa, US, and India use the term 'securities', UK and Australia use 'investments' and 'financial products', respectively.[36] Its meaning, too, has varied over time. As observed in an old English case, 'The word [securities] is not a term of art, but only a word of description. It is a commercial word which will vary with the history of commerce.'[37] Thus, initially, only those financial instruments qualified as securities that 'were supported by security interests or were otherwise "secure" (e.g.

---

[35] Joanna Benjamin, *Interests in Securities: A Proprietary Law Analysis of the International Securities Market* (Oxford University Press 2000), at p. 4.

[36] Frederick H.C. Mazando, 'The Taxonomy of Global Securities: Is the U.S. Definition of a Security too Broad?' (2012) 33 Northwestern Journal of International Law and Business 121, at p. 131.

[37] *In Re: Rayner*, [1904] 1 Ch. 176.

because they were obligations of the government)'.[38] Railroad bonds in the US are a classic example of the original securities. With the success and proliferation of the corporate form of business organization, shares and debentures, whether secured or unsecured, also came to be recognized as securities.

Presently, it is the statute that dictates the meaning and scope of securities; we examine this a little later. But before we do that, securities (or security) must be distinguished from security interest (commercially also referred to as security). Security interest is a right given to one party in the asset of another party to secure payment or performance by that other party or by a third party.[39] Such a right is created by a debtor for the benefit of the creditor in a transaction involving financial assistance such as loans. The primary purpose of creating a security interest is to reduce credit risk and obtain priority over other creditors in the event of the debtor's bankruptcy or winding-up.[40] Common forms of security interest are mortgage, charge, hypothecation, pledge, and lien. The general law on contract and property, including the Indian Contract Act, 1872 and the Transfer of Property Act, 1882, governs the creation of security interest. The Companies Act governs the creation and enforcement of certain types of security interest by companies. Further, to improve recovery and enforcement of security interest, the Recovery of Debts Due to Banks and Financial Institutions Act, 1993 and the Securitisation and Reconstruction of Financial Assets and Enforcement of Security Interest Act, 2002 (or the SARFAESI Act) have been enacted.

In India, 'securities' has been defined under the Securities Contracts (Regulation) Act, 1956 (or the SCRA).[41] Defining securities is important for the simple reason that they are the subject matter of extensive

---

[38] Geoffrey Fuller, *The Law and Practice of International Capital Markets* (LexisNexis 2009), at p. 5.

[39] Roy Goode, *Legal Problems of Credit and Security* (3rd edn, Sweet & Maxwell 2003), at p. 11.

[40] Goode (n. 39), at p. 1.

[41] See clause (h) of section 2 of the SCRA. The Companies Act as well as the Securities and Exchange Board of India Act, 1992 (or the SEBI Act) incorporate by reference the definition contained in the SCRA. See clause (81) of section 2 of the Companies Act and clause (i) of section 2 of the SEBI Act.

regulation.[42] Before examining the definition, it must be remembered that the function of all types of securities is not just to provide capital. The scope of securities under the SCRA extends to a much wider category of instruments, many of which are created and traded for other objectives such as pooling of investments, hedging risk, and so on. The reason for such a wide definition is that the SCRA is a legislation to prevent undesirable transactions in securities by regulating the business of dealing therein. Clause (h) of section 2 of the SCRA defines 'securities' as follows:

'securities' include—
(i) shares, scrips, stocks, bonds, debentures, debenture stock or other marketable securities of a like nature in or of any incorporated company or other body corporate;
[1][(ia) derivative;
(ib) units or any other instrument issued by any collective investment scheme to the investors in such schemes;]
[2][(ic) security receipt as defined in clause (zg) of section 2 of the Securitisation and Reconstruction of Financial Assets and Enforcement of Security Interest Act, 2002;]
[3][(id) units or any other such instrument issued to the investors under any mutual fund scheme;]
[4][Explanation.—For the removal of doubts, it is hereby declared that "securities" shall not include any unit linked insurance policy or scrips or any such instrument or unit, by whatever name called, which provides a combined benefit risk on the life of the persons and investment by such persons and issued by an insurer referred to in clause (9) of section 2 of the Insurance Act, 1938 (4 of 1938);]
[5][(ie) any certificate or instrument (by whatever name called), issued to an investor by any issuer being a special purpose distinct entity which possesses any debt or receivable, including mortgage debt, assigned to such entity, and acknowledging beneficial interest of such investor in such debt or receivable, including mortgage debt, as the case may be;]
[6][(ii) Government securities;
(iia) such other instruments as may be declared by the Central Government to be securities; and]

---

[42] See sections 13 to 19 of the SCRA and Notification no. LAD-NRO/GN/2013-14/26/6667, dated 3 October 2013 issued by SEBI.

(iii) rights or interest in securities;

[1] Inserted by the Securities Laws (Amendment) Act, 1999, Sec. 2, w.e.f. 22-02-2000.

[2] Inserted by the Securitisation and Reconstruction of Financial Assets and Enforcement of Security Interest Act, 2002, Sec. 41 and Schedule, w.r.e.f. 21-06-2002.

[3] Inserted by the Securities Laws (Amendment) Act, 2004, Sec. 2, w.e.f. 12-10-2004.

[4] Inserted by the Securities and Insurance Laws (Amendment and Validation) Act, 2010, Sec. 4, w.r.e.f. 09-04-2010.

[5] Inserted by the Securities Contracts (Regulation) Amendment Act, 2007, Sec. 2, w.e.f. 28-05-2007.

[6] Substituted by Securities and Exchange Board of India Act, 1992, Sec. 33 and Schedule, Pt II, for sub-clause (ii), w.r.e.f. 30-01-1992.

Two aspects of this definition must be noted. First, the definition is not a conceptual one; instead, it identifies instruments that will constitute securities. An understanding of the concept of securities under the SCRA (which is the only statute that defines securities) is however, essential to understanding the types of securities that are issued by a company to raise finance, and the laws and regulations governing such issuances. We, therefore, examine these instruments as well as their conceptual underpinnings. Second, the definition is an inclusive one, and it takes within its purview not only the matters specified therein but also all other types of securities as commonly understood. The courts have, thus, generally given an expansive meaning to securities.[43] An inclusive definition of securities is consistent with the approach adopted by the legislature of other common law countries such as the UK, US, South Africa, Australia, and New Zealand. The intent behind an inclusive definition is that securities, being an instrument of investment, are the subject matter of continuous change and innovation depending on the commercial needs of the economy. Such a nature of securities is sufficiently exemplified by the fact that the definition of securities has

---

[43] *Sudhir Shantilal Mehta v. Central Bureau of Investigation*, (2009) 8 SCC 1; *Sahara India Real Estate Corporation Limited and Ors v. Securities and Exchange Board of India and Anr*, (2013) 1 SCC 1.

undergone numerous amendments as and when new types of securities begin to be generally sold as investment instruments. The definition thus generally follows an approach of economic reality rather than a set of *per se* rules. This approach has the advantage of permitting the regulator and the courts sufficient flexibility to ensure that those who market investments are not able to escape the coverage of securities law by creating new instruments that would not be covered by a more determinate definition.[44] One could question whether, at the expense of the goal of clarity, the legislature has overvalued the goal of avoiding manipulation by the clever and the dishonest.[45] However, the regulation and enforcement of securities law in India would demonstrate that an inclusive definition has helped in better regulation of the securities markets and protection of the interests of gullible investors. An example of this is the judgment of the Supreme Court of India in *Sahara India Real Estate Corporation v. Securities and Exchange Board of India*[46] on the regulation of optionally fully convertible debentures.

We now examine each of the types of securities that have been expressly specified in the SCRA.

'(i) shares, scrips, stocks, bonds, debentures, debenture stock, or other marketable securities of a like nature in or of any incorporated company or other body corporate;'

The first three types of instruments namely shares, scrips, and stocks belong to the family of shares as a class of security; the next three, namely bonds, debentures, and debenture stock fall within the category of debentures. In terms of legal theory, shares and debentures are the two primary types of corporate securities. We examined the meaning of shares earlier. A debenture is an instrument executed by a company evidencing a debt that is normally, but not necessarily, secured by a charge

---

[44] *Bob Reves v. Ernst & Young*, 494 U.S. 56 (1990); *Sudhir Shantilal Mehta v. Central Bureau of Investigation*, (2009) 8 SCC 1; *PCS Industries Limited v. Securities and Exchange Board of India*, 2001 SCC OnLine SAT 29.

[45] *Bob Reves v. Ernst & Young*, 494 U.S. 56 (1990).

[46] (2013) 1 SCC 1.

on the assets of the company.[47] A debenture holder is, therefore, a creditor of the company having contractual rights *against* the company, unlike a shareholder, who is a member of the company having rights *in and against* the company.[48] Due to this legal distinction, company law rules restricting dealings in share capital such as capital maintenance are not applicable to debentures. Debentures may be issued at a discount, may be redeemed, and interest on it may be paid out of the company's share capital.[49] However, there is an element of imprecision in the definition of debenture, as not every type of indebtedness constitutes a debenture. In terms of legal characterization, it is not clear how the line between an ordinary loan and a debenture should be drawn.[50] In practice, however, it is easy to distinguish between the two. The creditor of an ordinary loan would not normally seek to trade in that loan (though the loan can be assigned for a consideration), whereas a debenture holder will seek to do so.[51] Debentures are, therefore, easily transferable, and can be listed and traded on stock exchanges unlike an ordinary loan for which there

---

[47]   Clause (30) of section 2 of the Companies Act defines a debenture as follows: "'debenture' includes debenture stock, bonds and any other instrument of a company evidencing a debt, whether constituting a charge on the assets of the company or not'. The Companies (Amendment) Bill, 2016, introduced in the lower house of the Parliament on 16 March 2016, seeks to amend the definition of 'debenture' and exclude money market instruments from its scope.

[48]   To maintain this legal distinction, a company is prohibited from issuing debentures carrying any voting rights. See sub-section (2) of section 71 of the Companies Act. See also *R.D. Goyal v. Reliance Industries Limited*, (2003) 1 SCC 81; *Narendra Kumar Maheshwari v. Union of India*, 1990 (Supp) SCC 440; *Cochin International Airport Limited v. Presiding Officer, Debt Recovery Tribunal*, (2010) 173 DLT 247 (Del).

[49]   Gower (n. 16), at p. 402.

[50]   Paul L. Davies, *Gower and Davies' Principles of Modern Company Law* (8th edn, Sweet & Maxwell 2008), at p. 1141. See also *National Rayon Corporation Ltd. v. Commissioner of Income Tax*, [1997] 227 ITR 764 (SC); *Commissioner of Income Tax v. Secure Meters Ltd.*, [2010] 321 ITR 611 (Raj); *Commissioner of Income Tax v. Industrial Credit and Development Syndicate Ltd.*, [2006] 285 ITR 310 (Kar); *Commissioner of Income Tax v. Shree Rajasthan Syntex Ltd.*, [2004] 269 ITR 461 (Raj).

[51]   Alastair Hudson, *Securities Law* (Sweet & Maxwell 2008), at p. 13.

may not be a ready market. Ordinary loans can, however, be turned into securities through securitization—a process that we examine later in this section.

Scrips, bonds, stocks, and debenture stock are variants of shares and debentures. Scrips are certificates representing fractions of shares issued to represent instalments paid on the shares; when all the instalments are paid, the scrip is exchanged for a share certificate.[52] They are no longer issued. Similarly, 'bonds' is a term of the past and was commonly used, both in law and practice, to refer to debentures that were secured by a mortgage on the property of the company.[53] Now bonds are less a term of law and more a term of commerce.

Stocks are securities that arise upon conversion of shares. A company may, by ordinary resolution, convert any fully paid-up shares into stock and reconvert any stock into paid-up shares of any denomination.[54] The holders of stock may transfer it or any part thereof in the same manner as the shares from which the stock arose.[55] Granting stockholders the right to transfer any part of stock has the effect that the stock is freely divisible into fractions of any amount. The necessity and purpose for the provision of conversion of shares into stock appears to have arisen primarily for its administrative value for both investor and the company—the investor has convenience in trading the shares which has been converted into stock and the company has convenience in maintaining a record of allotment of shares and its subsequent transfer through trading. From the company's point of view, stocks greatly simplified the work of maintaining the share register and issuing share certificates. Prior to conversion, a company was obligated to maintain a register to keep track of each share identified by a separate number, while the conversion of such share into stock no longer caused this difficulty, as the company merely had to register the amount of stock held by each member. Under the Companies Act, 1956, where a company had converted any of its shares into stock, and given notice

[52] John Moody, *The Investor's Primer* (The Moody Corporation 1907), at p. 118.

[53] *Commissioner of Income Tax v. Enam Securities (P) Ltd.*, [2012] 345 ITR 64 (Bom).

[54] Clause (c) of sub-section (1) of section 61 the Companies Act.

[55] Regulation 37 of Table-F of Schedule I to the Companies Act.

of the conversion to the registrar of companies, all the provisions of the Companies Act, which were applicable to shares only, ceased to apply to as much of the share capital as was converted into stock.[56] However, with time the relevance of stock greatly reduced in practice, evidently because the nominal value of any share is fixed at such rate that its division into fractions becomes more cumbersome and purposeless rather than the convenience it originally sought to provide. Further, having regard to the development of the depository system, with the companies no longer being obligated to distinguish each of their shares by its appropriate number,[57] and with the growth of the technology of record keeping, it is difficult to see what practical purpose is served by converting shares into stock.

Debenture stock is conceptually similar to stocks. Thus, debentures can be aggregated into debenture stock and any fraction of the debenture stock can be transferred. However, while stocks cannot be issued directly and have to be created through conversion of shares, the Companies Act does not impose such a requirement for debenture stock. Debenture stock can thus be issued directly by a company. While this aspect of a debenture stock does make it of some practical value as compared to stocks, companies in India do not generally issue such instruments.

The expression 'or other marketable securities of a like nature' is a residual category and consists of securities in the nature of shares and debentures that are marketable. Numerous judicial decisions have examined the meaning of 'marketable' and held that (a) marketability of a security denotes the ease with which a security can be sold; (b) what is freely transferable is marketable; and (c) what is saleable is also marketable.[58] Thus, optionally fully convertible debentures issued by a public

---

[56] Section 96 of the Companies Act, 1956.

[57] Section 45 of the Companies Act.

[58] *Dahiben Umedbhai Patel v. Norman James Hamilton and Ors*, [1985] 57 Comp Cas 700; *B.K. Holdings Private Limited v. Prem Chand Jute Mills and Ors*, [1983] 53 Comp Cas 367; *Mysore Fruit Products Limited and Ors v. The Custodian and Ors*, 2005 (107) BomLR 955. The Whole Time Member of SEBI, in its order in the matter of issuance of optionally fully convertible debentures by Sahara India Real Estate Corporation Limited and Sahara Housing Investment Corporation Limited, reviewed many of these judicial decisions and provided the meaning and scope of 'other marketable securities

company have been held to be categorized as 'other marketable securities of a like nature'.[59] Hybrid securities—securities that combine the elements of two or more different securities—would fall under this residual category.[60] However, shares of a private company do not fall within the purview of this phrase as they have been held to be not marketable.[61]

Securities specified in clause (i) are qualified by 'in or of any incorporated company or other body corporate'. An incorporated company is a company formed and registered under the Companies Act. 'Body corporate', in contrast, is a wider category and includes a company incorporated outside India; but excludes a cooperative society registered under any law relating to cooperative societies, and any other body corporate (not being a company defined under the Companies Act), which the central government has, by notification in the Official Gazette specified in this behalf.[62] Thus, units issued by a mutual fund will not come with the ambit of clause (i) since a mutual fund being a trust is not a company or a body corporate.[63]

---

of a like nature' which was affirmed on appeal by the Securities Appellate Tribunal and the Supreme Court of India. See Order dated 23 June 2011 of the Whole Time Member of SEBI in the Matter of Issuance of Optionally Fully Convertible Debentures by Sahara India Real Estate Corporation Limited and Sahara Housing Investment Corporation Limited, para 14.5.6.

[59] *Sahara India Real Estate Corporation Limited & Ors v. Securities and Exchange Board of India and Anr*, (2013) 1 SCC 1.

[60] Hybrid securities are securities that combine two or more different financial instruments. They generally combine the characteristics of equity shares and debentures. See *Sahara India Real Estate Corporation Limited and Ors v. Securities and Exchange Board of India and Anr*, (2013) 1 SCC 1.

[61] *Naresh K. Aggarwala and Co. v. Canbank Financial Services Limited and Anr*, AIR 2010 SC 2722; *Dahiben Umedbhai Patel v. Norman James Hamilton and Ors*, [1985] 57 Comp Cas 700; *Mysore Fruit Products Limited and Ors v. The Custodian and Ors*, (2005) 107 BomLR 955.

[62] Clause (11) of section 2 of the Companies Act. As per section 2A of the SCRA, words and expressions used therein and not defined in the SCRA but defined in the Companies Act or the SEBI Act or the Depositories Act, shall have the same meanings as respectively assigned to them in those Acts.

[63] *PCS Industries Limited v. Securities and Exchange Board of India*, 2001 SCC OnLine SAT 29.

'(ia) derivative'

The SCRA defines the term 'derivative' as:

'derivative' includes—(A) a security derived from a debt instrument, share, loan, whether secured or unsecured, risk instrument or contract for differences or any other form of security; (B) a contract which derives its value from the prices, or index of prices, of underlying securities; (C) commodity derivatives; and (D) such other instruments as may be declared by the central government to be derivatives.[64]

This definition is not helpful for understanding the meaning of the term 'derivative' and, perhaps, illustrates the difficulty in defining it. We, therefore, examine the natural meaning, nature, and function of derivatives. The courts, too, have adopted such an approach since the above definition is inclusive and the natural meaning of derivative is not lost.[65]

A derivative is a special type of contract between two parties, an end user (usually a financial institution or an institutional investor) and a dealer (a bank or a securities firm). The contract has a fixed expiration date, mostly in the range of 3–12 months from the date of commencement of the contract.[66] Typically, the end user enters into the contract to hedge, or to protect itself against adverse changes in the value of certain assets or liabilities such as equity shares, exchange rate, and interest rate (called the 'underlying'). The dealer enters into the contract and offers protection to the end user by assuming the risk with the expectation to profit from non-occurrence of the adverse change. The dealer, therefore, is engaged in a speculative activity, but this speculation serves an important economic purpose—providing a facility for hedging in the most cost-efficient way against market risk.[67] Hedgers and speculators, thus, co-exist and the derivatives market's capacity to absorb buying and

---

[64] Clause (ac) of section 2 of the SCRA.

[65] *Rajshree Sugars and Chemicals Limited* v. *Axis Bank Limited and Anr*, AIR 2011 Mad 144.

[66] Securities and Exchange Board of India, *Report of the Committee constituted by the Securities and Exchange Board of India on 'Derivatives'* (March 1998), at paragraph 10 of chapter one.

[67] Report of the Committee on Derivatives (n. 66), at paragraph one of the Executive Summary.

selling by hedgers is directly dependent on the availability of speculators to act as counter-parties to hedgers. [68] Despite an element of speculation, derivative contracts have been held to be not in breach of sections 23 and 30 of the Indian Contract Act, 1872 so as to render them void.[69]

The reason why derivative contracts have come to occupy an important position is due to expansion in the volume of financial instruments and globalization of the financial markets. In such a scenario, the primary risks that market participants face are unpredictable movements in foreign exchange, interest rates, and prices of equities and commodities.[70] Derivative contracts with these assets or liabilities as the underlying help in mitigating these risks over which market participants have no control. Growth of such contracts can be gauged by the fact that the turnover in the equity derivative segment rose from Rs 47,575,571 crore in the financial year 2013–14 to Rs 75,969,290 crore in the financial year 2014–15, and became the most traded and valued segment in the capital markets in India.[71]

The meaning and function of derivative contracts can be further understood by examining two standard derivative contracts, namely futures and options.[72] A futures contract

is an agreement between two parties to buy or sell an underlying asset at a specified price and future date. This agreement creates a pair of

[68] Report of the Committee on Derivatives (n. 66), at paragraph 17 of chapter one.

[69] *Rajshree Sugars and Chemicals Limited* v. *Axis bank Limited and Anr*, AIR 2011 Mad 144. Section 23 of the Indian Contract Act, 1872 renders void every agreement of which the object is unlawful and section 30 of the Indian Contract Act renders void agreements by way of wager.

[70] Joseph L. Motes, 'A Primer on the Trade and Regulation of Derivative Instruments' (1996) 49 Southern Methodist University Law Review 579, at p. 585.

[71] Securities and Exchange Board of India, *Annual Report* (2014–15).

[72] Although derivative contracts are of multiple types with several permutations and combinations, almost all of them fall into one of four major categories: forwards, futures, options, and swaps. See Edward S. Adams and David E. Runkle, 'The Easy Case for Derivatives Use: Advocating a Corporate Fiduciary to the use of Derivatives' (2000) 41 William and Mary Law Review 595, at p. 600.

obligations: The buyer must purchase the underlying asset from the seller at the contract's maturity date; and the seller must sell the asset to the buyer at the agreed-upon price regardless of current fair market value.[73]

Due to the advance price fixation, the risk of loss from adverse price changes is reduced. However, it also reduces the possibility of gain from positive price changes.[74] Such contracts are traded on the stock exchange and are standardized in terms of size, expiration date, and all other features. Due to the exchange-traded nature of futures contracts, trading is transparent, subject to financial safeguards and protection from defaults.[75] A futures contract that is not exchange-traded and where the contract terms, such as asset quantity and contract duration, are negotiated individually between the counterparties is called a forward contract.[76] And a forward contract where the counterparties 'agree to exchange a series of payments according to agreed-upon terms over a set period of time' is called a swap.[77]

An option contract, on the other hand, is similar to a futures contract except for the fact that it provides the end user or the holder 'with the right rather than an obligation, to buy or sell the underlying asset at a predetermined price on or before a particular date.'[78] Option contracts are of two types: '[A] call option provides the holder the right to purchase the underlying asset at a specified price whereas a put option gives the holder the right to sell the underlying asset at a specified price.'[79] In order to acquire the right of option, the end user pays the dealer (known as the 'option writer') a premium or a fee. In an options contract, the end user can lose no more than the option premium paid but his possible gain is unbounded. On the other hand, the dealer's possible loss is unbounded but his maximum gain is limited to the premium. The

---

[73] Adams and Runkle (n. 72), at pp. 603 and 605.

[74] Adams and Runkle (n. 72), at p. 604.

[75] *Report of the Committee on Derivatives* (n. 66), at paragraph 4 of chapter one.

[76] Adams and Runkle (n. 72), at p. 604.

[77] Joseph Motes (n. 70), at p. 590.

[78] Adams and Runkle (n. 72), at p. 609.

[79] Adams and Runkle (n. 72), at p. 609. See also *In Re: Royal Bank of Scotland*, [2010] 323 ITR 380 (AAR); *In Re: Morgan Stanley & Co. International Limited*, [2005] 272 ITR 416 (AAR).

most critical aspect of options contracts, therefore, is the evaluation of the fairness of the premium.[80]

Three key features of derivative contracts must be noted: First, the value of the contract is derived from and dependent on the value of the underlying asset. After entering into the contract, if the value of the underlying asset does not change, the contract value is zero. However, if the market price of the underlying asset changes, the value of the contract also undergoes a change.[81] Second, based on the mode of trading, derivative contracts can be categorized into exchange-traded derivatives and derivatives traded outside the stock exchange. The latter is commonly referred to as over-the-counter (OTC) derivatives. Thus, futures and options are exchange-traded derivatives. Third, since the object of derivative contracts is protection against adverse changes or fluctuations in the value of certain assets or liabilities, these assets or liabilities ordinarily are corporate securities such as equity shares, commodities such as agricultural produce and metals, foreign exchange such as dollars and pounds, and interest rates.

With the aid of the foregoing discussion on the meaning, nature, and function of derivatives, we now revisit its definition under SCRA. First, derivatives were recognized as 'securities' only with effect from 22 February 2000. However, much before this date, some form of derivative contracts were being transacted under the SCRA and Forward Contracts (Regulation) Act, 1952 (FCRA). Under the SCRA, from its enactment until 22 February 2000, corporate securities, and government securities were broadly the two recognized classes of 'securities'. With these as the underlying, option contracts were prohibited since enactment of the SCRA because these were viewed as purely speculative activities and hence undesirable.[82] This prohibition was lifted with effect from 25 January 1995 because the stock exchanges were seen to be capable to regulate them under the supervision of the Securities and Exchange Board of India (SEBI). Forward contracts, on the other hand, were permitted since the enactment of the SCRA. However, the

---

[80] *Report of the Committee on Derivatives* (n. 66), at paragraph 15 of chapter one.

[81] Adams and Runkle (n. 72), at p. 604.

[82] Section 20 of the SCRA.

central government prohibited these with effect from 27 June 1969.[83] Later, recognizing the utility of forward contracts, the central government modified the prohibition and permitted forward contracts in a phased manner from 1 June 1994 and onwards.[84] Under the FCRA, forward contracts with commodities (other than corporate securities and government securities) as the underlying were permitted since inception. However, option contracts were, on lines identical to the SCRA, prohibited.[85] Finally, derivative contracts with foreign exchange and interest rate as the underlying appears to have been transacted earlier than 22 February 2000. Given that the legislature never intended to regulate such derivatives under the SCRA, they were expressly brought within the regulatory jurisdiction of the Reserve Bank of India.[86]

We now examine the definition of derivative itself. The scope of definition is important because only exchange-traded derivatives are legal and valid, and entering into non-exchange-traded derivative contracts is an offence.[87] Clearly the first part of the definition of 'derivative' is

---

[83] Central government notification S.O. no. 2561 dated 27 June 1969. See also *Desh Bandhu Gupta v. Delhi Stock Exchange Association Limited*, (1979) 4 SCC 565.

[84] See central government notifications S.O. no. 425(E) dated 1 June 1994; S.O. no. 750(E) dated 18 October 1994; S.O. no. 434(E) dated 13 June 1996; S.O. no. 764(E) dated 6 November 1997; S.O. no. 225(E) dated 18 March 1998; S.O. no. 345(E) dated 24 April 1998; and S.O. no. 581(E) dated 14 July 1999. Central government rescinded all these notifications vide notification no. S.O. 186(E) dated 1 March 2000 upon the introduction of derivatives as a separate class of securities to be regulated by the stock exchanges and SEBI.

[85] Section 19 of the FCRA.

[86] See, chapter IIID of the Reserve Bank of India Act, 1934 and the Foreign Exchange Management (Foreign Exchange Derivative Contracts) Regulations, 2000 framed by the RBI under the Foreign Exchange Management Act, 1999 (or FEMA).

[87] Section 18A of the SCRA on 'Contracts in derivatives' states:-

Notwithstanding anything contained in any other law for the time being in force, contracts in derivative shall be legal and valid if such contracts are—

(a) traded on a recognised stock exchange;
(b) settled on the clearing house of the recognised stock exchange;
    in accordance with the rules and bye-laws of such stock exchange;

broad and vague. Instead of a derivative being considered a contract, it is defined as being a 'security', the underlying asset of which could be a 'risk instrument', a 'contract for differences' in addition to a debt instrument, loan, and share. Derivative could also be 'any other form of security'. [88] The second part of the definition is more meaningful: Derivatives are contracts whose underlying asset is either prices of securities such as equity shares, or index of prices of securities. The third part defines a derivative to include commodity derivatives. Commodity derivatives are defined under clause (bc) of section 2 of the SCRA and are essentially derivative contracts wherein the underlying assets are notified movable property, such as fibres, spices, edible oil and oil seeds, pulses, metals, and bullion.[89] The fourth part is an open-ended category empowering the central government to declare other instruments as derivatives.

(c) between such parties and on such terms as the Central Government may, by notification in the Official Gazette, specify.

Clause (d) of sub-section (1) of section 23 of the SCRA prescribes penalty for entering into any contract in derivative in contravention of section 18A of the SCRA.

[88] This aspect was also the subject matter of parliamentary debate. A member of the house pointed out that the definition ought to have defined what exactly a derivative is instead of stating that derivatives includes such and such things, and that too ambiguously. This approach makes the legislative provisions on derivatives susceptible to judicial review, especially because section 18A of the SCRA makes all non-exchange-traded derivatives illegal and invalid. See Lok Sabha Debates, 'Securities Laws (Amendment) Bill, 1999' (30 November 1999).

[89] Clause (bc) of section 2 of the SCRA states:

'commodity derivatives' means a contract– (i) for the delivery of such goods, as may be notified by the Central Government in the Official Gazette, and which is not a ready delivery contract; or (ii) for differences, which derives its value from prices or indices of prices of such underlying goods or activities, services, rights, interests and events, as may be notified by the Central Government, in consultation with the Board, but does not include securities as referred to in sub-clauses (A) and (B) of clause (ac) [of section 2 of the SCRA].

Earlier FCRA regulated commodity derivatives and the Forward Markets Commission, a statutory body established and constituted under the FCRA, was the advisory body for the administration of this Act. The Finance Act, 2015

'(ib) units or any other instrument' and '(id) units or any other such instrument'

Due to conceptual similarity, we analyse these two kinds of securities together. These securities are the outcome of an investment strategy commonly called pooling of investment. Small investors, who generally lack expertise to invest on their own in securities or in other kinds of assets, prefer pooling in their marginal resources, invest in the specified asset, and distribute the returns therefrom among themselves on cooperative principles.[90] Under law, pooled investment cannot be a free-standing object, meaning that it cannot in and of itself be a legal person or entity. Legal title to the pooled investment or assets purchased by the pooled investment has to be somewhere extrinsic, namely in an investment vehicle.[91] The pooled investment vehicle could be a trust, company, LLP, etc. The legal form of the pooled investment vehicle is generally shaped by economic costs and benefits as well as the express provisions of law that regulate the pooled investments. A manager typically manages the pooled investment vehicle, and investors benefit in terms of reduced risk and higher returns arising from the professional expertise of the fund managers. This way, investors also get an opportunity to invest in a wide variety of assets. In India, pooled investment vehicles are broadly of five kinds: mutual funds, collective investment schemes (CISs), alternative investment funds (AIFs), infrastructure investment trusts (InvITs), and real estate investment trusts (REITs). Of these, we examine mutual funds and CISs here because financial instruments issued by them fall under sub-clauses (id) and (ib) of clause (h) of section 2, respectively.

---

inserted sections 29A and 29B in the FCRA by way of an amendment. With effect from 29 September 2015, section 29A repealed the FCRA and dissolved the Forward Markets Commission. Section 29B transferred the undertaking of the Forward Markets Commission and vested it with SEBI. In consequence of the Finance Act, 2015 amending several other provisions of FCRA and SCRA, buying, selling, or dealing in commodity derivatives are now regulated by SEBI.

[90] National Stock Exchange of India Limited, *Indian Securities Market, A Review-1999*.

[91] Charles E. Rounds, Jr and Andreas Dehio, 'Publicly-Traded Open End Mutual Funds in Common Law and Civil Law Jurisdictions: A Comparison of Legal Structures' (2007) 3 NYU Journal of Law & Business 473, at pp. 484–5.

We examine the remaining pooled investment vehicles towards the end of this section.

A mutual fund, regulated under Securities and Exchange Board of India (Mutual Funds) Regulations, 1996 (or the SEBI [MF] Regulations), is a pooled investment vehicle which raises money from the public under schemes launched by it for investing in securities, money market instruments, gold or gold-related instruments, or real estate assets. The legal form in which a mutual fund can be established in India is that of a trust[92] and money is raised from the public through the issuance of units.[93] A unit is the interest of unitholders in a scheme, each unit representing one undivided share in the assets of a scheme.[94] This, therefore, is the meaning of units under sub-clause (id) of clause (h) of section 2 of the SCRA and the scope and meaning of 'or any other such instrument' would be an investment instrument in the nature of a unit issued to the investors under any mutual fund scheme.

The Explanation to sub-clause (id) of clause (h) of section 2 of the SCRA was inserted to put to rest a regulatory tussle between SEBI, and the Insurance Regulatory and Development Authority of India (IRDA). In the Explanation, a 'unit linked insurance policy' (ULIP) is a life insurance policy that provides a combination of risk cover and investment. The investment portion of all the ULIPs is pooled together to set up an investment fund (commonly called a unit fund) and the policyholders bear the risk of the investment out of the unit fund.[95] Historically,

---

[92] The legal framework for such trusts is the Indian Trusts Act, 1882. A mutual fund is set up in the form of a trust, which has sponsor(s), trustees, an asset management company (AMC), and a custodian. The trust is established by a sponsor (or several sponsors) who is like the promoter of a company. The trustees of the mutual fund hold its property for the benefit of the unitholders. An AMC approved by SEBI manages the funds by making investments in various types of securities or other permitted assets. The custodian, who is registered with SEBI, holds the assets of various schemes of the fund in its custody. The trustees are vested with the general power of superintendence and direction over the AMC. They monitor the performance of the mutual fund and its compliance with the SEBI (MF) Regulations.

[93] Clause (q) of regulation 2 of the SEBI (MF) Regulations.

[94] Clause (z) of regulation 2 of the SEBI (MF) Regulations.

[95] 'Frequently Asked Questions' dated 23 October 2007 issued by IRDA.

insurance companies offered ULIPs and the IRDA regulated their offering. However, in April 2010, SEBI passed an order directing several insurance companies not to issue ULIPs for subscription, as ULIPs were a combination of investment and insurance and the investment component was in the nature of mutual funds (which are under SEBI's purview and therefore ULIPs fell under SEBI's jurisdiction).[96] Soon thereafter, the IRDA passed an order that notwithstanding SEBI's order, insurance companies could continue to carry out insurance business as usual including offering, marketing, and servicing ULIPs.[97] The explanation was therefore introduced to clarify that ULIPs would not fall within the definition of securities, and would be outside the regulatory purview of SEBI.

A CIS, as a pooled investment vehicle, is very similar to a mutual fund and is regulated under Securities and Exchange Board of India (Collective Investment Schemes) Regulations, 1999 (or the SEBI [CIS] Regulations). Due to historical reasons,[98] a CIS is defined very widely under Securities and Exchange Board of India Act, 1992 (the

[96] Order no. WTM/PS/IMD/06/APR/2010 dated 9 April 2010 passed by the whole time member, SEBI.

[97] Order no. 56/IRDA/Legal/ULIP-MF dated 10 April 2010 passed by the Chairman, IRDA.

[98] In the past, CIS, as a form of investment vehicle, was launched and managed in a manner detrimental to the interest of the investors. For example, large sums of monies used to be collected by persons without sufficient experience in the proposed investment activity, high risks were associated with the venture, and inadequate information was provided to the investors to enable them to make an informed decision. See Securities and Exchange Board of India, *Report of the Committee on Collective Investment Schemes* (5 April 1999); *P.G.F. Limited v. Union of India*, (2015) 13 SCC 50; *Sachin Gupta v. Securities and Exchange Board of India*, (2014) 183 Comp Cas 47 (Del). To safeguard the interest of the investors and the orderly development of the market, a complete legal framework to regulate CISs was put in place. The SEBI Act was amended and SEBI framed the SEBI (CIS) Regulations, 1999. Inadequacy in the legal framework was once again felt in the year 2013 in the wake of detection of ponzi schemes and chit fund scams. This led to further amendments to the legal framework governing collective investment schemes through the Securities Laws (Amendment) Act, 2014. The definition and scope of a CIS was further generalized in order to include those schemes.

SEBI Act).[99] The definition has four limbs. The first limb defines a CIS broadly to mean a scheme or arrangement offered by any person under which contributions made by investors are pooled with a view to receive profits, income, produce, or property. The property, contribution, or investment forming part of the scheme is managed on behalf of the investors and the investors do not have day-to-day control over the management and operation of the scheme or arrangement. The second limb

[99] A CIS is defined in section 11AA of the SEBI Act as follows:

(1) Any scheme or arrangement which satisfies the conditions referred to in sub-section (2) or sub-section (2A) shall be a collective investment scheme: Provided that any pooling of funds under any scheme or arrangement, which is not registered with the Board or is not covered under sub-section (3), involving a corpus amount of one hundred crore rupees or more shall be deemed to be a collective investment scheme.

(2) Any scheme or arrangement made or offered by any person under which,—

   (i)   the contributions, or payments made by the investors, by whatever name called, are pooled and utilized for the purposes of the scheme or arrangement;

   (ii) the contributions or payments are made to such scheme or arrangement by the investors with a view to receive profits, income, produce or property, whether movable or immovable, from such scheme or arrangement;

   (iii) the property, contribution or investment forming part of scheme or arrangement, whether identifiable or not, is managed on behalf of the investors;

   (iv) the investors do not have day-to-day control over the management and operation of the scheme or arrangement.

(2A) Any scheme or arrangement made or offered by any person satisfying the conditions as may be specified in accordance with the regulations made under this Act.

(3) Notwithstanding anything contained in sub-section (2) or sub-section (2A), any scheme or arrangement—

   (i)   made or offered by a co-operative society registered under the Co-operative Societies Act, 1912 (2 of 1912) or a society being a society registered or deemed to be registered under any law relating to co-operative societies for the time being in force in any State;

   (ii) under which deposits are accepted by non-banking financial companies as defined in clause (f) of section 45-I of the Reserve Bank of India Act, 1934 (2 of 1934);

then excludes certain categories from the definition which are governed by specific laws such as cooperative societies, non-banking financial companies, pension schemes, deposits under the Companies Act, and mutual fund schemes. The third limb of the definition creates a deeming fiction to widen the scope of a CIS further. Thus, any pooling of funds under any scheme or arrangement, which is not registered with SEBI or is not covered under the second limb, that involves a corpus amount of Rs 100 crore or more is deemed a CIS. As per the fourth and the last limb, a CIS is also any scheme or arrangement made or offered by any person satisfying the conditions as may be specified in regulations made by SEBI under the SEBI Act.

A trust is the legal form in which a CIS can be constituted.[100] A collective investment management company launches the scheme and collects funds from the public through issuance of units. A unit is, therefore, defined to include any instrument issued under a scheme, by whatever name called, denoting the value of the subscription of a unitholder,[101] which is what 'units' mean under sub-clause (ib) of clause (h) of section 2 of the SCRA. Given the historical background of CISs,

---

    (iii)   being a contract of insurance to which the Insurance Act, 1938 (4 of 1938), applies;

    (iv)   providing for any Scheme, Pension Scheme or the Insurance Scheme framed under the Employees Provident Fund and Miscellaneous Provisions Act, 1952 (19 of 1952);

    (v)   under which deposits are accepted under section 58A of the Companies Act, 1956 (1 of 1956);

    (vi)   under which deposits are accepted by a company declared as a Nidhi or a mutual benefit society under section 620A of the Companies Act, 1956 (1 of 1956);

    (vii)   falling within the meaning of Chit business as defined in clause (d) of section 2 of the Chit Fund Act, 1982 (40 of 1982);

    (viii)   under which contributions made are in the nature of subscription to a mutual fund;

    (ix)   such other scheme or arrangement which the Central Government may, in consultation with the Board, notify,

shall not be a collective investment scheme.

[100] Regulation 16 of the SEBI (CIS) Regulations.

[101] Clause (dd) of sub-regulation (1) of regulation 2 of the SEBI (CIS) Regulations.

the definition of securities in the said clause also includes 'or any other instrument' so as to bring within the statutory and regulatory purview any other investment instrument issued by CISs.

Though conceptually similar, mutual funds and CISs cater to distinct needs of investors. A CIS cannot be launched for the purpose of investing in securities,[102] whereas a mutual fund can invest in securities.[103] Securities are an attractive investment target for pooled investments in general. For investing in securities, mutual funds offer a wide array of schemes that cater to different needs based on age, financial position, risk tolerance, and returns expectations. The dominance of mutual funds among the public as a pooled investment vehicle can be gauged by the fact that as on 31 March 2015, there was only one CIS registered with SEBI and it had not launched any CIS. On the other hand, 47 registered mutual funds had mobilized gross resources of Rs 11,086,259 crore during the financial year 2014–15 through their different schemes.[104]

A mutual fund and a CIS (and the units that they issue) must be distinguished from a conventional chit fund, prize chit and money circulation scheme, none of which fall within the regulatory purview of SEBI. Chit (meaning a written piece of paper) transactions originated in the rural parts of India during the nineteenth century. A small group of people well known to each other would agree to contribute periodically a certain amount of grain or money and to distribute the entire collection, termed as fund, to one of the members. The collected fund may be given either by draw of lots or by bidding and the member whose name appeared on the winning chit received the entire collection without any deduction. He, however, would continue to pay his subscriptions but his name would be removed from subsequent lots. Thus every member got a chance to receive the whole amount of the chit fund.[105] This conventional chit transaction or chit fund served two legitimate demands of rural people:

---

[102] Clause (c) of regulation 13 of the SEBI (CIS) Regulations.

[103] Clause (q) of regulation 2 read with sub-regulation (1) of regulation 43 of the SEBI (MF) Regulations.

[104] Securities and Exchange Board of India, *Annual Report* (2014–15).

[105] *Registrar of Firms, Societies and Chits, Uttar Pradesh* v. *Secured Investment Co. Lucknow*, 1988 (Supp) SCC 248. See judgment of the Supreme Court of India in *Shriram Chits and Investment (P) Ltd.* v. *Union of India*, 1993 Supp (4) SCC 226 for the history, regulation, and functioning of chit fund. See also *Delhi*

(a) a necessity for a lump sum amount to meet some unusual expenditure and (b) to provide a form of accumulated saving when people had no banking facilities.[106] They are therefore permitted today but subject to extensive regulation under the Chit Funds Act, 1982. A conventional chit fund is different from a mutual fund and a CIS in the sense that, though there is pooling of money, it is not for the purposes of making an investment. Instead, all members pool money so that it is distributed to one of them on the basis of a lot, auction, tender, etc.

Unlike a conventional chit fund, prize chit and money circulation scheme are banned under the Prize Chits and Money Circulation Schemes (Banning) Act, 1978. In a prize chit, the organizer collects money in lump sum or instalments, pursuant to a scheme or arrangement, and he/she utilizes the money as he/she fancies, and for (a) awarding periodically or otherwise to a specified number of subscribers, prizes in cash or kind, and (b) refunding to the subscribers the whole or part of the money collected on the termination of the scheme or otherwise.[107] A money circulation scheme is essentially a scheme for making quick or easy money by collecting money from subscribers of the scheme and then paying them back some money collected from the next set of subscribers, and so on. The legislative definition of money circulation scheme is quite wide,[108] and the courts have often struggled in applying

---

Chit Fund Association v. Union of India, [2013] 32 STT 955 (Del); All Kerala Association of Chit Funds v. Union of India, [2013] 40 STT 500 (Ker); Bilahari Investments (P.) Ltd. v. Commissioner of Income Tax, [2007] 288 ITR 39 (Mad).

[106] Registrar of Firms case (n. 105)

[107] Srinivasa Enterprises v. Union of India, (1980) 4 SCC 507. See also clause (e) of section 2 of the Prize Chits and Money Circulation Schemes (Banning) Act, 1978.

[108] Clause (c) of section 2 of the Prize Chits and Money Circulation Schemes (Banning) Act, 1978 defines 'money circulation scheme' to mean 'any scheme, by whatever name called, for the making of quick or easy money, or for the receipt of any money or valuable thing as the consideration for a promise to pay money, on any event or contingency relative or applicable to the enrolment of members into the scheme, whether or not such money or thing is derived from the entrance money of the members of such scheme or periodical subscriptions'.

it in the facts of particular cases.[109] Naturally, prize chit and money circulation scheme are banned given their exploitative nature.

'(ic) security receipt' and '(ie) any certificate or instrument'

Securities specified in sub-clause (ic) (to be referred to as 'security receipt') and those specified in sub-clause (ie) (to be referred to as 'securitized debt instrument') warrant a side-by-side analysis since both these securities are the outcome of a financing transaction referred to as securitization.

Securitization, in its simplest form, is the purchase of payment rights by a special purpose entity resulting in the issue of securities (which funds the purchase of the payment rights) whose value is determined by the payment rights so purchased.[110] The payment rights could arise out of mortgages, car loans, or student loans owing to the initial payee who made the loan (and who is thus typically referred to as an 'originator').[111] In India, statutory recognition of securitization came about in the year 2000, when the National Housing Bank Act, 1987 was amended to provide for the creation of special purpose vehicles in the form of trusts by the National Housing Bank (NHB) for

---

[109] See *State of West Bengal v. Swapan Kumar Guha*, (1982) 1 SCC 561; *Kuriachan Chacko v. State of Kerala*, (2008) 8 SCC 708; *Lambert Kroger v. NCT of Delhi*, (2003) 108 DLT 150; *Commissioner of Income Tax v. Amarjeet Kaur*, [2006] 283 ITR 71 (Kar).

[110] Jonathan C. Lipson, 'Re: Defining Securitization' (2012) 85 Southern California Law Review 1229, at p. 1233. Securitization (also spelt as securitisation in several jurisdictions) as a financial transaction has flourished in the US. According to some estimates, more than 75 per cent of the global securitization volumes are accounted for by the US. Consequently, securitization including its definition has been the subject matter of extensive discussion in academic writings. We have, therefore, borrowed a definition of securitization that best explains its constituents. For more on the definition of securitization, see Steven L. Schwarcz, 'What is Securitization? And for what purpose?' (2012) 85 Southern California Law Review 1283, and Jonathan C. Lipson, 'Why (and How to) Define Securitization? A Sur-Reply to Professor Schwarcz' (2012) 85 Southern California Law Review 1301.

[111] Lipson (n. 110), at p. 1239.

purchasing loans secured by mortgages and issuing mortgage backed securities (MBSs) to fund such purchase.[112] The MBSs could be in the form of debt obligations, trust certificates of beneficial interest, or other instruments.[113]

Later, to provide the legal framework for facilitating securitization of financial assets (and thus extend securitization to payment rights other than mortgages) of banks and financial institutions, Parliament enacted the SARFAESI Act.[114] Briefly stated, in a securitization under the SARFAESI Act,[115] a securitization company acquires debts or receivables of any bank.[116] The securitization company, then, sets up a trust for holding the acquired assets. To fund the acquisition, the trust offers (other than by offer to the public) security receipts to qualified

[112] The National Housing Bank (Amendment) Act, 2000, which came into force on 12 June 2000.

[113] Clause (ec) of section 14 of the National Housing Bank Act, 1987.

[114] The SARFAESI Act also provides for reconstruction of financial assets and enforcement of security interest by banks and financial institutions.

[115] Securitization, under clause (z) of section 2 of the SARFAESI Act, is widely defined to mean 'acquisition of financial assets by any securitisation company or reconstruction company from any originator, whether by raising of funds by such securitisation company or reconstruction company from qualified institutional buyers by issue of security receipts representing undivided interest in such financial assets or otherwise'.

[116] Section 5 of the SARFAESI Act. Securitization can be undertaken by a reconstruction company also. A securitization company or a reconstruction company is a company formed and registered under the Companies Act, 1956 for the purpose of securitization or reconstruction, respectively. As per section 3 of the SARFAESI Act, a securitization company or a reconstruction company has to compulsorily obtain a certificate of registration from the RBI to commence or carry on the business of securitization. However, as per sub-para (iii) of para 4 of the Securitisation Companies and Reconstruction Companies (Reserve Bank) Guidelines and Directions, 2003 issued by the RBI in exercise of its powers under the SARFAESI Act, 'any entity not registered with the Bank under section 3 of the Act may conduct the business of securitisation or asset reconstruction outside the purview of the Act'. The validity of this direction vis-à-vis section 3 of the SARFAESI Act has not been examined by any court under the principles of administrative law.

institutional buyers for subscription[117] and holds the acquired assets for the benefit of the security receipt holders.[118] A security receipt, therefore, means a receipt or other security, issued by a securitization company to qualified institutional buyers pursuant to a scheme, evidencing the purchase or acquisition by the holder thereof, of an undivided right, title, or interest in the financial asset involved in the securitization.[119] The originator of the financial assets, therefore, accesses the capital markets by undertaking a securitization transaction such that investment instruments in the form of security receipts are issued to investors. The essential function that securitization performs for the originator is that, based on the economics of the transaction, an originator is able to obtain lower cost funding for carrying on its business by divesting certain of its financial assets. Investors, on the other hand, receive returns on the security receipt that they hold as and when the financial asset is realized.

Over time, two important limitations came to be noticed in relation to securitization under the SARFAESI Act: (a) the security receipts could only be issued to a small class of investors other than by way of offer to the public, and (b) concerns were raised regarding the viability of such securities to be listed on the stock exchanges.[120] To overcome

[117] Qualified institutional buyers are a class of sophisticated investors and have been defined under section 2(u) of the SARFAESI Act to mean

> a financial institution, insurance company, bank, state financial corporation, state industrial development corporation, trustee or securitisation company or reconstruction company which has been granted a certificate of registration under sub-section (4) of section 3 or any asset management company making investment on behalf of mutual fund or a foreign institutional investor registered under the Securities and Exchange Board of India Act, 1992 or regulations made thereunder, or any other body corporate as may be specified by [SEBI].

[118] Section 7 of the SARFAESI Act read with para 8 of the Securitisation Companies and Reconstruction Companies (Reserve Bank) Guidelines and Directions, 2003.

[119] Clause (zg) of section 2 of the SARFAESI Act.

[120] See Ministry of Finance, Government of India, *Report of High Level Committee on Corporate Bonds and Securitization* (23 December 2005). The Ministry of Finance had set up this committee to look into the legal, regulatory, tax, and market design issues in the development of the corporate bond market in India.

these limitations and to provide further boost to securitization, the SCRA was amended in 2007 and a legal framework for the public issue and listing of securities issued in a securitization was set up.[121] SEBI was given the regulatory jurisdiction over such public issuance and listing.[122] Accordingly, SEBI framed the Securities and Exchange Board of India (Public Offer and Listing of Securitised Debt Instruments) Regulations, 2008 (or the Securitised Debt Instruments Regulations). The Securitised Debt Instruments Regulations provide for the manner in which, to fund a securitization,[123] the special purpose entity, in the form of a trust (referred to as the special purpose distinct entity[124]), can make a public offer of securities and/or seek listing of such securities. Therefore, 'securitized debt instrument' means any certificate or instrument, by whatever name called, of the nature referred to in sub-clause (ie) of clause (h) of section 2 of the SCRA issued by a special purpose distinct entity.[125]

Security receipts and securitized debt instruments are, therefore, kinds of securities that are issued under and in accordance with the SARFAESI Act and the Securitised Debt Instruments Regulations, respectively, pursuant to a securitization.

---

[121] Securities Contracts (Regulation) Amendment Act, 2007.

[122] Sub-section (1) of section 17A of the SCRA.

[123] Clause (r) of sub-regulation 1 of regulation 2 of the Securitised Debt Instruments Regulations defines 'securitisation' to mean 'acquisition of debt or receivables by any special purpose distinct entity from any originator or originators for the purpose of issuance of securitised debt instruments to investors based on such debt or receivables and such issuance'.

[124] Clause (u) of sub-regulation 1 of regulation 2 of the Securitised Debt Instruments Regulations defines 'special purpose distinct entity' to mean 'a trust which acquires debt or receivables out of funds mobilized by it by issuance of securitised debt instruments through one or more schemes, and includes any trust set up by the National Housing Bank under the National Housing Bank Act, 1987 (53 of 1987) or by the National Bank for Agriculture and Rural Development under the National Bank for Agriculture and Rural Development Act, 1981 (61 of 1981)'.

[125] Clause (s) of sub-regulation 1 of regulation 2 of the Securitised Debt Instruments Regulations.

'(ii) Government securities'

The SCRA defines 'government security' to mean a security created and issued by the central government or state government for the purpose of raising a public loan and having one of the forms specified in clause (2) of section 2 of the Public Debt Act, 1944 (or the Public Debt Act).[126] The form of government security specified in the Public Debt Act is a stock transferable by registration in the books of the RBI, a promissory note payable to order, a bearer bond payable to the bearer, and in any other form as may be prescribed.[127] The RBI issues government securities on behalf of the central or a state government generally to finance its fiscal deficit. Government securities should also be understood in the context of the Indian debt market. The debt market in India can be classified into two categories—the government securities market and the corporate bond market. While government securities fall under the definition of 'securities' by virtue of sub-clause (ii) of clause (h) of section 2 of the SCRA, corporate bonds fall within the definition of 'securities' by virtue of sub-clause (i) of clause (h) of section 2 of the SCRA. Government securities are the most dominant category of debt markets and form a major part of the market in terms of outstanding issues, market capitalization, and trading value. For example, in the year 2014–15, the government and the corporate sector collectively mobilized Rs 1,424,400 crore from the primary debt market. Of this, the central and the state governments had raised about 69 per cent through government securities, while the corporate sector had mobilized the balance through corporate bonds.[128]

It must be noted that over the years, the Public Debt Act began to be considered rigid and deficient for achieving the statutory purpose. Many of its provisions had ceased to be relevant in the present context. Parliament, therefore, enacted the Government Securities Act, 2006 (or the Government Securities Act) in place of the Public Debt Act. The Government Securities Act is applicable to government securities created and issued, whether before or after the commencement of the

---

[126] Clause (b) of section 2 of the SCRA.

[127] Sub-section (2) of section 2 of the Public Debt Act.

[128] National Stock Exchange of India Limited, *Indian Securities Market, A Review* (2015).

Government Securities Act, by the central government or a state government.[129] The form of government security specified in the Government Securities Act is wider than that in the Public Debt Act.[130] Therefore, the definition of 'government security' in the SCRA requires an amendment to the effect that reference to the Public Debt Act is substituted with reference to the Government Securities Act.

'(iia) such other instruments'

This is a residual clause giving power to the central government to declare any other instrument to be 'securities'. The need for such a clause is understandable given the dynamic nature of the securities market, which leads to the development of newer forms of investment instruments that ought to be regulated. Applying the *noscitur a sociis* rule,[131] the scope of 'such other instruments' would be limited to the types of instruments mentioned in the preceding sub-clauses. The central government has exercised its power under this sub-clause only once. On 1 August 2014, the central government declared onshore rupee bonds issued by multilateral institutions like the Asian Development Bank

[129] Sub-section (2) of section 1 of the Government Securities Act.

[130] As per section 3 of the Government Securities Act,

[a] Government security may, subject to such terms and conditions as may be specified, be in such forms as may be prescribed or in one of the following forms, namely: (i) a Government promissory note payable to or to the order of a certain person; or (ii) a bearer bond payable to bearer; or (iii) a stock; or (iv) a bond held in a bond ledger account. A 'stock' means a Government security,- (i) registered in the books of the [RBI] for which a stock certificate is issued; or (ii) held at the credit of the holder in the subsidiary general ledger account including the constituents subsidiary general ledger account maintained in the books of the [RBI], and transferable by registration in the books of the [RBI].

[131] The principle, *noscitur a sociis*, is a latin maxim stating a linguistic canon of interpretation of statutes. As per this principle, a statutory term is recognized by its associated words. The maxim *noscitur a sociis* states this contextual principle, whereby a word or phrase is not to be construed as if it stood alone but in the light of its surroundings. F.A.R. Bennion, *Bennion on Statutory Interpretation* (4th edn, LexisNexis 2002), at p. 1225. See also *Rohit Pulp and Paper Mills Limited v. Collector of Central Excise, Baroda*, AIR 1991 SC 754; *Prabhudas Damodar Kotecha v. Manhabala Jeram Damodar*, AIR 2013 SC 2959.

and the International Finance Corporation as securities under this sub-clause.[132]

'(iii) rights or interest in securities'

The expression 'rights or interest in securities' would mean rights or interest in any of the investment instruments preceding sub-clause (iii) of clause (h) of section 2 of the SCRA. Letters of allotment for preference shares issued by a listed company are, thus, securities because 'the letter of allotment that [the person] received created a right in him and his interest in the specific shares which had actually been allotted'.[133] Global depository receipts (GDRs)—an investment instrument issued outside India by a foreign depository on the footing of security issued by an Indian company and deposited with a domestic Indian custodian in India—also fall under this category.[134] Similarly, share warrants issued under the Companies Act would be securities since the share warrant entitles the bearer thereof to specified shares and the shares can be transferred by the delivery of the warrant.[135] Share warrants may also

[132] Notification No. SO 1978(E) dated 1 August 2014, issued by the Ministry of Finance, Government of India.

[133] *Alok Khetan v. Securities and Exchange Board of India*, 2007 SCC OnLine SAT 33.

[134] *Securities and Exchange Board of India v. Pan Asia Advisors Ltd.*, AIR 2015 SC 2782. In this judgment, Supreme Court held GDRs to be 'securities' upon a conjoint application of sub-clauses (i) and (iii) of clause (h) of section 2 of the SCRA. For detailed discussion on GDRs, see the section 'Raising Capital by Issue of Securities' in the later part of this chapter.

[135] Share warrant is a financial instrument issued by a company with respect to any of its fully paid-up shares stating that the bearer of the warrant is entitled to the shares specified therein. The instrument could provide, by coupons or otherwise, for the payment of the future dividends on the shares specified in the warrant. On the issue of a share warrant, the company strikes out of its register of members, the name of the member then entered therein as holding the shares specified in the warrant as if he had ceased to be a member, and enters in that register the particulars of the share warrant. The function of a share warrant is that it converts shares from being a registered security to a bearer security and allows for much smoother transferability. Shares can be transferred by delivery

be classified as securities under sub-clause (i) of clause (h) of section 2 of the SCRA.

Generally speaking, the expression would also mean rights or interest in *existing* securities as opposed to *future* securities. The application of this proposition by courts has been inconsistent in the context of warrants which are financial instruments that give the warrant holder a right without an obligation to convert it into securities of a company, generally equity shares.[136] Such instruments are different from share warrants issued by a company. Share warrants are issued with respect to any fully paid-up shares of the company. Warrants, on the contrary, are not issued against any fully paid-up shares of the company. Instead, they are issued as instruments that may be converted into equity shares at the option of the warrant holder.[137]

---

of the warrant and without the need to register the transfer of shares through an instrument of transfer. At the same time, the bearer of the share warrant is entitled, on surrendering the warrant to the company for cancellation, to have his name entered as a member in the register of members. Sections 114 and 115 of the Companies Act, 1956 contained the statutory provisions on share warrants, which have not been carried into the Companies Act, 2013. This could be due to the fact that share warrants have lost their utility over the years due to dematerialization of shares and an easier registration process upon transfer of shares. However, it is not clear whether share warrants can still be issued. On the one hand, the Companies Act, 2013 does not prohibit their issuance and contains some stray references to them (see section 57 of the Companies Act, 2013). But, on the other hand, share warrants could be issued under the Companies Act, 1956 if authorized by the articles of association of the company and with the previous approval of the central government. It is unlikely that the central government would now entertain an application for approval given that the statutory basis for such an application is lost. See *Commissioner of Income Tax v. Juliet M. Fateh*, [1979] 116 ITR 368 (Bom).

[136] *Commissioner of Income Tax, Bangalore v. Infosys Technologies Limited*, (2008) 2 SCC 272.

[137] See *Orissa Sponge Iron & Steel Limited and Ors v. Bhushan Energy Limited and Ors*, [2011] 167 Comp Cas 497 (Ori); *BNS Steel Trading Private Limited and Ors v. Orissa Sponge Iron and Steel Limited and Ors*, [2010] 154 Comp Cas 357 (Company Law Board).

In this regard, the Income Tax Appellate Tribunal (ITAT), while adjudicating upon the financial year in which perquisites on account of equity warrant certificates issued by a listed company arose to the assessee under an employee stock option plan, rejected the contention of the assessee that warrants were rights or interest in securities under sub-clause (iii) of clause (h) of section 2 of the SCRA. The ITAT held that the warrants merely made the assessee eligible to exercise an option to obtain shares in future. The warrants are not convertible into equity shares automatically and thus, are not securities under the SCRA.[138] On the contrary, SEBI has observed that warrants are securities under the SCRA.[139] The Securities and Exchange Board of India (Foreign Portfolio Investors) Regulations, 2014 (or the SEBI [FPI] Regulations) too recognize warrants as securities in which foreign portfolio investors (FPIs) can make investment.[140] Similarly, the RBI too considers warrants as securities for foreign investment purposes under the Foreign Exchange Management (Transfer or Issue of Security by a Person Resident outside India) Regulations, 2000.

Before we move to the next section, we examine some financial instruments that are issued or sold as investments and thus are securities but have not been expressly stated to be so in clause (h) of section 2 of the

---

[138] *Deputy Commissioner of Income Tax, New Delhi v. Vijay Gopal Jindal*, [2009] 120 ITD 859. See also *ACIT v. Tripti Sharma*, (2010) 1 ITR (Trib) 471.

[139] The observation of SEBI seems to suggest that warrants are securities under sub-clause (i) of clause (h) of section 2 of the SCRA. See Order dated 23 September 2010 of the Whole Time Member of SEBI in the matter of *MCX Stock Exchange Limited*, para 60. Whether warrants are securities, was not a fact in issue, and on appeal, this issue was not discussed by the High Court. See *MCX Stock Exchange Limited v. Securities and Exchange Board of India*, 2012 (114) BomLR 1002.

[140] Clause (a) of sub-regulation (1) of regulation 15 of SEBI (FPI) Regulations. Warrants are permitted to be issued in public issues, rights issues, preferential issues, and qualified institutions place under the Securities and Exchange Board of India (Issue of Capital and Disclosure Requirements) Regulations, 2009 (or the ICDR Regulations). However, it is not clear whether this SEBI regulation views warrants to be a separate class of securities or merely as a sweetener to equity shares and debentures.

SCRA. These are units issued by AIFs, InvITs, and REITs; and certain money market instruments like certificates of deposit and commercial paper.

Recall our earlier discussion on pooling of investment in the context of mutual funds and CISs.[141] Alternative investment funds, InvITs and REITs are species of pooled investment vehicles constituted to achieve specific commercial objectives that are not otherwise achievable under the existing framework of mutual funds and CISs. They are of recent origin and have evolved given the robust economic growth of India.

An AIF refers to any fund which is a privately pooled investment vehicle and collects funds from investors, whether Indian or foreign, for investing in accordance with a defined investment policy for the benefit of its investors. An AIF, as a vehicle for pooling of investment, is distinct from a mutual fund and a CIS in two ways: (a) unlike mutual funds and CISs, it is for sophisticated and high net-worth investors,[142] and (b), investments can be pooled only on a private placement basis.[143] The Securities and Exchange Board of India (Alternative Investment Funds) Regulations, 2012 (or the the SEBI [AIF] Regulations) regulate these funds.[144] The legal form in which these can be constituted is a fund established or incorporated in India in the form of a trust, a company, an LLP, or a body corporate. Mutual funds and CISs have been excluded from the ambit of AIFs.[145] Funds are raised from investors by issue of

---

[141] See the discussion "'(ib) units or any other instrument" and "(id) units or any other such instrument'" in the earlier part of this section.

[142] An AIF is not permitted to accept from an investor, an investment of a value less than Rs 1 crore. See, clause (c) of regulation 10 of the SEBI (AIF) Regulations.

[143] Clause (g) of regulation 10 of the SEBI (AIF) Regulations.

[144] However, SEBI regulated venture capital funds, one of the many types of alternative investment funds, existed since a much earlier stage under the Securities and Exchange Board of India (Venture Capital Funds) Regulations, 1996.

[145] Clause (b) of sub-regulation (1) of regulation 2 of the SEBI (AIF) Regulations defines an 'alternative investment fund' as follows:

> 'Alternative Investment Fund' means any fund established or incorporated in India in the form of a trust or a company or a limited liability partnership or a body corporate which,—

units, which means beneficial interest of the investors in the AIF or a scheme of the AIF and includes shares or partnership interests.[146]

It must be noted that these units issued by AIFs have not been expressly included as a class of securities in clause (h) of section 2 of the SCRA. However, if the units are in the form of shares issued by an AIF constituted as a public company, these will be considered as securities under sub-clause (i) of clause (h) of section 2 of the SCRA. It is not clear whether units issued by an AIF constituted in the form of a private company, an LLP, or a trust would fall within the definition of

---

(i) is a privately pooled investment vehicle which collects funds from investors, whether Indian or foreign, for investing it in accordance with a defined investment policy for the benefit of its investors; and

(ii) is not covered under the Securities and Exchange Board of India (Mutual Funds) Regulations, 1996, Securities and Exchange Board of India (Collective Investment Schemes) Regulations, 1999 or any other regulations of the Board to regulate fund management activities:

Provided that the following shall not be considered as Alternative Investment Fund for the purpose of these regulations,-

(i) family trusts set up for the benefit of 'relatives' as defined under Companies Act, 1956;

(ii) ESOP Trusts set up under the Securities and Exchange Board of India (Employee Stock Option Scheme and Employee Stock Purchase Scheme), Guidelines, 1999 or as permitted under Companies Act, 1956;

(iii) employee welfare trusts or gratuity trusts set up for the benefit of employees;

(iv) 'holding companies' within the meaning of Section 4 of the Companies Act, 1956;

(v) other special purpose vehicles not established by fund managers, including securitisation trusts, regulated under a specific regulatory framework;

(vi) funds managed by securitisation company or reconstruction company which is registered with the Reserve Bank of India under Section 3 of the Securitisation and Reconstruction of Financial Assets and Enforcement of Security Interest Act, 2002; and

(vii) any such pool of funds which is directly regulated by any other regulator in India;

[146] Clause (y) of sub-regulation (1) of regulation 2 of the SEBI (AIF) Regulations.

securities. The fact that the SEBI (AIF) Regulations permits listing of units of AIFs[147] gives an indication that these units may be termed as 'securities' since instruments are listed on stock exchanges generally if they are 'securities'.[148]

An InvIT is a pooled investment vehicle for investing in infrastructure projects such as roads and bridges, ports, urban public transport, electricity projects, oil pipelines, waste management projects, and telecommunication projects. The legal form of InvIT is a trust under the Indian Trusts Act, 1882 and it is regulated under the Securities and Exchange Board of India (Infrastructure Investment Trusts) Regulations, 2014. The InvIT invites subscription from investors by issuing units—beneficial interest of the InvIT—which are transferable investment instruments. Similar to an InvIT is a REIT, with the difference being that a REIT is a pooled investment vehicle for investing in real estate. In both InvIT and REIT, investors benefit by having an additional investment option and a regular income stream, and the infrastructure operators and real estate owners benefit by accessing wider and long-term finance and refinance, freeing up of current capital for reinvestment into new projects and reducing bank loan exposure. In structure and operation, InvIT and REIT are similar to a mutual fund. Units issued by InvIT and REIT must therefore fall within the inclusive definition of securities under clause (h) of section 2 of the SCRA. Similar to an AIF, the fact that SEBI regulations on InvIT and REIT permit listing of the units also indicates that the units are securities.

Money market instruments are investment instruments issued and traded in the money market—a market for trading in short-term financial instruments that are close substitutes of money. We examine the nature of money market a little later.[149] Some money market instruments like certificates of deposit and commercial papers have the characteristic of securities. Certificate of deposit is an investment instrument issued in dematerialized form or as a promissory note by banks and other eligible financial institutions against funds deposited with them for a specified

---

[147] Regulation 14 of the SEBI (AIF) Regulations.

[148] Section 21 of the SCRA.

[149] See the section 'Securities Market' in the later part of this chapter.

time period. Commercial paper is an unsecured borrowing issued as an investment instrument in dematerialized form or as a promissory note by eligible companies and financial institutions. To the extent these money market instruments are issued by companies, they would constitute debenture and thus 'securities' under sub-clause (i) of clause (h) of section 2 of the SCRA.[150] Otherwise, the legislative intention appears to be to not bring them under the ambit of 'securities' and regulate them under the SCRA because the RBI regulates them under Chapter IIID of the Reserve Bank of India Act, 1934. Taking note of this scenario, at least the Companies Act exempts these investment instruments from regulation by it.[151]

Form of Securities

Traditionally, securities were issued as paper-based instruments and held by the investor directly. As the volume of trading in securities grew on the stock exchanges, physical paper began causing problems such as risk of loss, theft, and mutilation of paper certificates. Settlement of trade became a time-consuming process as huge bundles of paper had to pass from one broker to another via the clearing house. At times, the exchanges would be closed for a day or two to complete the settlement work. There was, thus, an urgent need to develop a system that would reduce the problems of paper-based settlement.[152] Dematerialization was introduced to solve this problem. Dematerialization is the process

---

[150] See the earlier analysis of shares and debentures under this section. However, the Companies (Amendment) Bill, 2016, introduced in the lower house of the Parliament on 16 March 2016, seeks to amend the definition of 'debenture' and exclude money market instruments from its scope.

[151] Rule 18 of Companies (Share Capital and Debentures) Rules, 2014 lays down rules for the issue of debentures by companies. Sub-rule (9) of this rule states that 'Nothing contained in this rule shall apply to any amount received by a company against issue of commercial paper or any other similar instrument issued in accordance with the guidelines or regulations or notification issued by the Reserve Bank of India.'

[152] M.T. Raju and Prabhakar R. Patil, 'Dematerialisation: A Silent Revolution in the Indian Capital Market' (2001) *Securities and Exchange Board of India Working Paper Series No. 4*, at paragraph 2.1.

of converting securities held in physical form to electronic form or, upon subscription of securities, receiving them directly in electronic form. This new process required statutory support since the rules of traditional company law and property law generally require the use of paper instruments, which had to be first disapplied by a statute.[153] Accordingly, the Depositories Act, 1996 was enacted and amendments were made to the Companies Act, 1956. It must be noted that dematerialization does not fundamentally alter the legal nature of securities since securities are intangible property, both in physical form and dematerialized form.[154] The instrument, whether in physical or electronic form, merely represents the securities and does not constitute the securities. Loss or destruction of the instrument does not mean that the securities have ceased to exist. However, dematerialization does affect the legal rights and entitlements over the dematerialized securities. To understand this, it would be useful first to understand how and by whom the process of dematerialization is carried out under the Depositories Act.

Depositories carry out dematerialization. They are constituted as companies registered under the Companies Act[155] and have to obtain a certificate of registration from SEBI under the Securities and Exchange Board of India (Depositories and Participants) Regulations, 1996 to deal in securities.[156] Currently, there are two depositories in India. The National Securities Depository Limited was the first to be set up, followed by the Central Depository Services (India) Limited. Depositories function through depository participants who are its agents.[157] A security holder, through the depository participant, can enter into an agreement with the depository to maintain a depository account.[158] The security holder can then surrender the certificate of security to the company, which had issued the security. The company then cancels the security certificate and substitutes in its records the name of the depository as a registered owner in respect of that security and informs the depository

---

[153] Benjamin (n. 35), at p. 25.
[154] Benjamin (n. 35), at p. 25.
[155] Clause (e) of sub-section (1) of section 2 of the Depositories Act.
[156] Sub-section (1A) of section 12 of the SEBI Act.
[157] Sub-section (1) of section 4 of the Depositories Act.
[158] Section 5 of the Depositories Act.

accordingly. The depository then enters the name of the person who had surrendered the security certificate in its records as the beneficial owner.[159] Depositories also carry out dematerialization at the stage of subscription of securities itself. A person who has a depository account and has subscribed to securities has the option to either receive the security certificates or hold the securities with the depository.[160] If the person opts to hold a security with the depository, the entity issuing the securities intimates the depository the details of allotment of the security, and on receipt of the information, the depository enters in its records the name of the allottee as the beneficial owner of that security.[161] It must be noted that dematerialization is not an irreversible action. The beneficial owner has the option to opt out in respect of any dematerialized security.[162]

Depositories also carry out other necessary activities incidental to dematerialization, such as registering the transfer of securities,[163] recording the creation of pledge or hypothecation of securities,[164] and furnishing of information to the company that had issued the securities.[165]

In terms of legal characterization of the securities, the depository is the registered owner of the securities for the purposes of effecting the transfer of ownership of the securities on behalf of a beneficial owner. However, this is the only limited legal right that the depository has over the securities. The depository does not have any voting rights or any other rights in respect of the securities held by it. It is the beneficial owner who is entitled to all the rights and benefits and is subject to all the liabilities in respect of his securities held by the depository.[166] For this, every depository must maintain a register and an index of beneficial owners, and this register is deemed to be the register of members, debenture holders, and any other security holders of the company whose securities have been dematerialized.[167]

---

[159] Section 6 of the Depositories Act.

[160] Sub-section (1) of section 8 of the Depositories Act.

[161] Sub-section (2) of section 8 of the Depositories Act.

[162] Section 14 of the Depositories Act.

[163] Section 7 of the Depositories Act.

[164] Section 12 of the Depositories Act.

[165] Section 13 of the Depositories Act.

[166] Section 10 of the Depositories Act.

[167] Section 11 of the Depositories Act and section 88 of the Companies Act.

Corporate Securities

From a review of the types of securities, it is evident that a company intending to finance its business through issuance of securities would raise capital by issuing shares and debentures (or a combination of the two). Issue of security receipts and securitized debt instruments through the process of securitization are also methods of raising capital, but they involve divestment of asset. Derivatives are not securities for raising finance. Pooling investments, by issuance of units by mutual funds and CISs, are again not for utilizing it to engage in ordinary business activities of production of goods or services. To the extent that pooled investments are invested into securities by the managers, such investments are utilized by the companies intending to finance their business by issuing securities. Government securities are issued by the central and state governments, and thus fall outside the purview of corporate finance. Therefore, the principal forms of securities that we examine and study in this book are shares and debentures.

As stated earlier, in terms of legal theory, shares and debentures are the two primary types of corporate securities as well as the two classes in which other corporate securities fall. It is axiomatic that a company limited by shares must issue some shares having a nominal value constituting its share capital. In theory, shares can have different nominal values (and hence different liability), though this is rarely the case in practice. Beyond this, the Companies Act prevents share capital to be moulded into different kinds.

Share capital of a public company can only comprise two kinds: equity shares and preference shares; the three rights and entitlements of shares (dividend, voting, and return on capital) exist in different variants in them. Preference shares are that part of the issued share capital of the company which carry a preferential right to dividend at a fixed amount or rate, and a preferential right to the repayment of the amount of share capital paid-up in the case of winding up of the company or repayment of capital. Equity shares are shares, which are not preference shares. Though both equity shareholders and preference shareholders are members of the company, a crucial difference between the two is that preference shares carry limited voting rights. Equity shareholders have a right to vote on every resolution placed before the company.[168] Due to this crucial difference, company law rules on capital maintenance are relaxed for preference shares. A company limited by shares may, if so authorized by its articles of association, issue redeemable preference shares in the manner provided under section 55 of the Companies Act.

Other than the restriction on kinds of share capital, rights attached to equity shares, preference shares, and debentures are a matter of freedom of contract and not of the Companies Act. Depending on the memorandum and articles of association of the company, as well as on the terms of issue, equity shares, preference shares, and debentures can be of different types. Equity shares can be further classified into equity shares with voting rights; and equity shares with differential rights as to dividend, voting, or otherwise. However, a company whose equity shares are listed on a recognized stock exchange is prohibited from issuing shares in any manner, which may confer on any person, superior

---

[168] Section 47 of the Companies Act on 'Voting Rights' reads:

(1) Subject to the provisions of section 43 and sub-section (2) of section 50,—

    (a) every member of a company limited by shares and holding equity share capital therein, shall have a right to vote on every resolution placed before the company; and

    (b) his voting right on a poll shall be in proportion to his share in the paid-up equity share capital of the company.

(2) Every member of a company limited by shares and holding any preference share capital therein shall, in respect of such capital, have a right to vote only on resolutions placed before the company which directly affect the rights attached to his preference shares and, any resolution for the winding up of the company or for the repayment or reduction of its equity or preference share capital and his voting right on a poll shall be in proportion to his share in the paid-up preference share capital of the company:

Provided that the proportion of the voting rights of equity shareholders to the voting rights of the preference shareholders shall be in the same proportion as the paid-up capital in respect of the equity shares bears to the paid-up capital in respect of the preference shares:

Provided further that where the dividend in respect of a class of preference shares has not been paid for a period of two years or more, such class of preference shareholders shall have a right to vote on all the resolutions placed before the company.

rights as to voting or dividend vis-à-vis the rights on equity shares that are already listed.[169]

Preference shares, being part of the company's share capital, are subject to the same rules regarding dividend as equity shares—the principle being that a company can pay dividend only out of its profits. However, due to absence of profit or inadequate profit in a financial year, the terms of issue of the preference shares may provide that the missed dividend shall be made up in subsequent years. Alternatively, it may be that once the dividend is missed, it is lost for all time. In other words, preference shares may be either cumulative or non-cumulative.[170] Preference shares may also be, partly, fully, optionally, or mandatorily, convertible into equity shares, thereby making them convertible or non-convertible preference shares. Preference shares may be non-participating or participating, in respect of either or both dividend and capital. A participating preference share means that it carries, in addition to its customary preferential rights, a right to share in distribution of residual or surplus profits after payment of their preference dividend; and, in respect of capital, it has a right to participate along with equity share capital, in any surplus which may remain after the entire capital has been repaid.

As far as debentures are concerned, the board of directors of a company has the power to borrow money and issue debentures, which it may decide to undertake on several occasions. When several debentures are issued in succession, it forms a series and each debenture of the series confers like rights. A series of debentures may be unsecured or secured by way of charge (that includes mortgage under company law), fixed or floating, and on the properties and assets of the company. It is uncommon for companies to issue unsecured debentures due to their lack of appeal among investors and because such debentures may constitute a 'deposit', thereby attracting compliance with Chapter V of the Companies Act and the Companies (Acceptance of Deposits) Rules,

---

[169] Sub-regulation (3) of regulation 41 of Securities and Exchange Board of India (Listing Obligations and Disclosure Requirements) Regulations, 2015 (or the LODR Regulations).

[170] Gower (n. 16), at p. 413.

2014.[171] Like preference shares, debentures may also be partly, fully, optionally, or mandatorily, convertible into equity shares of the company.

It is evident that a company can issue various types of equity shares, preference shares, and debentures to apportion the elements of risk, income, and control involved in the enterprise.[172] However, too many types of securities can lead to a complex capital structure and, at times, merge the conceptual distinction between the different corporate securities. In practice, therefore, it is uncommon for companies to have more than one or two types of equity shares and debentures. Preference shares are uncommon for a different reason. A holder of preference shares, though a member of the company, has very limited rights in the company. It is the holder of the majority of equity shares that is commonly referred to as the controlling shareholder of a company. Preference shares seem more like debentures or hybrid securities.[173] In fact, preference shares, which are not convertible into equity shares, are considered to be borrowings under the foreign investment laws of India.[174]

Free Transferability of Corporate Securities

A company is the most suitable form of business organization if a business is to be organized in a manner that the management and ownership

[171] Clause (c) of sub-rule (1) of rule 2 of Companies (Acceptance of Deposits) Rules, 2014 defines deposit to include 'any receipt of money by way of deposit or loan or in any other form by a company, but does not include—' and then excludes several types of amount received by a company that are pursuant to ordinary business activities or does not affect the public at large.

[172] Hastings Lyon, *Corporation Finance* (Houghton Mifflin Company 1912), at p. 2.

[173] However, in terms of legal characterization, they continue to be different. Debentures form part of the loan capital of the company and preference shares form part of the share capital of the company. See *Commissioner of Income Tax v. Enam Securities (P) Ltd.,* [2012] 345 ITR 64 (Bom); *Hindustan Gas and Industries Limited v. Commissioner of Income Tax, West Bengal,* [1979] 117 ITR 549 (Cal).

[174] The Foreign Exchange Management (Borrowing or Lending in Foreign Exchange) Regulations, 2000 framed by the RBI under FEMA.

are distinct and separate, and ownership can change hands without the legal and practical limitations of other business organizations such as partnerships. As we see in the next chapter, this has been one of the reasons for partnerships to evolve into the modern company. The Companies Act, therefore, provides that shares and debentures shall be movable property transferable in the manner provided in the articles of association of the company.[175] A private company, through its articles of association, should provide some restriction on the right to transfer its shares to comply with the statutory definition of what denotes a private company. This restriction is desirable if such a company is to retain its character of a private business organization.[176] However, the articles of association of a public company cannot provide such a restriction, and shares and debentures of a public company are freely transferable.[177] However, whether shareholders can *inter se* restrict transferability of shares of a public company through private contracts has not been satisfactorily settled by judicial decisions, and this issue merits some discussion.

It is quite common for shareholders of a public company to enter into agreements in respect of transfer of their shares. The agreements may be either among two or more shareholders (shareholders' agreements) or among shareholders and third parties. Sometimes the company too is a party to such agreements. In these agreements, restrictions on transfer of shares are generally shaped as 'right of first refusal' and 'right of first offer' clauses (also referred to as 'right of pre-emption' clauses) which are means to ensure that other shareholders (or third parties) will have an opportunity to purchase any shares that any of the shareholders desire to sell.[178] A 'right of first refusal' requires a shareholder intending to sell its shares to present an offer made by a potential third-party purchaser that it proposes to accept, to the other shareholders, who then have an opportunity to purchase the shares at the same price and terms.[179] A

---

[175]   Section 44 of the Companies Act.

[176]   Gower (n. 16), at p. 107.

[177]   Sub-section (2) of section 58 of the Companies Act.

[178]   The Corporation Law Committee of the Association of the Bar of the City of New York, 'The Enforceability and Effectiveness of Typical Shareholders Agreement Provisions' (2010) 65 The Business Lawyer 1153, at p. 1178.

[179]   Corporation Law Committee (n. 178).

'right of first offer' requires the selling shareholder to first solicit offers from the other shareholders, and if the selling shareholder prefers to seek better offers from third parties, they may do so. But they may not sell the shares to a third party at a price lower or on other terms that are less favourable to the selling shareholder than those offered by the other shareholders.[180]

The propositions of law that have emerged through judicial decisions on the enforceability of contractual restrictions on the transfer of shares of public companies are: (a) if clauses in the articles of association provide for such a restriction, such clauses will be void, and (b) if clauses in agreements involving shareholders provide for such a restriction, such clauses will be void as against the contracting parties.[181] While the first proposition is justified under company law, the second proposition is not.

One of the grounds[182] on which the second proposition is based is the (erstwhile) sub-section (2) of section 111A of the Companies Act, 1956 that provides for free transferability of shares of a public company. Courts have held that the principle of free transferability must be given a broad interpretation; restriction, if any, on free transferability is solely

[180]   Corporation Law Committee (n. 178).

[181]   *Mafatlal Industries Ltd. v. Gujarat Gas Co. Ltd. and Ors*, [1999] 97 Comp Cas 301 (Guj); *Smt. Pushpa Katoch v. Manu Maharani Hotels Limited and Ors*, [2006] 131 Comp Cas 42 (Del); *Jer Rutton Kavasmanek and Anr v. Gharda Chemicals Limited and Ors*, (2011) 113 BomLR 2487.

[182]   The second proposition is also based, to a large extent, on the application of the decision of the Supreme Court of India in *V.B. Rangaraj v. V.B. Gopalakrishnan*, (1992) 1 SCC 160 wherein in the context of a private company, it was held that the only restriction on the transfer of the shares of a company is as laid down in its articles of association and a restriction which is not specified in the articles of association is not binding either on the company or on the shareholders. It is submitted that the *Rangaraj* case has not laid down the law correctly. While a complete discussion and critique of the *Rangaraj* case is not within the scope of this book, suffice to say that K.S. Radhakrishnan J. in *Vodafone International Holdings B.V. v. Union of India and Anr*, (2012) 6 SCC 613, observed, in obiter, that the court does not subscribe to the view taken by the Supreme Court in the *Rangaraj* case. For a critique of the *Rangaraj* case, see V. Niranjan and Umakanth Varottil, 'Enforceability of Contractual Restrictions on the Transfer of Shares' (2012) 5 Supreme Court Cases (Journal), at p. 1.

a legislative function.[183] Such a view ignores an important legal incident of shares as property, namely the power to use the property for one's own benefit and the right to create fetters on the transferability of one's property through the freedom of contract. The power to use one's property conventionally included creation of interests in the property in favour of third parties.[184] The legislature seems to have put to rest the controversy around the second proposition by making a provision under the new Companies Act. Now securities or other interest of any member in a public company is freely transferable, provided that any contract or arrangement between two or more persons in respect of the transfer of securities is enforceable as a contract.[185]

Free and full transferability of securities of a public company must be distinguished from free tradability and the freedom to acquire securities. Securities generally become freely tradable when they enter the securities market such as on the stock exchange through the process of listing. Even then, trading of securities is subject to laws governing the securities market. Further, the Securities and Exchange Board of India (Substantial Acquisition of Shares and Takeovers) Regulations, 2011, restrict and regulate the freedom to acquire listed shares to protect the interests of the

[183] *Western Maharashtra Development Corporation Ltd. v. Bajaj Auto Limited*, [2010] 154 Comp Cas 593 (Bom).

[184] The Bombay High Court in *Messer Holdings Limited v. Shyam Madanmohan Ruia and Ors*, (2010) 112 BomLR 4005 has given effect to contractual restrictions on the transfer of shares by partly approaching this issue from the perspective of property rights and the freedom of contract. The court held that section 111A of the Companies Act, 1956

> is a provision mandating the Board of Directors of the company to transfer shares in the name of the transferee, subject to stipulations in Section 111A of the Act. The expression 'freely transferable' therein is in the context of the mandate against the Board of Directors to register the transfer of specified shares of the members in the name of the transferee, unless there is not sufficient cause for doing so. The said provision cannot be construed to mean that it also intends to take away the right of the shareholder to enter into consensual arrangement/agreement with the purchaser of their specified shares.

This decision of the Bombay High Court is currently on appeal before the Supreme Court of India.

[185] Sub-section (2) of section 58 of the Companies Act.

shareholders of a publicly listed company. Free transferability of corporate securities must also be distinguished from a company's involvement in the transfer of its securities. A company's involvement in the transfer of its securities arises from the simple fact that corporate securities are registered securities—the name of the holder of the securities is recorded in a register and transfer of securities involves an amendment of the register.[186] The transferor and transferee of corporate securities must execute a proper instrument of transfer and deliver it to the company. The company may refuse to register the transfer of its securities if it is not in accordance with prescribed norms like stamping of the instrument, details of the parties, etc.[187]

Raising Capital by Issue of Securities

To understand raising of capital through issue of securities, we enquire into two areas of company law. First, which organ of a company has the power to issue securities, and second, how and to whom must a company issue the securities. The power to issue securities, and whether to issue securities at all, generally lies with the board of directors of a company. The articles of association of most companies provide that

> the shares in the capital of the company shall be under the control of the Directors who may issue, allot or otherwise dispose of the same or any of them to such persons, in such proportion and on such terms and conditions and either at a premium or at par and at such time as they may from time to time think fit.[188]

Similarly, the power to issue debentures is with the board of directors.[189]

---

[186] Section 88 of the Companies Act.

[187] See sections 56 and 58 of the Companies Act. A company's involvement is not necessary in the transfer of securities between persons both of whose names are entered as holders of beneficial interest in the records of a depository. In these cases, the transferor and transferee must comply with the Depositories Act, and the rules and regulations framed thereunder.

[188] Article 1 of the 'Articles of Association of a Company Limited by Shares' as contained in Table F of Schedule I to the Companies Act.

[189] Clause (c) of sub-section (3) of section 179 of the Companies Act.

However, when it comes to the choice of how and to whom must the company issue securities, the Companies Act and securities laws impose significant restrictions on the power of the board of directors to prevent abuse of power and to protect shareholders, creditors, and the investing public. Some of these restrictions have a doctrinal basis while others owe their origin to specific instances of misuse of the company form to raise large-scale capital for wrongful purposes. Together these restrictions determine the different methods of issuing corporate securities that we commonly come across.

The principal restriction is that where, at any time, a company having a share capital proposes to increase its subscribed capital by the issue of further shares, such shares must be offered to persons who, at the date of the offer, are holders of equity shares of the company.[190] The offer must be made in proportion, as nearly as circumstances admit, to the paid-up share capital on the equity shares by sending a letter of offer. The offer must be made by notice specifying the number of shares offered and limiting a time not being less than 15 days and not exceeding 30 days from the date of the offer within which the offer, if not accepted, shall be deemed to have been declined. Further, unless the articles of association of the company otherwise provides, the offer shall be deemed to include a right exercisable by the person concerned to renounce the shares offered to him or any of them in favour of any other person. After the expiry of the time specified in the notice, or on receipt of earlier intimation from the person to whom such notice is given that he declines to accept the shares offered, the board of directors can dispose of the shares on offer in such manner which is not disadvantageous to the shareholders and the company. Such an issuance of shares is referred to as a rights issue.[191]

---

[190] Clause (a) of sub-section (1) of section 62 of the Companies Act. This restriction is not applicable to the increase of the subscribed capital of a company caused by the exercise of an option as a term attached to the debentures issued or loan raised by the company to convert such debentures or loans into shares in the company. However, the terms of issue of such debentures or loans containing such an option must have been approved before the issue of such debentures or the raising of the loan by a special resolution passed by the company in general meeting. See sub-section (3) of section 62 of the Companies Act.

[191] *In Re: Mafatlal Industries Limited*, [1996] 87 Comp Cas 705 (Guj); *Navin Jindal v. Assistant Commissioner of Income Tax*, [2010] 320 ITR 708 (SC).

Rights issue is based on the doctrine of pre-emptive right of the equity shareholders to subscribe to new shares. As per this doctrine, equity shareholders, as the ultimate co-proprietors (in the commercial sense) of the business, must have proper protection against a dilution, without their consent, of their existing interests in the company's assets and earnings, and of their proportionate voting control.[192] The doctrine of pre-emptive right is not applicable to the issue of debentures, and the Companies Act does not obligate the company to offer the debentures to the existing shareholders or the debenture holders.[193] Further, this pre-emptive right of the equity shareholders is not absolute. Depending upon the scale of capital being raised or if the company seeks to achieve some other objective such as providing incentives to its employees, the company may choose to issue shares to some other person. However, as we see in the succeeding paragraphs, in each such case, the shareholders must be adequately informed and their consent and authority obtained.

Another method of issuing further shares is to offer them to the employees under an employees' stock option scheme.[194] It means that the directors, officers, or employees of a company, or of its holding company or subsidiary company, have the benefit or right to purchase, or to subscribe for, the shares of the company at a future date at a pre-determined price.[195] The stock option takes effect through stages. The company formulates a scheme pursuant to which it grants options to the employees. After the options have been granted, there is a vesting period at the end of which the option vests with the employee. Thereafter, there is an exercise period during which the employee can exercise vested options and receive the shares. Else, the vested option lapses. The purpose of

[192] Henry S. Drinker, Jr, 'The Preemptive Right of Shareholders to Subscribe to New Shares' (1930) 43 Harvard Law Review 586, at p. 586.

[193] The obligation may however arise on account of express provision to this effect in the articles of association or in contracts entered into by the company. See *Commissioner of Income Tax v. Abhinandan Investment Limited*, [2015] 376 ITR 153 (Del).

[194] Clause (b) of sub-section (1) of section 62 of the Companies Act and rule 12 of the Companies (Share Capital and Debentures) Rules, 2014.

[195] Clause (37) of section 2 of the Companies Act.

issue of shares through employees' stock option is not to raise capital for business and operations, but to remunerate the employees and give them a stake in the prospects of the company.

Given the scope for misuse and the fact that share issuance leads to dilution of existing shareholding, there are several limitations to the exercise of this power.[196] The principal limitations are that company law excludes controlling shareholders and their relatives, and directors having, directly or indirectly, substantial equity shareholding from the scope of 'employees'. Shareholders must have approved the issue of the employees' stock option scheme by passing a special resolution, and the explanatory statement to the notice for passing the special resolution must contain detailed information about the scheme. If the company's shares are listed on a stock exchange, it must also comply with the Securities and Exchange Board of India (Share Based Employee Benefits) Regulations, 2014.

Other than the above, a company may issue further shares to any persons, either for cash or for a consideration other than cash, if it is authorized by a special resolution and if the price of such shares is determined by the valuation report of a registered valuer.[197] Under this residual category are other methods of issue of shares, namely sweat equity shares, bonus issue, private placement (or preferential offer) of shares, and public offer of shares, each of which are also subject to separate rules of their own.

Sweat equity shares means 'equity shares as are issued by a company to its directors or employees at a discount or for consideration, other than cash, for providing their know-how or making available rights in the nature of intellectual property rights or value additions, by whatever name called'.[198]

Bonus issue is the issue of fully paid shares by a company to its members by capitalizing its profits, meaning that the profit, instead of being

---

[196] See rule 12 of the Companies (Share Capital and Debentures) Rules, 2014.

[197] Clause (c) of sub-section (1) of section 62 of the Companies Act.

[198] Clause (88) of section 2 of the Companies Act. Section 54 of the Companies Act and rule 8 of the Companies (Share Capital and Debentures) Rules, 2014 regulate the manner of issue of sweat equity shares.

distributed as dividend, is turned into shares.[199] It must not be confused with rights issue as it is not a method of raising new capital and members of the company do not pay for the bonus shares. The High Court of Karnataka in *In Re: Astra Zeneca Pharma Limited*,[200] explaining bonus issue, observed:

> When a company prospers and earns profits it may do one of two things with the profits. It may either distribute the profits by way of dividend among the shareholders or accumulate them. Ordinarily, these undistributed profits are employed in the business either in acquisition of fixed assets or as working capital and really represent an increase in the capital employed in the business. When these increase to a considerable extent, the issued capital of the company ceases to bear a true relation to the real capital employed in the business. The company may, in such a case, decide to bring its issued capital into a true relationship with the capital actually employed in the business and may for that purpose capitalise its accumulated profits and issue fully paid-up shares.

Consequently, an issue of bonus shares is an issue for a consideration other than cash, and a copy of the resolution passed in the general meeting authorizing the issue of such shares must be delivered to the registrar of companies along with the return of allotment.[201] For the company, the advantage of a bonus issue is that it pays undistributed profits to the shareholders not in cash but in the form of bonus shares and retains the money for its business and operations.[202]

The other two methods—private placement (or preferential offer) and public offer—are methods of issue of all corporate securities, and

---

[199] *Khoday Distilleries Limited* v. *Commissioner of Income Tax*, [2008] 307 ITR 312 (SC); *Commissioner of Income Tax* v. *General Insurance Corporation*, [2006] 286 ITR 232 (SC); *Hunsur Plywood Works Limited* v. *Commissioner of Income Tax*, [1998] 229 ITR 112 (SC); *Escorts Farms (Ramgarh) Limited* v. *Commissioner of Income Tax*, [1996] 222 ITR 509 (SC). Section 63 of the Companies Act governs bonus issues.

[200] (2008) 2 Comp LJ 72 (Kar).

[201] Sub-rule (6) of rule 12 of the Companies (Prospectus and Allotment of Securities) Rules, 2014.

[202] *Escorts Farms (Ramgarh) Limited*, v. *Commissioner of Income Tax*, [1996] 222 ITR 509 (SC).

not just shares. We examine these methods in detail in Chapter 3 of this volume. At this stage, it will suffice to say that private placement is an issue of securities to a select group of persons, and a public offer is issue of securities to the public at large through the issue of a prospectus. Where the private placement is of equity shares or other securities convertible into or exchangeable with equity shares, the method of issue is also called a preferential offer and it attracts additional rules.[203] Else, conceptually there is no other difference between private placement and preferential offer.[204] For the issue of shares, private placement and public issue methods are in addition to what we discussed above; however, for issue of debentures, the Companies Act provides only these two methods.[205] This is not to say that debentures cannot be issued on a rights basis or bonus issue of debentures cannot be made. These can be done to fulfil a company's contractual obligations and may require the sanction of the National Company Law Tribunal.[206]

The legal character of these methods is unaffected by whether a company issues securities to an Indian or foreign investor. Foreign investors can participate in these securities offerings on an equal footing with Indian investors. However, at times, companies may desire to raise capital by issue of securities only to foreign investors in the foreign securities market so as to access a larger pool of investible capital as opposed to being limited by the capacity of the Indian securities market. For this, there are two mechanisms—global depository receipts (GDRs) and foreign currency convertible bonds (FCCBs).

A GDR is an investment instrument issued outside India by a foreign depository on the footing of securities issued by an Indian company and deposited with a domestic custodian in India.[207] Here an Indian

---

[203] Rule 13 of the Companies (Share Capital and Debentures) Rules.

[204] For details, see the section titled 'Prospectus' in Chapter 3 of this volume.

[205] Section 23 of the Companies Act does contemplate rights issue and bonus issue of debentures in accordance with the provisions of the Act. However, provisions of the Companies Act on rights issue and bonus issue are restricted in their application to only shares.

[206] See *In Re: Astra Zeneca Pharma Limited*, (2008) 2 Comp LJ 72 (Kar) and section 230 of the Companies Act.

[207] This is less of a definition and more of a description of what GDRs are. For definitions, see clause (44) of section 2 of the Companies Act and clause (a)

company issues its securities to a foreign depository through any of the methods that we discussed earlier and deposits them with a domestic custodian, who is an agent of the foreign depository. The foreign depository then issues depository receipts to foreign investors by way of a public offering, private placement, or in any other manner as is permissible in the foreign securities market. Proceeds of the subscription of the depository receipts go to the Indian company. GDRs may also be issued on the back of existing Indian securities. In this exercise, the Indian company gets holders of existing securities to sell them to the foreign depository, who in turn issues depository receipts to the foreign investors. Proceeds of the subscription of the depository receipts go the security holders who had sold their securities to the foreign depository. Lastly, issue of depository receipts may be unsponsored. This method is similar to the previous method barring the fact that there is no formal arrangement between the Indian company and the foreign depository. An existing securities holder typically, without involving the Indian company, transfers the securities to the foreign depository, who in turn issues depository receipts to the foreign investors.

Section 41 of the Companies Act, the Companies (Issue of Global Depository Receipts) Rules, 2014, and the Depository Receipts Scheme, 2014 framed by the central government constitute the principal legal framework for issue of GDRs. Issue of GDRs being a capital account transaction in terms of the Foreign Exchange Management Act, 1999 (or FEMA),[208] this act and regulations framed under it by the RBI, chiefly the Foreign Exchange Management (Transfer or Issue of Security by a Person Resident Outside India) Regulations, 2000 are also applicable.

Global Depository Receipts must not be confused with Indian Depository Receipts (IDRs). Conceptually identical to GDRs, issuance

---

of sub-paragraph (1) of paragraph 2 of the [Central Government] Depository Receipts Scheme, 2014. See also *Securities and Exchange Board of India v. Pan Asia Advisors Ltd.*, AIR 2015 SC 2782.

[208] Clause (e) of section 2 of the FEMA defines a capital account transaction to mean 'a transaction which alters the assets or liabilities, including contingent liabilities, outside India of persons resident in India or assets or liabilities in India of persons resident outside India, and includes transactions referred to in sub-section (3) of section 6'.

of IDRs is a method by which foreign companies can access the Indian securities market exclusively. IDRs are, therefore, investment instruments in the form of a depository receipt created by a domestic depository in India and authorized by a company incorporated outside India making an issue of such depository receipts. Sections 390 and 391 of the Companies Act; rule 13 of the Companies (Registration of Foreign Companies) Rules, 2014; and the Securities and Exchange Board of India (Issue of Capital and Disclosure Requirements) Regulations, 2009 (or the ICDR Regulations) principally govern the issue of IDRs.

Foreign currency convertible bonds refer to bonds issued by Indian companies and subscribed by non-residents, and convertible into ordinary shares of the issuing company in any manner, either in whole, or in part. These bonds are denominated in foreign currency, which means that both the principal and interest is payable in foreign currency. Here 'bonds' is a misnomer because quite often the FCCBs are unsecured debentures instead of secured ones. Indian companies can issue FCCBs in the foreign securities market under the Central Government Issue of Foreign Currency Convertible Bonds and Ordinary Shares (Through Depository Receipt Mechanism) Scheme, 1993.[209] Companies are also permitted to issue FCCBs that, instead of being convertible into ordinary shares of the issuing company, are exchangeable into ordinary shares of another company under the Central Government Foreign Currency Exchangeable Bonds Scheme, 2008. Similar to GDRs, FCCBs too are a capital account transaction and the Indian company must comply with foreign exchange laws, chiefly the Foreign Exchange Management (Borrowing or Lending in Foreign Exchange) Regulations, 2000.

Securities Market

A company intending to raise capital by issue of its securities must access the securities market, which, as the name implies, means a place or an institution where the business of selling or buying of securities is carried out.[210] In most countries, the dominant segment of the securities market

---

[209] The [Central Government] Depository Receipts Scheme, 2014 has repealed this scheme except to the extent relating to FCCBs.

[210] *Karnavati Fincap Limited and Alka Spinners Limited v. Securities and Exchange Board of India*, [1996] 87 Comp Cas 186 (Guj).

is the stock exchange. Stated in simple terms, a stock exchange is an entity that assists, regulates, and controls the business of buying, selling, or dealing in securities.[211] As and when the scope of 'securities' grows, the scope of stock exchanges too grows. In this regard, recall our discussion of derivatives in the earlier part of this chapter.[212] Until recently, entities called 'association' registered under the FCRA regulated and controlled the business of the sale or purchase of forward contracts with commodities as the underlying. Now that these contracts, called commodity derivatives, have been recognized as 'securities', the associations qualify as stock exchanges.[213] Outside the stock exchange, the securities market exists in the form of an over-the-counter (OTC) market where transactions take place for securities that are not listed on the stock exchange or that can be traded off the stock exchange as well.[214] In India, legislative fiat significantly regulates the OTC securities market and prohibits its operation in certain circumstances.[215] Securities market can also be divided on the basis of the tenure of the securities. Securities with tenure of less than one year, that is, short-term securities, such as government treasury bills, cash management bills, certificates of deposit, and commercial papers, are dealt with in the *money markets*.[216] Securities with tenure of more than one year, that is, medium-term or long-term securities, such as dated government securities and corporate securities, are dealt with in the *capital markets*.

The importance of stock exchanges in a securities offering transaction necessitates a broader enquiry into what stock exchanges are by looking at their functions. Fleckner describes the functions of stock exchanges as market organizers, information distributors, market regulators, and finally, to an increasing degree, as business enterprises.[217] As market

---

[211] Clause (j) of section 2 of the SCRA.

[212] See the section 'Concept of Securities' of this chapter.

[213] See section 28A of the FCRA and section 131 of the Finance Act, 2015.

[214] Mila Freire and others (eds), *Subnational Capital Markets in Developing Countries* (World Bank and Oxford University Press 2004), at p. 122.

[215] See sections 13–19 of the SCRA.

[216] See Chapter IIID of the Reserve Bank of India Act, 1934.

[217] Andreas M. Fleckner, 'Stock Exchanges at Crossroads' (2006) 74 Fordham Law Review 2541, at p. 2546. Fleckner's analysis of the functions of a stock exchange is largely universal and the Bombay High Court approved it in

organizers, stock exchanges provide a marketplace where securities can be easily bought, sold, and dealt with.[218] The buying, selling, and dealing in securities is done by members of the stock exchange called stockbrokers. Traditionally, the marketplace provided by the stock exchange was a defined physical place, called the trading floor. With increase in the volume of securities trading and modernization, the level of infrastructure has grown. It now consists of an online screen-based trading system through a nationwide network and an online surveillance capability that monitors positions, prices, and volumes of securities in real time.

This marketplace can be divided into two categories: primary market and secondary market. The primary market is where issue and subscription of new securities or sale and purchase of unlisted securities (that is, securities that are not listed on the stock exchange) takes place. In the secondary market, subsequent trading of the securities, which have reached the buyers, sellers, and dealers of securities through the primary market, takes place.[219] In their primary market segment, stock exchanges, thus, bring together those who demand capital (companies) and those who supply capital (investors).[220] Investors get an opportunity to invest in a variety of companies and securities, thereby reducing their risk. This investment can then be realized in the secondary market segment of the stock exchange. The presence of stock exchanges where securities can be disposed of easily without incurring much cost also increases an interest in securities on the part of the public.

Next, stock exchanges function as information distributors by publishing information about securities transactions such as volume and price (and in certain cases, the parties involved), and information about the price at which market participants are willing to buy or sell the listed securities.[221] Stock exchanges also function as market regulators by supervising and managing the marketplace, by regulating the persons

---

MCX Stock Exchange Limited v. Securities and Exchange Board of India and Ors, (2012) 114 (2) BomLR 1002, at 1030.

[218] Fleckner (n. 217).

[219] Philip R. Wood, *Law and Practice of International Finance: Regulation of International Finance,* Vol. 7 (Sweet & Maxwell 2007), at p. 324.

[220] Fleckner (n. 217).

[221] Fleckner (n. 217) at p. 2547.

that trade in the marketplace, and by exercising control over contracts in securities transacted in the marketplace. Stock exchanges also regulate, through the listing agreement, the entities that have accessed the primary market and listed their securities. A listing agreement is an agreement that entities desirous of getting their securities listed on a stock exchange must enter into with the stock exchange and comply with on a continuous basis.[222] The agreement, by applying Securities and Exchange Board of India (Listing Obligations and Disclosure Requirements) Regulations, 2015 (or the LODR Regulations), covers several matters including corporate governance norms, minimum public holding requirement, and disclosure of unpublished price sensitive information. Finally, by carrying out the foregoing functions, stock exchanges carry on a *business enterprise* with the objective of earning profit.

The market organizing function of the stock exchange has witnessed a crucial change in the year 2012. Traditionally, stock exchanges facilitated execution of contracts for buying and selling of securities as well as their settlement. Settlement of the trades involves ensuring that parties to the trade do not default in performing their obligations and applying measures for mitigating its effects in case they do. Its importance must not be understated as the reputation and credibility of a stock exchange depends on it. For better and efficient settlement of trades, stock exchanges were permitted to transfer this function to a specialized body called the clearing corporation. Clearing corporations are entities that are established to undertake the activity of clearing and settlement of trades in securities that are dealt with or traded on stock exchanges. With the enactment of the Securities Contracts (Regulation) (Stock Exchanges and Clearing Corporations) Regulations, 2012, transferring the settlement function is no longer elective; it is mandatory that such function is performed by a clearing corporation set up as a company limited by shares.

Securities Law

By now, the chapter has referred to several statutory provisions. These fall under the rubric of securities law. However, for the sake of completeness,

---

[222] See section 21 of the Securities Contracts (Regulation) Act, 1956 and regulations 109 of the LODR Regulations.

we must fully understand what securities law is. Securities law is a mixture of substantive laws and regulations on securities and the securities market. We do not use the expression 'regulations' in its ordinary sense, which is delegated legislation. Instead, we use it as it is understood in law and economics. The term 'regulation' in law and economics means a 'sustained and focused control exercised by a public agency over activities that are valued by a community'[223] and can be understood in the backdrop of two systems of economic organization, namely the market system and collectivist system. Under the market system, 'individuals and groups are left free, subject only to certain basic restraints, to pursue their own welfare goals'.[224] The legal system supports these arrangements mainly through private law such as contract law, and regulation has no significant role.[225] Under the collectivist system, 'the state seeks to direct or encourage behaviour which (it is assumed) would not occur without such intervention'.[226] The objective of this system is to correct perceived deficiencies in the market system in meeting collective or public interest goals.[227]

Under the category of substantive law fall the general laws (such as contracts, properties, torts, and crime, which have a bearing on securities and the securities market) and specific laws (such as the Companies Act; the SCRA; the Depositories Act, 1996; and other statutes enacted from time to time on securities and the securities market). These substantive laws fit into our notion of law as traditionally understood. They are enacted by the legislature or laid down by courts of record, are largely static, and are enforced in the ordinary courts, though tribunals are slowly taking over this function of the ordinary courts. The latter category of 'regulations' comprises the SEBI Act, and the regulations (in

---

[223] P. Selznick, 'Focusing Organizational Research on Regulation', in R. Noll (ed.), *Regulatory Policy and the Social Sciences* (1985), at p. 363 as cited from Anthony Ogus, *Regulation: Legal Form and Economic Theory* (Hart Publishing 2004), at p. 1.

[224] Anthony Ogus, *Regulation: Legal Form and Economic Theory* (Hart Publishing, 2004) at p. 1.

[225] Ogus (n. 224).

[226] Ogus (n. 224), at pp. 1–2.

[227] Ogus (n. 224), at pp. 1–2.

terms of delegated legislation), circulars, general orders, informal guidance, clarifications, and guidelines that SEBI issues from time to time. These are the outcome of the process that we examined earlier when discussing the meaning of regulation in law and economics. Under this division of securities law, we have a principal legislation, the SEBI Act, that has established an autonomous securities regulator. The legislation identifies the objectives of regulation and empowers the regulator to frame 'regulations' on the specifics. The Securities and Exchange Board of India, therefore, frames and issues the regulations, modifies them and introduces newer ones quite regularly, and enforces them by acting as a quasi-judicial body. The regulations are very detailed in character as compared to substantive law and form the bulk of securities law.

2. Evolution of Regulation of Public Offerings

We now know that securities are investment instruments issued by companies, pooled investment vehicles, and the government. Companies issue securities principally to raise capital to finance their business and operations, and raising capital on a large scale generally involves offering securities to the public. Before looking at the law and regulation of the public offering of corporate securities, it would be helpful to examine its history; for this is an aspect of securities law that cannot be properly understood without reference to its historical background. The history will also help us understand why certain laws exist, influences that have gone into shaping these laws, and their current relevance. This history is inevitably tied to the history of company law since it is companies that create and issue securities in return for capital provided by subscribers of securities. Some of the cornerstone legal principles, such as investor protection through disclosure of material information, have their origin in the evolution of company law. Finally, the history of raising capital through issue of securities is also linked to the history of the securities market. This chapter, therefore, begins with a review of the history of company law in India and the genesis of the disclosure philosophy. It then examines the emergence of regulation of public offerings under company law, and the general law regulating the raising of capital. The origin of the Indian securities market and its regulation is examined next. The chapter then summarizes the remarks.

History of Company Law

In India, the company form of business organization, as we know it today, owes its origin to foreign influences and developments during the early seventeenth century. The English East India Company, Dutch East India Company, and French East India Company were established in 1600, 1602, and 1604 respectively. Operation of these and other European companies ushered in the company form of business organization to Indian merchants.[1] Laws passed during the British colonial rule firmly established it by providing the legal framework for its existence and operation. These laws were almost entirely based on the then existing company law of the UK.[2] The company law of the UK was in turn the

---

[1] Radhe Shyam Rungta, *Rise of Business Corporations in India, 1851–1900* (Cambridge University Press 1970), at p. 1. Prior to the seventeenth century, there is evidence of business organizations constituted along territorial or religious lines, akin to the modern company, being in existence during the early periods of ancient India. For example, 'nigam' or 'sreni' (as they were called in Sanskrit) were guilds that have been traced as far back as 800 BC. These guilds shared some functional similarity with the company form of business organization in terms of ownership of property, employment of individuals, etc. However, such organizations seem to have withered away by the end of the fifteenth century in the wake of the political disturbances preceding and following the advent of European merchants in India. See Radhe Shyam Rungta, *Rise of Business Corporations in India, 1851–1900* (Cambridge University Press 1970), at pp. 1 and 272. See also Ramesh Chandra Majumdar, *Corporate Life in Ancient India* (The Oriental Book Agency 1922).

[2] Department of Economic Affairs, Ministry of Finance, Government of India, *Report of the Company Law Committee* (1952) (also called the 'Bhabha Committee Report'). This was a common phenomenon in the then colonies

result of indigenous developments. We, therefore, look to the history of company law in the UK.

Company Law in the UK

Any discussion on the history of company law in the UK must begin with a reference to the corporate form—the principal feature of a company—which means conferring a legal personality upon an entity distinct from individuals. In the UK, the corporate form has medieval roots. Initially, it was a means for holding and organizing the property of public, educational, charitable, and ecclesiastical offices through a perpetual succession of incumbents—the borough, bishopric, university, etc.[3] It was not a feature relevant in the commercial realm simply because there was no need for it. Guilds of merchants were the prevalent form of organization to carry on commercial activities. Conferring a legal personality upon guilds was hardly needed since each member traded on his own account, subject only to compliance with the regulations of the

---

of the UK. An imperial conference held in New Zealand in 1911 had a segment on uniformity in company law in the British dominions. The need for the uniformity arose because 'As British Companies are increasingly carrying on operations in New Zealand and other overseas Dominions, it is desirable that there should be uniformity in respect of [the] main principles connected with [the] formation and operation of mercantile companies. With this object legislation should be prepared by Imperial Government and should be submitted to overseas Dominions for consideration and approval.' See Government of New Zealand, *Imperial Conference* (1911), at pp. 163–4. See also Secretary of State for the Colonies, *Report of the East Africa Commission* (April 1925). This report states that up to the end of 1921, the legislation regarding companies in Kenya and Uganda was the Indian Companies Act, 1882, and various subsequent Indian amending acts. At the end of 1920, the Indian Companies Act, 1913 was applied to Tanganyika Territory.

[3] W.R. Cornish and G. de N. Clark, *Law and Society in England 1750–1950* (The book was originally published by Sweet & Maxwell, London in 1989 and is now out-of-print in book form. The digital version has been made available by the surviving author and is available at <http://www.law.cam.ac.uk/faculty-resources/summary/law-and-society-in-england-1750-1950/2624> accessed on 15 September 2015), at p. 313.

guild. Trading on joint account, as opposed to individual trading subject to the rules of the guild, was carried on through partnerships.[4]

With time, the guild form of business organization began to change. Upon the expansion of British foreign trade and settlement during the sixteenth century, merchant bodies began to be constituted for trading overseas which, for the first time, were referred to as 'company'. Initially, companies were an extension of the guild where each member traded with his own stock and on his own account. Subsequently, the partnership principle of trading on joint account began to dominate this form of enterprise and the companies became joint commercial enterprises instead of trade protection associations. They started to operate on a joint account and with a joint stock.[5] This led to the establishment of 'joint stock companies' such as the East India Company of 1600.[6] This was the first major step towards the evolution of companies. These joint stock companies were formed as partnerships by agreement under a seal, providing for the division of the undertaking into shares that were transferable by the original partners according to the terms of the partnership agreement.[7]

It was only towards the second half of the seventeenth century that incorporated joint stock companies began to be differentiated from the unincorporated ones due to the obvious benefits. However, incorporation of joint stock companies could be had only through the grant of a royal charter or by a specific act of Parliament, which was a rare event. Nevertheless, towards the end of the seventeenth century, there was an immense growth of joint stock companies in the UK—a growth fuelled by availability of capital looking for profitable investment. This kind of partnership was also useful in accomplishing undertakings for which

---

[4] L.C.B. Gower, *The Principles of Modern Company Law* (3rd edn, Stevens & Sons 1969), at p. 23.

[5] Gower (n. 4), at p. 24.

[6] The East India Company is the common name of one of the earliest chartered trading companies, namely 'the Governor and Company of Merchants of London trading to the East Indies' which was granted the royal charter on 31 December 1599. See Geroge Cawston and A.H. Keane, *The Early Chartered Companies* (Edward Arnold 1896).

[7] Gower (n. 4), at p. 25.

individual capital and enterprise were inadequate, or where the risk was beyond that usually incurred in private trade like in mining ventures.[8]

Soon malpractices crept into the formation and management of joint stock companies. Two causes seem to have led to this. First, there was no legislation on joint stock companies. Partnership law, which formed the basis for setting up of joint stock companies (except where the joint stock company was constituted by an act of the legislature or under a charter), did not provide a solution to many unique challenges presented by a joint stock company. For example, the innumerable holders of capital that had been minutely divided could not exercise an effective control over the management, which, in ordinary partnerships, could be exercised with comparative ease and advantage.[9] Second, the legal system, in order to afford individuals to withdraw their capital from joint stock companies and others to invest in it, permitted the transfer of shares. But members of companies, not content with the ordinary and legitimate profits of their capital, sought a further profit by the sale of their shares. The transfer of shares (or what was then called stock-jobbing) itself became a trade, which soon slid into speculative trading.[10] Ker's report notes that 'in order to supply the market for shares, it was necessary that companies should be multiplied, not with a view to bona fide employment of capital or industry, but merely to enable the trader in shares to speculate in their rise and fall, to effect sales at a premium, and to shift the ultimate loss upon the last purchaser'.[11]

In the first and the second decades of the eighteenth century, there was, thus, a frenetic boom in company flotation. The clamour against these flighty practices finally led to legislative intervention. Unfortunately, the legislature directed its ire not against the market abuse, but against joint stock companies in general. The Bubble Act, 1720 (or the Bubble Act), was passed which made a large class of joint stock companies illegal and

---

[8] Report on Partnership made in 1837 by Bellenden Ker at the direction of the Board of Trade, United Kingdom and printed in the Appendix to the House of Commons, United Kingdom, *First Report of the Select Committee on Joint Stock Companies* (1844), at p. 247.

[9] George Taylor, *A Practical Treatise on the Act for the Registration, Regulation, and Incorporation of Joint Stock Companies* (William Benning & Co. 1847), at p. 2.

[10] Ker (n. 8), at p. 247.

[11] Ker (n. 8), at p. 248.

void, and laid down other stringent measures such as penalties because such companies 'manifestly tend to the prejudices of the public trade and commerce of the kingdom.'[12]

The Bubble Act, however, proved to be ineffectual as it took the extreme step of impeding the formation of joint stock companies as opposed to regulating them. Further, in certain aspects, the provisions of the Bubble Act were vaguely worded and while every type of existing unincorporated company had not been declared illegal, the extent to which partnerships could be formed was not clear. Commercial needs and legal ingenuity, therefore, led to the development of 'deed of settlement companies.' Taking the aid of private law like contract law and trust law, people conferred on unincorporated joint stock companies nearly all the advantages of incorporation.[13] In a deed of settlement company,

> the company would be formed under a deed of settlement (approximating to a cross between the modern articles of association and a debenture trust deed) under which the subscribers would agree to be associated in an enterprise with a prescribed joint stock divided into a specified number of shares; the provisions of the deed would be variable with the consent of a specified majority of the proprietors; management would be delegated to a committee of directors; and the property would be vested in a separate body of trustees; some of whom would often be directors also.[14]

The Bubble Act thus did not lead to the suppression of the company form of business organization and was repealed in 1825.

Although the Bubble Act was repealed, there was a strong sentiment among the legislators that something ought to be done to regulate joint stock companies. This culminated in the last step in the evolution of company law akin to what we are familiar with today with the setting up of a select committee in the UK, '[t]o enquire into the state of the laws respecting Joint Stock Companies (except Banking Companies), with a view to greater security to the public.'[15] The committee, also

---

[12] Gower (n. 4), at p. 29.

[13] Gower (n. 4), at p. 33.

[14] Gower (n. 4), at p. 34.

[15] The House of Commons, United Kingdom, *First Report of the Select Committee on Joint Stock Companies* (1844) (also called the 'Gladstone Committee Report'), at p. iii.

known as the Gladstone Committee after its chairman, published its report in March 1844, which led to the enactment of the 'Act for the Registration, Incorporation, and Regulation of Joint Stock Companies, 1844' (henceforth referred to as the 1844 Act) in the UK. The 1844 Act laid the foundation for modern company law in the UK as well as in India—then one of the colonies of the UK. The 1844 Act introduced three main principles that have constituted the basis of modern company law.[16] First, it made the distinction between partnerships and joint stock companies clear by providing for the registration of all new companies with more than 25 members. Second, it made incorporation generally available through an administrative process. Third, it provided for publicity of information by companies.[17] The privilege of limited liability was, however, not provided by the 1844 Act and the members were jointly and severally liable for the debts of the company. This was subsequently introduced by way of the Limited Liability Act, 1855. English company law has since undergone several changes by way of new enactments. The foundations of modern company law had, however, been laid by this time.

Company Law in India

Around this very time, company law made its way into India and an 'Act for the Regulation of Registered Joint Stock Companies' was passed in 1850.[18] Though joint stock companies had come into existence in India by the late eighteenth century,[19] this act marked the first stage in

---

[16] Gower (n. 4), at p. 42.

[17] Gower (n. 4), at p. 42.

[18] Act No. XLIII of 1850 passed by the President of the Council of India. See also *S.V. Kondaskar, Official Liquidator v. V.M. Deshpande, Income-tax Officer*, [1972] 83 ITR 685 (SC).

[19] In fact, there are records of joint stock companies having come into existence about the middle of the seventeenth century in South India due to considerable expansion of trade and commerce between India and Europe. However, the problems being faced by the joint stock company form in India were many. The joint stock company did not have a separate legal personality, which could only be obtained by a royal charter or an act of the legislature. The

the development of a body of law to regulate companies.[20] It was not a codifying statute and regulated limited aspects of joint stock companies registered under the act. Registration was not compulsory and every unincorporated company of partners associated under a deed containing a provision that the shares in the stock or business of the company are transferable without the consent of all the partners, became entitled to registration under the act. However, registration in return for some privileges like the ability to sue and be sued, as if it were an incorporated company, put several restrictions and conditions like holding of periodic general meetings, prohibiting the company from purchasing its own shares, compulsory audit of the company's financial statements, etc. Importantly, the act did not confer the privilege of limited liability on the members of the company and did not regulate the methods of raising capital by issue of securities.

Soon, in 1857, the act was repealed and replaced with an act 'for the incorporation and regulation of Joint-Stock Companies and other Associations, either with or without limited liability of the members thereof'.[21] This act made incorporation mandatory and prohibited more than 20 persons to carry on in partnership, any trade or business having gain for its object unless they were registered as a company under the act or had legal authorization.[22] The act also provided for the privilege

---

difficulties were compounded for the British companies that sought to operate in India. This was on account of opposition by the East India Company, which was consulted on all such matters. In India, only five acts of incorporation proper were passed up to 1850. The common law rules of partnership and trust were inadequate to deal with management of the company. Liability of the shareholders was unlimited. Creditors did not have enough protection as the paid-up capital of the company could be reduced to nothing at the will of the management. There was no proper winding-up law. For details, see Rungta (n. 1), at p. 36.

[20] Rungta (n. 1), at p. 45.

[21] Act No. XIX of 1857 passed by the Legislative Council of India.

[22] Section II of the act read as follows:

Not more than twenty persons shall after the first day of January 1858 carry on in partnership, in any part of the territories in the possession and under the Government of the East India Company, any trade or business having gain for

of limited liability and introduced several new provisions for regulating companies, which continue to exist even today.[23] These provisions include registering of memorandum of association and articles of association and their legal effects, free transferability of shares, payment of dividend out of profits, winding-up by court and voluntary winding-up, and official liquidators.

Then following the English Act of 1862, a comprehensive Act was passed in India in 1866 that repealed earlier legislation on companies, and consolidated and amended 'the laws relating to the incorporation, regulation and winding-up of Trading companies and other associations'.[24] This was the first enactment to bear the short title 'The Indian Companies Act'. Subsequently, the Indian Companies Act, 1882[25] was passed, which recast the 1866 Act embodying the amendments that were made in the company law in England up to that time.[26] Thereafter, following the English Companies (Consolidation) Act, 1908, the Indian Companies Act, 1913 was passed, which was a close reproduction of the English acts.[27] After the Independence, on the recommendation of

---

its object, unless they are registered as a Company under this Act, or are authorized so to carry on business by an Act of Parliament, or by Royal Charter or Letters Patent, or by an Act of the Governor General of India in Council; and if any persons carry on business in partnership contrary to this provision, every person so acting shall be severally liable for the payment of the whole debts of the partnership, and may be sued for the same without the joinder in the action or suit of any other members of the partnership.

[23] Section I of the act. The privilege of limited liability was not extended to any company formed for the purpose of banking and insurance. Banking companies were extended this privilege by Act No. VII of 1860 passed by the Legislative Council of India.

[24] The Indian Companies Act, 1866 (Act No. X of 1866) passed by the Governor General of India in Council.

[25] Act No. VI of 1882 passed by the Governor General of India.

[26] Bhabha Committee Report (n. 2), at p. 17. The Government of India constituted the Company Law Committee in 1950 to consider and report the amendments necessary in the Indian Companies Act, 1913. The report of this committee is commonly referred to as the Bhabha Committee Report after the name of C.H. Bhabha, the chairman of the committee. The Bhabha Committee Report formed the basis for the enactment of the Companies Act, 1956.

[27] Bhabha Committee Report (n. 2), at p. 17.

the Bhabha Committee,[28] the Companies Act, 1956 was passed. The Companies Act, 1956 was in force for about 55 years and was amended several times in the duration. In August 2013, the Companies Act, 2013 was enacted to replace the 1956 Act in view of the changes in the national and international economic environment.

Disclosure Philosophy

A significant development in the evolution of company law was the statutory requirement of disclosure of information by companies. This development, having its origin principally in the Gladstone Committee Report, has defined and shaped the contours of regulation of the public offering of corporate securities. Recall the earlier discussion that the Bubble Act, 1720, failed to suppress the formation of companies and was thus repealed in 1825. At this stage, large numbers of companies were raising capital to defraud the public. For example,

> some half-dozen adventurers, any one of whom, in his individual capacity, would have found it difficult to obtain credit to the most limited extent, boldly announced to the world the formation of an imaginary Assurance Company, with a capital of one million sterling...tempting inducements to the ignorant and unwary...to defraud the public, in the course of about four years, to the extent of upwards of 200,000 sterling.[29]

[28] Bhabha Committee Report (n. 2).

[29] Taylor (n. 9), at p. 10. Reported court decisions of cases during this period further illustrate this practice. In *Gerhard v. Bates*, [1853] 2 E&B 476, the directors of the company had stated in the prospectus that they did not hesitate to guarantee a minimum dividend of 33 per cent. Soon thereafter in *New Brunswick and Canada Railway and Land Co. v. Muggeridge*, 1 Dru. & Sm. 363 (1860), the court laid down what later began to be called the 'golden rule' for preparing a prospectus. The court held that:

> Those who issue a prospectus, holding out to the public the great advantages which will accrue to persons who will take shares in a proposed undertaking, and inviting them to take shares on the faith of the representations therein contained, are bound to state everything with strict and scrupulous accuracy, and not only to abstain from stating as fact that which is not so, but to omit no one fact within their knowledge the existence of which might in any degree affect the nature or extent or quality of the privileges and advantages which the prospectus holds out as inducements to take shares.

The House of Commons of the UK, therefore, appointed the Gladstone Committee to enquire into the state of the laws respecting joint stock companies with a view to greater security to the public.[30]

The Gladstone Committee divided the bubble or the unsuccessful companies into three classes: (a) faulty companies as these were founded on unsound calculations; (b) ill-constituted companies so as to render it probable that they will be mismanaged; and (c) companies formed for defrauding others.[31] The first class was held to be beyond legislative cure, though measures aimed at the second and third classes would undoubtedly be useful in controlling such undertakings at the outset.[32] For the second class, the committee proposed the remedy of periodic holding of meetings, periodic audit and publication of accounts, and making the directors and officers more immediately responsible to the shareholders.[33] It was the third class that received the significant attention of the committee, and the remedy proposed for this class was publication of information—publication of the directors, shareholders, deed of settlement, amount of share capital. The committee was of the view that 'publication…would baffle every case of fraud which has come under the notice of your committee. The public would have the means of knowing with whom they deal; and agents and bankers would be enabled to avoid participating in the discredit of such concerns, by giving the sanction of their names to questionable undertakings'.[34]

Although the foregoing was an ambitious statement, publication of information about the affairs of the company has since then formed the fundamental basis of company regulation to prevent fraud and protect investors. At this stage of the evolution of company law, the other rationale for the disclosure philosophy was incorporation and limited liability. Disclosure of information was the price that a company had to

---

The House of Lords approved this rule in *The Central Railway Company of Venezuela v. Kisch*, (1867) LR 2 HL 99, at p. 113.

[30] See the earlier section 'History of Company Law', of this chapter.

[31] Gladstone Committee Report (n. 15), at p. iv.

[32] Gladstone Committee Report (n. 15), at p. v.

[33] Gladstone Committee Report (n. 15), at p. v.

[34] Gladstone Committee Report (n. 15), at p. v.

pay for these twin privileges.[35] Over the years, the disclosure philosophy has entrenched itself in company law of almost every common law country including India. Newer justifications have emerged for the increased disclosure of information such as accountability of the directors and managers, corporate democracy, efficiency, and public interest.[36]

Today, disclosure of information by companies and its publicity has three underlying themes. The first theme is that the assumption behind many disclosure requirements is that mere disclosure of information and its publicity influences behaviour irrespective of negative prohibition or positive regulation.[37] The types of information to be disclosed and to whom the information must be disclosed are the second and the third themes.[38] These themes have manifested themselves into provisions of company laws beginning with the Act for the Regulation of Registered Joint Stock Companies, 1850, and subsequently, in the last two decades, into provisions of securities laws. Some examples of these themes are: the requirement that the names of the directors and shareholders of the company and any change thereof be filed with the relevant government authority;[39] the board of directors of the company provide to the shareholders the financial statements of the company and the auditor's report, and also file them with the relevant governmental authority.[40] The information disclosed has been made public such that

---

[35] Leonard Sealy, 'The Disclosure Philosophy and Company Law Reform' (1981) 2 Company Lawyer 51.

[36] See Charlotte Villiers, *Corporate Reporting and Company Law* (Cambridge University Press 2006).

[37] John H. Farrar and Brenda Hannigan, *Farrar's Company Law* (4th edn, Butterworths 1998), at p. 463. Although Farrar has identified these themes in the context of British company law, these are equally present under Indian company law and securities law on account of their legal origins and the contemporary structure.

[38] Farrar's Company Law (n. 37), at p. 464.

[39] See section X of the Regulation of Registered Joint Stock Companies Act, 1850. This requirement has continued in the subsequent company laws including the Companies Act, 2013.

[40] See section VIII of the Regulation of Registered Joint Stock Companies Act, 1850 and Chapter IX of the Companies Act, 2013.

the records can be inspected and copies obtained by the members of the public.[41]

Regulation of Public Offering under the Company Law

Regulation of the public offering of corporate securities is an offshoot of company law. The reason is obvious—companies create and issue securities to raise capital. However, this was not the case initially. In India, the legislature showed great concern for the protection of creditors of the company while investor protection measures remained absent. During this period, that is, between the enactment of the Act for the Regulation of Registered Joint Stock Companies, 1850 and the enactment of the Indian Companies Act, 1882, a company could issue shares to all persons to whom shares could be allotted.[42] Issue of corporate securities was entirely within the domain of contracts, torts, and fiduciary law.

It was probably during this period that companies, taking a cue from practices then prevalent in the UK, began inviting subscriptions for their securities from investors on the basis of a 'prospectus.'[43] The prospectus was marketing material containing relevant information about the company and its business (quite often exaggerated and pompously presented) that sought to induce the investors to enter into a contract for subscription of its securities. The unregulated nature of the prospectus changed with the enactment of the Indian Companies Act, 1882, which for the first time sought to regulate the issue of shares by companies through disclosure of information and introduced the statutory law on prospectus. It appears that the change was prompted more on account of changes being made to the company law in the UK and less on account of fraudulent prospectuses in India. Section 88 of the Indian Companies Act, 1882 declared that every prospectus of a company, and every notice inviting persons to subscribe for shares in any joint stock company, must specify the dates and the names of the parties to any agreement

---

[41] See section XIV of the Regulation of Registered Joint Stock Companies Act, 1850 and section 399 of the Companies Act, 2013.

[42] Section XIII of the act 'for the incorporation and regulation of Joint-Stock Companies and other Associations, either with or without limited liability of the members thereof', 1857.

[43] Alastair Hudson, *Securities Law* (Sweet & Maxwell 2008), at p. 23.

enforceable by law which the company, or the promoters, directors, or trustees thereof, may have entered into before the issue of such prospectus or notice. The scope of agreements was limited to agreements which might reasonably influence a person in determining whether he would or would not become a shareholder in the company. Any prospectus or notice not specifying the names was deemed fraudulent on the part of the promoters, directors, and officers of the company knowingly issuing the same, as regards any person taking shares in the company on the faith of such prospectus, unless he had notice of such agreement.[44]

The succeeding company legislation contained several provisions regulating the issue of prospectuses to the public, most of which continue until today. Disclosure-based securities regulation through prospectus was entrenched into our company law with the enactment of the Companies Act, 1956. In this regard, the Bhabha Committee Report noted:

> Recent developments in company law have emphasised the importance of the fullest possible disclosure in prospectuses or statements in lieu of them...it is now increasingly recognised that full disclosure of the facts and circumstances relating to the formation of a company and the manner in which it is worked as reflected in its accounts, constitutes the best safeguard against abuse of the process of the law by unscrupulous company promoters and managers.[45]

Two aspects of disclosure-based regulation of the public offering of securities under company law must be noted. One, this regulation is confined to primary issuance of securities. It does not concern itself with the trading of securities post their issue and allotment. The reason for this is obvious. Upon issue and allotment of securities, they become the property of the holder who is expected to deal with them in accordance with the law governing the buying and selling of securities. The company has no role to play in it. Two, disclosure-based regulation must

---

[44] Section 88 of the Indian Companies Act, 1882. Curiously, this single provision was enacted under the heading 'Meetings' in Part III of the 1882 Act on 'Management and Administration of Companies and Associations under this Act'.

[45] Bhabha Committee Report (n. 2), at p. 41.

be contrasted with merit-based regulation. Merit-based regulation is based on the belief that statutory authorities and regulatory bodies are better able to assess the merits of an offer of securities to the public and mere disclosure of information to the public is not enough. Under this approach, companies submit information in a draft form to the statutory authority who then decides on the business viability of the offering. It may ask the company to modify the information or supply additional information; may either approve the proposed offer or reject it, thereby preventing the company from going public, in the best interest of potential investors and the market as a whole.[46] While the nature of initial regulation of the public offering of corporate securities was disclosure based, merit-based regulation too became a part of the legal and regulatory framework of securities law, as can be seen later.

Control over Capital Issues

To prevent fraud and protect investors, public offerings of securities by companies began to be regulated under company law. During the 1940s, another concern associated with the public offering of corporate securities was diversion of limited investible resources to non-essential projects. As a result, the government imposed control over capital issues in May 1943 as a war measure and extended the imposition from time to time, leading to the enactment of the Capital Issues (Control) Act, 1947 (or the Capital Issues Control Act). After Independence, the legislature permanently adopted this legislation. In addition to the original purpose, the need for such legislation was also felt as an aid and complement to the new company law and the Industries (Development and Regulation) Act, 1951.[47] The latter act had been enacted to provide the central government with the means of implementing their industrial policy based on a planned socialist economy.

---

[46] S.M. Solaiman, 'Disclosure Philosophy for Investor Protection in Securities Markets: Does one size fit all?' (2007) 28 (5) Company Lawyer 135, at p. 138.

[47] Rajya Sabha Debates, 'The Capital Issues (Continuance of Control) Amendment Bill, 1956' (9 March 1956); *Narendra Kumar Maheshwari* v. *Union of India*, 1990 (Supp) SCC 440.

The Capital Issues Control Act and the exemption orders and rules framed thereunder controlled the raising of capital and issue of securities. Companies were prohibited from making an issue of capital or public offer of securities except with the prior consent of the central government. The central government had wide discretionary powers in granting consent such as imposition of conditions, price at which the securities could be issued, and revocation of the consent.[48] The central government also controlled the circulation or advertisement of offer of securities to the public including to existing holders of securities.[49] Such control also extended to the purchasers of securities. Thus, persons were prohibited from accepting or giving any consideration for any securities, or selling, purchasing, or transferring any securities issued by a company, in respect of an issue of capital unless such an issue was consented to by the central government.[50] Depending on the policies of the central government and needs of the securities market, the powers under the Capital Issues Control Act were also used to prevent fraudulent capital issues entering the securities market and prevent undue speculation on the stock exchanges by deciding the rates of dividend/interest and premium on and timing of capital issues. The Capital Issues Control Act, thus, embodied the philosophy of merit-based regulation. The Controller of Capital Issues within the Ministry of Finance, Government of India administered the Capital Issues Control Act.[51] Over time, relaxations were granted from the extreme rigour of the Capital Issues Control Act through the Capital Issues (Exemption) Order, 1969. In July 1991, the Government of India adopted a new industrial policy based on liberalization. In the wake of liberalization, government control over the issue of capital and its pricing became irrelevant.[52] Accordingly, the Capital Issues Control Act was repealed with effect from May 1992.

[48] Section 3 of the Capital Issues Control Act. See also *In Re: Navjivan Mills Co. Ltd.*, (1972) 42 Comp Cas 265 (Guj).

[49] Section 4 of the Capital Issues Control Act.

[50] Section 5 of the Capital Issues Control Act.

[51] On the powers, functions and role of the erstwhile Controller of Capital Issues, see *Narendra Kumar Maheshwari v. Union of India*, 1990 (Supp) SCC 440.

[52] Rajya Sabha Debates, 'The Capital Issues (Control) Repeal Bill, 1992' (10 August 1992).

The Indian Securities Market and Its Regulation

Company law and the Capital Issues Control Act primarily regulated the public offering of corporate securities. Because such offerings involved accessing the securities market, laws governing trading in the securities market also incidentally regulated it. Evolution of such laws is intrinsically linked to the evolution of the securities market itself. Globally the emergence of the securities market is attributed to government borrowings represented by transferable securities. In fact, as Ronald Mitchie notes, if a particular event can be taken to represent the beginnings of the global securities market, it was the forced loan that Venice imposed on its inhabitants in 1171–2.[53] Government securities comprised an important element of the securities market in Europe, and prior to the 1840s, governments had issued most of the securities in existence for the financing of wars. However, India was unaffected by this trend because government debt was held in London and not in India. Under British influence, limited trading of government securities and bank shares took place in Calcutta (now Kolkata), and contemporary newspapers gave quotes of securities prices.[54] Instead of government securities, it was company securities that provided an impetus for the securities market in India. A 1948 Government of India report links the creation and development of a securities market in India to the rise in commercial activities and floating of joint stock companies around the middle of the nineteenth century.[55]

After the Government of India came under the British Crown in 1858, there was an abundance of British capital in India, possibly because there was neither any opposition by the East India Company nor any checks on such movement of capital. This resulted in the opening and proliferation of company enterprise in India. These enterprises received a fillip when the American Civil War stopped cotton supplies to Lancashire, UK; prices of Indian cotton went up to record heights, bringing much money into the hands of cotton dealers of Bombay

[53] Ronald C. Mitchie, *The Global Securities Market: A History* (Oxford University Press 2006), at p. 17.

[54] Ministry of Finance, Government of India, *Report on the Regulation of the Stock Market in India* (1948), at p. 1.

[55] Government of India Report on Stock Market (n. 54).

(now Mumbai), some of which flowed into the shares of the numerous joint stock companies. Share dealing thus became popular in Bombay. Though the boom burst in 1865 and several companies failed, a regular securities market had been created.[56]

The transition from a fragmented securities market to an organized one came about with the setting up of stock exchanges. Among the stock exchanges, the Native Share and Stock Brokers' Association of Bombay (renamed as the Bombay Stock Exchange; now known as BSE Limited) was the first to be set up; it was formally constituted in 1887.[57] Subsequently, the Ahmedabad Share & Stock Brokers' Association and the Calcutta Stock Exchange Association were set up in 1894 and 1908, respectively.[58] The Native Share and Stock Brokers' Association of Bombay and the Ahmedabad Share & Stock Brokers' Association were constituted as private associations: unincorporated but registered non-profit associations. Stock exchanges were also constituted as companies incorporated under the prevailing statute on company law. As of 1948, the largest of such stock exchanges was the Calcutta Stock Exchange Limited; the others in this category were the Bengal Share & Stock Exchange Limited, Stock Exchange Association of Bengal Limited, Indian Stock Exchange Limited, Madras Stock Exchange Limited, Punjab Stock Exchange Limited, Punjab Stock & Share Brokers' Association Limited, Lahore Stock Exchange Limited, Lahore Central Stock Exchange Limited, All-India Stock Exchange Limited, Delhi Stock Exchange Limited, U.P. Stock Exchange Limited, and Nagpur Stock Exchange Limited.[59] Memorandum of association and articles of association governed the regulation of these incorporated stock exchanges.

[56] Government of India Report on Stock Market (n. 54).

[57] By an indenture dated 3 December 1887, the Native Share and Stock Brokers' Association of Bombay was formally constituted. It is recited in this indenture that its formal constitution followed a resolution of certain Bombay brokers on 9 July 1875 'to form an association for protecting the character, status and interest of Native share and stock brokers and for providing a hall or building for the use of the members of the Association'. See Government of Bombay, *Report of the Bombay Stock Exchange Enquiry Committee* (9 January 1924), at p. 3.

[58] Government of India Report on Stock Market (n. 54), at p. 2.

[59] Government of India Report on Stock Market (n. 54), at p. 10.

Whether constituted as an association or a company, the stock exchanges were mutualized bodies—the members of the association or the shareholders who owned and managed the stock exchange were the ones who had the right of access to trading. In this respect, stock exchanges emerged in India and functioned in a manner no different from other industrial economies. As has been noted in a paper of the International Monetary Fund:

> Exchange began as private clubs, or curbside meetings, that eventually adopted a more formal structure. Eventually rules were developed setting time and place of trading, priority of trades, and price-setting mechanisms. Exchanges formalized their ownership structure by granting 'seats' to members—a seat entitled the owner to trade on the floor of the exchange (or 'sit' on the exchange) and each seat holder had an equal vote on the exchange's affairs. Only those with seats were entitled to vote. The mutuality of this structure was generally reinforced by a prohibition on members trading elsewhere—that is, for the purpose of the securities traded on the exchanges, members pledged to trade only with each other and only through the exchange. Nonmembers could not trade on the exchange or with members.[60]

Thus, membership of stock exchanges constituted as associations, so as to act as stockbrokers, could either be acquired by the purchase of a card or be inherited by the legal heir of a deceased member. Similarly, share qualification was the basis of membership of the incorporated stock exchanges.

Setting up of stock exchanges did not just lead to an organized securities market, it also led to regulation of the securities market, the form of regulation being self-regulation. Self-regulation, in the legal context, may be understood to mean regulation (formulating rules of conduct, enforcing the rules, and adjudication) of a collective association by a body drawn exclusively or predominantly from members of the collective association itself.[61] Self-regulation, in this legal sense, is consensual

---

[60] Jennifer Elliott, 'Demutualization of Securities Exchanges: A Regulatory Perspective' (2002) IMF Working Paper WP/02/119, 3 <http://www.imf.org/external/pubs/ft/wp/2002/wp02119.pdf> accessed on 12 March 2016.

[61] Anthony Ogus, *Regulation: Legal Form and Economic Theory* (Hart Publishing 2004), at p. 107; Bronwen Morgan and Karen Yeung, *An Introduction*

and co-operative in nature, and does not emanate from the government. It is seen to originate 'in the realisation by a group of individuals or institutions that regulation of their activities is desirable in the common interest, and their acceptance that rules for the performance of functions and of duties should be established and enforced'.[62]

Stock exchanges, thus, began to self-regulate the securities market. For example, the aims and objects of the Native Share and Stock Brokers' Association of Bombay were to 'promote honourable practice; to suppress malpractices; to settle disputes among brokers; [and] to decide all questions of usage and courtesy in conducting brokerage business'.[63] Being a mutualized body, the stock exchange had rules for admission to membership, and the members were subject to the rules and regulations of the stock exchange. A managing committee, consisting of at least 12 members of the stock exchange, and the members of the stock exchange at general meeting, exercised the powers of management and control of the stock exchange including framing by-laws and rules for the guidance of the members. From time to time, the managing committee and the members at general meeting passed resolutions to empower the managing committee to prevent fraud in securities transactions, to lay down norms for settlement of trade, to check excessive speculation in securities, etc. In addition to regulating the conduct of their own members, stock exchanges also regulated certain aspects of the conduct of companies that desired to admit their securities for dealing on the exchange. Regulation of listed companies was, strictly speaking, not self-regulatory because the companies were not regulating themselves through the stock exchange like stockbrokers. However, the justification for such regulation was the protection of its members and the marketplace and the basis of regulation was contractual—the listing agreement. Listing of securities was a matter of importance as it gave the company

to *Law and Regulation: Text and Materials* (Cambridge University Press 2007), at p. 92.

[62] Alan C. Page, 'Self-Regulation: The Constitutional Dimension' (1986) 49 (2) *Modern Law Review* 141, at p. 144 citing *Second Stage Evidence to the* [U.K.] *Wilson Committee Vol. 4* (1977), at p. 89.

[63] Clause (XV) of the indenture dated 3 December 1887 constituting the Native Share and Stock Brokers' Association of Bombay.

facilities of dealing and publicity. As a result, the stock exchange scrutinized the affairs of the company before admission and enforced certain conditions on a continuous basis. There was prohibition of all dealings in the market in the shares of a company which had not been registered and in which allotment to the public had not been made.[64]

The self-regulatory framework of the stock exchange came up for scrutiny following the stock market crashes in the 1920s. On 14 September 1923, the Government of Bombay appointed a committee chaired by Sir Wilfrid Atlay 'to enquire into the constitution, customs, practices, rules, regulations and methods of business of the Native Share and Stock Brokers' Association of Bombay and to investigate any…complaints of the public…and thereafter with a view to protect the investing public against the interested or irregular control of business.'[65] The committee came up with glaring findings: laxity in the administration of the stock exchange, difficulty in ascertaining the rules and regulations of the stock exchange, weak enforcement of the rules and regulations, and lack of disciplinary action against erring members. The situation of other stock exchanges was no better, if not worse. Then came the market crash in June 1925 because of large-scale speculative activities in Bombay.

The June 1925 market crash provided the impetus for the first government regulation of the securities market. The Government of Bombay thus enacted the Securities Contracts Control Act of 1925. The scope of this legislation was very limited: It was applicable only to the Presidency of Bombay; provided for recognition of stock exchanges; and regulated certain contracts for the purchase and sale of securities. But its importance cannot be understated. This act, for the first time, provided a legislative framework for the regulation of certain aspects of the securities market, and its provisions found their way into the Securities Contracts (Regulation) Act, 1956 (or the SCRA)—the legislation that is in force till today.

The reform and regulation of the securities market in the Presidency of Bombay provided the impetus for such measures on an all-India basis. Adding to this was the post-war boom in the stock exchanges from the end of 1945 to the beginning of 1946 and its aftermath. The Government of

---

[64] Government of Bombay Report on Stock Exchange (n. 57), at p. 17.

[65] Government of Bombay Report on Stock Exchange (n. 57), at p. 31.

India undertook intensive study of this area through departmental enquiry: first through a committee set up under the chairmanship of P.J. Thomas and later a committee set up under the chairmanship of A.D. Gorwalla.[66] The process culminated with the enactment of the SCRA.[67]

The object of the SCRA and the rules framed thereunder was, and continues to be, threefold: to regulate stock exchanges, the largest component of the securities market, through a process of recognition and exercise of administrative control; to limit, and in certain cases prohibit, securities market activities outside the ambit of the recognized stock exchanges; and to prohibit certain contracts in securities altogether.[68] But the SCRA did not do away with the self-regulation of the securities market by the stock exchanges; instead, it brought it within the oversight of the central government. Thus, the rules and by-laws of a stock exchange applying for registration had to be in conformity with prescribed conditions with a view to ensuring fair dealing and protecting investors. The legal framework under the SCRA in relation to both the

[66] Government of India Report on Stock Market (n. 54).

[67] Though the need to regulate the securities market at an all-India level was felt much earlier, legislation to this effect could be enacted only in 1956. The reasons for the delay were twofold: First, it was only after the adoption of the Constitution of India, which included 'stock exchange' in the Union List, that it was possible to consider legislation on an all-India basis; and second, there was a certain degree of inter-connectedness between the legislative bill for this legislation and the Companies Bill. As long as the Companies Bill was not passed, it was considered not advisable to pass the bill on regulation of the securities market. See Rajya Sabha Debates, 'Securities Contracts (Regulation) Bill, 1954' (5 December 1955); *Madhubhai Amathlal Gandhi v. Union of India*, AIR 1961 SC 21; *Dahiben Umedbhai Patel v. Norman James Hamilton*, [1985] 57 Comp Cas 700 (Bom); *Delhi Stock Exchange v. K.C. Sharma*, 98 (2002) DLT 234.

[68] See section 20 of the SCRA which prohibited options in securities because the legislature viewed them to be purely speculative. However, the prohibition was done away with in 1995 because the stock exchanges were seen to be capable to regulate them under the supervision of SEBI. Today the power to prohibit contracts in securities is exercisable by both the central government and SEBI under section 16 of the SCRA read with Central Government's notification no. S.O. 573(E) dated 30 July 1992. In this regard, see SEBI's notification no. LAD-NRO/GN/2013-14/26/6667 dated 3 October 2013.

objectives affected the public offering of securities. Certain contracts for or relating to the purchase or sale of securities were rendered illegal and void, and the listing agreement that the company enters into with the stock exchange subsequent to the public offering of securities was given statutory sanction.

In 2004, an amendment to the SCRA that introduced the process of corporatization and demutualization led to significant changes in the organization and regulation of stock exchanges. Corporatization means constituting the stock exchange as a company, and demutualization means segregating ownership and management from the trading rights of the members of the stock exchange. Impetus for these structural changes was provided by persistent and pervasive mismanagement of the stock exchanges such as conflicts of interest, lack of transparency and efficiency, and failure to safeguard investors. The root cause of these problems, as noted by the *Report of the Joint Parliamentary Committee on Stock Market Scam*, 2002, lay in the organizational structure of the stock exchanges.[69] Barring the National Stock Exchange of India Limited and the OTC Exchange of India, stock exchanges continued to function as mutualized bodies. Many had not even been incorporated including the then BSE Limited—one of the two largest stock exchanges in the country. Accordingly, the central government promulgated the Securities Laws (Amendment) Ordinance, 2004 (followed by the legislature making an amendment to the SCRA) to facilitate corporatization and demutualization.[70] Besides bringing in

---

[69] In the early part of 2001, stock exchanges witnessed extreme volatility in the stock index. Prices of equity shares of several companies, too, fluctuated abnormally. There was widespread apprehension that these were the result of pervasive market manipulation to the detriment of borrowed funds of banks and small investors. There were indications that the Calcutta Stock Exchange, the third largest exchange in the country, was facing problems for its payout as some major brokers had defaulted on their pay-in obligations. Taking note of these and other related events, Parliament constituted a Joint Committee in April 2001 to enquire into the stock market scam and matters relating thereto. The Report dated 12 December 2002 was presented before the Parliament on 19 December 2002. Recommendations of the Joint Committee Report formed the basis for several reforms in the securities market including strengthening of SEBI.

[70] Sections 4A and 4B of the SCRA.

crucial structural reforms, this process also had other benefits. To cope with competition, stock exchanges required funds. While member-owned stock exchanges had limitations in raising funds, corporatized and demutualized exchanges could access the securities markets. These changes to the Indian securities market were in sync with the international trend. Thus, 'an informal survey by the World Federation of Stock Exchanges (the FIBV) in 2000 showed that 100 percent of its member respondents were either demutualized, in the process of demutualizing, or actively considering demutualization'.[71] Accordingly, all the stock exchanges became corporatized and demutualized, and it became a condition precedent for granting of recognition to any new stock exchanges under the SCRA.

The Indian securities market and its regulation continue to evolve particularly due to evolution of the meaning and scope of securities. As we examined in Chapter 1, commodity derivatives have recently been recognized as 'securities' under the SCRA.[72] Thus entities that regulated and controlled the business of buying, selling, and dealing in commodity derivatives are now considered as stock exchanges and are regulated under the SCRA.[73]

***

Regulation of the public offering of securities has its genesis in company law. It got fortified with the enactment of the Capital Issues Control Act and the SCRA. These provided a sound legal framework for the regulation of the public offering of securities. However, in practice, enforcement of these laws was weak. The central government was plagued with problems of centralized bureaucracy, and lacked a coordinated and focused securities enforcement programme. Stock exchanges too failed in their task of effective and meaningful self-regulation. A paper published in 1979 on the regulation of the Indian securities market, after detailed survey and interviews, had this to say:

---

[71] Elliot (n. 60), at p. 3.

[72] See sections 'Concept of Securities' and 'Securities Market' in Chapter 1 of this volume.

[73] See section 28A of the Forward Contracts (Regulation) Act, 1952 and section 131 of the Finance Act, 2015.

Indian investors are being deceived by the myth of self-regulation. From appearances it seems that the exchanges are regulating their member-brokers and overseeing a corporate disclosure program, and that the Central Government is a participant and big brother to all of this.... The fact is that the Central Government does not oversee self-regulatory responsibilities and, despite the power and need to do so, has never regulated directly. The same three government individuals sit as members of the governing bodies of the eight exchanges. Along with their other duties, they do not have the time to properly monitor exchange activities. Examinations of the exchanges and the broker community have never been conducted. Likewise, no proceedings have been brought directly by the Central Government against the exchanges or any of their members.[74]

Economic reforms initiated by the Government of India pursuant to the economic crisis of 1990–1 led to significant changes in the legal framework governing securities. The Capital Issues Control Act was repealed and companies could raise capital from the market without seeking prior consent of the central government, and freely price such securities. Contemporaneously, SEBI, a specialized autonomous regulatory body enjoined to protect the interests of investors in securities and to promote the development of, and to regulate, the securities market, was established under the Securities and Exchange Board of India Act, 1992. In addition to SEBI's powers and functions under the parent statute, the powers of the central government under the SCRA were delegated to it. Subsequently, the Depositories Act, 1996 was enacted to provide for regulation of depositories. Regulation of the public offering of securities, thus, entered a new phase, which continues till today and is the subject matter of the following chapters of this volume.

[74] Robert C. Rosen, 'The Myth of Self-regulation or the Dangers of Securities Regulation without Administration: The Indian Experience' (1979) 2(4) Journal of Comparative Corporate Law and Securities Regulation 261, at p. 288.

3. Public Offer and Prospectus

B y now, we have examined in brief the case of companies raising capital by issue of securities. In Chapter 1, we observed that a company intending to finance its business through issue of securities would raise capital directly by issuing shares and debentures. Further, while private companies are prohibited from inviting the public to subscribe for any securities of the company, public companies can mobilize substantial capital by issue of shares or debentures to the public. This chapter looks at the concept of public offer of shares and debentures[1] and its legal context. The concept of public offer is intertwined with that of prospectus because a public company issues securities to the public through a document called prospectus. Therefore, the concept of prospectus is also the focus of this chapter. The chapter begins with exploring the reasons for a company making a public offer of its securities. Next, it examines the meaning and constituents of a

---

[1] References to securities in this chapter are, therefore, to shares and debentures only.

prospectus. The principal legal requirements that a prospectus attracts are then discussed, followed by the function of a prospectus and types of prospectuses that are issued in the securities market. Then the chapter examines what is listing of securities, types of public offerings, proponents of a public offer, and the concept of 'offer for sale'. The chapter ends with describing prospectuses issued in India of companies incorporated outside India.

Reasons to Go Public

A successful public offering—especially an initial public offering (IPO) of equity shares—is a milestone for a company, its management, and its shareholders. For most companies that go public, it is a once-in-a-lifetime event. Though not an irreversible event, it is a new stage in the life of a company: new opportunities as well as risks and challenges. It is important, therefore, to understand the reasons for going public by referring first to public offerings of equity shares and then to debentures and preference shares.

Equity Shares

Typically, public companies start off as being private and continue to remain so for a considerable period.[2] Subsequently, some of them decide to undertake a public issue of equity shares for various reasons. First, companies go public to raise additional equity capital. This additional

---

[2] In fact, only a small percentage of public companies 'go public'. As an illustration, there were 62,412 public limited companies as of 31 March 2014, out of which the number of companies that went public and were listed on BSE Limited, the National Stock Exchange of India Limited (NSE), and the Metropolitan Stock Exchange of India Limited were 5,336, 1,688, and 12, respectively. (These figures have not been adjusted for the fact that there may be some companies that have listed only their debentures and not equity shares, and companies that are listed on one stock exchange may also be listed on the other stock exchange(s)). See, Securities and Exchange Board of India, *Annual Report* (2013–14), and Ministry of Corporate Affairs, Government of India, *58th Annual Report on the Working & Administration of the Companies Act, 1956* (31 March 2014).

equity capital serves many purposes: It finances companies' growth and expansion; increases the bearers of risk-capital, if existing shareholders are reluctant to provide further equity capital; and paves the way for re-accessing equity markets easily through methods such as Qualified Institutions Placement (QIP).[3] Additional equity capital also reduces leverage, that is, ratio of debt to debt plus equity capital, which improves the chances of the company to obtain loans from banks at better rates.

Disinvestment is another reason for going public, and to understand it, some historical background is necessary. The Constitution of India empowers the central government and state governments to carry on any trade or business; acquire, hold, and dispose of property; and enter into contracts. Since the 1950s, the exercise of this power and implementation of socialist economic policies led to the setting up and operation of a large number of companies whose equity shares were entirely owned by the government, such government companies being commonly referred to as Public Sector Enterprises (PSEs). The central government generally owned the PSEs carrying large business and operations due to the policy of centralization, and greater power and resources with it. These Central PSEs (CPSEs) were predominant and continue to be so in most of the large-scale economic activities such as the public utilities and infrastructure sector consisting of railways, roads, ports, airports, power, telecommunications, etc., and the tradable goods sector consisting of coal, oil and natural gas, steel, fertilizer, aluminium, etc. By the end of 1990, the number of CPSEs had increased to 244 with a total investment of Rs 99,329 crore.[4]

In 1991, the Government of India adopted the new industrial policy, which included disinvestment, namely, sale of a part of its shareholding in the CPSEs. In ordinary terms, disinvestment is akin to the sale of shares of a company by a shareholder to a prospective purchaser.

[3] Qualified Institutions Placement means issue and allotment of equity shares by a listed company to qualified institutional buyers (a class of sophisticated investors such as mutual funds and foreign portfolio investors) on a private placement basis. The placement is undertaken in terms of the Securities and Exchange Board of India (Issue of Capital and Disclosure Requirements) Regulations, 2009 (or the ICDR Regulations).

[4] Department of Disinvestment, Ministry of Finance, Government of India, *White Paper on Disinvestment of Central Public Sector Enterprises* (31 July 2007).

However, the difference lies in the fact that it is a sovereign function and is driven by political considerations. Despite some variance, the objective of disinvestment has largely been to raise budgetary resources for the government, improving the operations and management of the CPSEs, and encouraging direct or indirect public holding of the equity shares in the CPSEs. The method of disinvestment, on the other hand, has witnessed significant changes. Initially, the government adopted the bundling system wherein a certain percentage of equity shares of CPSEs doing well, doing badly, and falling in between were bundled together, and sold to prospective purchasers. Auctioning the equity shares and sale of equity shares through the global depository receipt (GDR) mechanism followed this approach. Disinvestment was also made through strategic sale. Since 2009, the policy and approach to disinvestment have been to make public offerings of shares and list all the profitable CPSEs on the stock exchange.[5] As a result, a large number of CPSEs have gone public wherein the central government has offered for sale the equity shares owned by it in the CPSEs to the public.

In disinvestment, the government generally sells a small percentage of its shareholding in a government company while ensuring that its equity shareholding does not fall below 51 per cent. However, in companies in the private sector, an existing shareholder may instead look to exit from the company. Exit from the company is, thus, the next reason for a company going public. Shareholders with such a strategy are generally venture capital funds (VCFs) and private equity funds, which invest primarily in equity shares of start-ups or emerging companies ordinarily involved in new products, new services, or a new business model.[6]

---

[5] Ministry of Finance, Government of India, *Annual Report* (2010–11) and *Annual Report* (2014–15).

[6] Globally this model of investment is followed only by VCFs. Private equity funds, on the other hand, invest using a leveraged buyout model wherein the fund acquires a company principally through debt finance; the company's assets are used as collateral for the debt and its income is used to service the debt. The fund is then involved in helping the company grow, with the ultimate goal of either selling it to a strategic buyer or taking it public. However, in India, due to legal and regulatory restrictions, and other reasons, private equity funds largely follow the VCF model of investment. See Afra Afsharipour, 'The Indian Private Equity Model' (July 2013) NSE Working Paper <http://www.nseindia.com/research/content/nse_working_papers.htm> accessed on 9 April 2016.

With the fund's investment, the company grows thereby increasing the value of the initial investment, which is then realized through the sale of equity shares. Exit through offer for sale to the public is generally preferred since a public offering leads to share liquidity and attracts many buyers. Public offering also optimizes the value of the shares.

Other reasons for going public are share liquidity, macroeconomic conditions, and compliance with certain special legal requirements.[7] Equity shares are considered liquid if they can be easily sold for cash. After a successful public offering of shares, equity shares are listed and traded on stock exchanges, thereby making them liquid. Companies value such liquidity for a variety of reasons. First, potential liquidity attracts more investors. Second, companies with acquisition of other companies as a business strategy can use their liquid shares as a currency for acquisition even if they lack sufficient cash or borrowing capacity.[8] Third, companies can offer the liquid equity shares to employees as compensation through employee stock options schemes and employee stock purchase schemes.[9] These schemes have tax benefits and permit companies to provide financial assistance, thereby making them attractive to employees. Companies engaged in business activities, such as information technology and engineering services, for which employees are the principal assets, generally utilize such schemes as they aid in employee recruitment and retention.[10]

Macroeconomic conditions also affect the decision to go public. Since the early 1990s, the growth of the Indian economy has attracted unprecedented foreign investment. Companies have benefited from this inward investment and generally watch for those periods when the investment sentiment among foreign investors is positive and high. Such periods create optimal market conditions for going public.

[7] Share liquidity and macroeconomic conditions are not singular reasons for going public, but coupled with any of the foregoing reasons, they make it advantageous for a company to go public. While compliance with certain special legal requirements can be the sole reason for going public, such laws are occasionally introduced.

[8] William K. Sjostrom, Jr, 'Carving a New Path to Equity Capital and Share Liquidity' (2009) 50 Boston College Law Review 639, at p. 642.

[9] These and other schemes of listed companies are principally regulated by the Securities and Exchange Board of India (Share Based Employee Benefits) Regulations, 2014.

[10] Sjostrom, Jr (n. 8).

Companies also go public to comply with specific laws such as the Securities Contracts (Regulation) Rules, 1957 (or the SCRR)—rules framed under the Securities Contracts (Regulation) Act, 1956 (or the SCRA) to regulate stock exchanges. Every company making a public offer is required to,'before making [the] offer, make an application to one or more recognised stock exchange or exchanges and obtain permission for the securities to be dealt with in such stock exchange or exchanges'.[11] However, listing and dealing of securities on the stock exchange is not a matter of right. It is subject to fulfilling prescribed legal requirements, one of which is that a certain minimum percentage of the equity shares issued by a company should have been offered and allotted to the public. The justification for the minimum public[12] shareholding requirement is that a large number of shares distributed among a large number of shareholders provides greater liquidity to the investors and helps discover fair prices. The larger the number of shares and the number of shareholders, that is, the larger the public float, the less is the scope for price manipulation. A minimum offer is generally prescribed at the time of initial listing, which is contemporaneous with the public offer, while a minimum float is prescribed for continued listing on the stock exchange subsequent to the public offer.

Prior to June 2010, the percentage of minimum public offer for initial listing was 25 per cent, or 10 per cent subject to fulfilment of specified conditions.[13] Most of the companies going public preferred the 10 per

---

[11] Sub-section (1) of section 40 of the Companies Act.

[12] Here 'public' must be understood in contradistinction with 'promoters', namely persons in control of the company. Clause (d) of rule 2 of the SCRR defines public to mean 'persons other than— (i) the promoter and promoter group; (ii) subsidiaries and associates of the company. Explanation. – For the purpose of this clause the words "promoter" and "promoter group" shall have the same meaning as assigned to them under the Securities and Exchange Board of India (Issue of Capital and Disclosure Requirements) Regulations, 2009.'

[13] Clause (b) of sub-rule (2) of rule 19 of the SCRR. The percentage of minimum public shareholding for initial listing has had a chequered history. Prior to September 1993, clause (b) of sub-rule (2) of rule 19 of the SCRR required a minimum public offer of 60 per cent of the issued capital of a company for getting listed on a recognized stock exchange. On 20 September 1993, it was changed to 25 per cent to encourage listing and to broaden the market.

cent route, as 25 per cent of the capital could be a huge sum, which the company did not require, and the promoters were unwilling to allow public shareholding as high as 25 per cent. However, given that the benefits of a larger public float far outweighed the costs, the SCRR was amended with effect from 4 June 2010 and the 10 per cent route was largely done away with.[14] Thus, for initial listing, at least 25 per cent of each class or kind of equity shares issued by the company should have been offered and allotted to the public in terms of an offer document.[15] Companies already listed under the 10 per cent route were required to increase their public shareholding to 25 per cent within a period of three years in the specified manner. The manner specified for this purpose was primarily public issue, rights issue, and bonus issue.[16] Thus, many companies went public to comply with the SCRR. The minimum public shareholding rule under the SCRR was once again amended with effect from 18 November 2014 to provide some relief to companies for initial listing.[17] The 25 per cent rule was relaxed for companies whose post-public-issue capital calculated at offer price was very high. However,

---

In 1999, SEBI relaxed the norm for companies in the information technology sector and permitted them to obtain initial listing by making a minimum public offer of 10 per cent, and in April 2000, extended this relaxation to companies in various other sectors. Subsequently, through an amendment to clause (b) of sub-rule (2) of rule 19 of the SCRR with effect from 7 June 2001, the pre-June 2010 initial listing rule of minimum public offer of 25 per cent, or 10 per cent subject to fulfilment of specified conditions, was introduced.

[14] Securities Contracts (Regulation) (Amendment) Rules, 2010.

[15] Clause (b) of sub-rule (2) of rule 19 of the SCRR. The 10 per cent route was available under a limited circumstance subject to the condition that 25 per cent public shareholding must be achieved within a period of three years.

[16] Clause 40A of the erstwhile equity listing agreement—an agreement that companies enter into with stock exchanges at the time of initial listing of the equity shares—is now subsumed under regulation 38 of Securities and Exchange Board of India (Listing Obligations and Disclosure Requirements) Regulations, 2015 (or the LODR Regulations) and circular no. CIR/CFD/CMD/14/2015 dated 30 November 2015 issued by SEBI.

[17] Clause (b) of sub-rule (2) of rule 19 of the SCRR as amended by the Securities Contracts (Regulation) Third Amendment Rules, 2014 and Securities Contracts (Regulation) (Amendment) Rules, 2015.

these companies would have to increase their public shareholding to at least 25 per cent within a period of three years from the date of listing of the equity shares in the manner specified by the Securities and Exchange Board of India (SEBI).

Debentures and Preference Shares

Raising capital to finance business and operations is the principal reason for which a company makes a public offering of debentures or bonds, and preference shares. However, in practice, bonds issued by companies (or corporate bonds) are relatively fewer in number, compared to the overall size of the debt market. This too largely consists of bonds issued on a private placement basis.[18] During the financial year 2014–15, the number of private placements of corporate bonds reported to BSE Limited and National Stock Exchange of India Limited was 2,611 (total amount Rs 404,137 crore), while the number of public issues of corporate bonds stood at 24 (total amount Rs 9,413 crore).[19] Compared to debentures, preference shares have lagged much. Given the nature and limitations of preference shares, they have played a relatively insignificant role as a source of capital for Indian companies.

Reasons to go public must be juxtaposed with certain costs associated with public offering. Other than the monetary cost involved in a public offering programme, it engenders extensive disclosure requirements on a continuous basis and the actions of the company and its directors and officers are exposed to potential civil and criminal liabilities and regulatory actions under the securities laws.

Prospectus

Keeping in view the foregoing costs and benefits, a company may choose not to go public. However, if a company decides to issue securities to the public, it can only do so through a prospectus.[20] The Companies

---

[18] Government bonds largely dominate the Indian bond market. See Stephen Wells and Lotte Schou-Zibell, 'India's Bond Market: Developments and Challenges Ahead' (Asian Development Bank, December 2008), at p. 7.

[19] Securities and Exchange Board of India, *Annual Report* (2014–15).

[20] Clause (a) of sub-section (1) of section 23 of the Companies Act.

Act defines a 'prospectus' to mean 'any document described or issued as a prospectus and includes a red herring prospectus referred to in section 32 or shelf prospectus referred to in section 31 or any notice, circular, advertisement or other document inviting offers from the public for the subscription or purchase of any securities of a body corporate'.[21] The expression 'inviting offers from the public for the subscription or purchase of any securities of a body corporate' qualifies everything that precedes it. The prospectus, therefore, essentially is a document inviting offers from the public for the subscription or purchase of any securities of a body corporate. A document like an advertisement that merely announces the fact of publication of a prospectus by a company in connection with the issue of its securities without any invitation to the public to subscribe to them will not be a prospectus.[22] We can divide the definition of a prospectus into the following components: (a) any document described or issued as a prospectus and includes a red herring prospectus referred to in section 32 of the Companies Act or shelf prospectus referred to in section 31 of the Companies Act or any notice, circular, advertisement, or other document, (b) inviting offers from, (c) the public, (d) for the subscription or purchase of any securities of a body corporate. For conceptual clarity, we will examine each of these components, not necessarily in a sequential order.

'inviting offers from'

Issue or sale of securities pursuant to a public offering involves the formation and performance of a contract between the company and the applicant. Like any other contract, this contract too is formed by the acceptance of an offer or proposal. But the prospectus is generally not the offer; it is an 'invitation to treat'—a communication made by a party not as an offer, but as an invitation whereby he invites the other party to make an offer. Invitation to treat is distinguishable from an offer primarily on the ground that it is not made with the intention that it

---

[21] Clause (70) of section 2 of the Companies Act.

[22] Ministry of Finance, Government of India, *Report of the Companies Act Amendment Committee* (1957), at p. 19. There are, however, some limitations on issue of such advertisements. See the section titled 'Limitations on Publicity, Research Reports and Financial Assistance' in Chapter 5 of this volume.

becomes binding as soon as the person to whom it is addressed simply communicates his assent to its terms.[23] It is in this sense that the prospectus has been defined to mean a document 'inviting offers'. Offer, on the other hand, is the application made by an applicant to the company in response to the prospectus, and a contract of issue or sale of securities is formed when the company accepts this offer.

This analysis should, however, not be treated as decisive. A document that makes an offer for subscription or purchase of securities to the public would also be a prospectus. In fact, it is possible to draft a prospectus in the form of an offer capable of acceptance by recipients. The legislative history of the definition of a prospectus as well as other provisions of the Companies Act on a prospectus indicate that 'inviting offers' has not been used in the strict sense as understood in the law of contract. The Indian Companies Act of 1913, which introduced the definition of a prospectus in the statute book, defined a prospectus to mean, 'any prospectus, notice, circular, advertisement or other invitation, offering to the public for subscription or purchase any shares or debentures of a company'.[24] In this definition, both 'invitation' and 'offering' have been included as a function of the prospectus. The Companies Act of 1956 changed this definition to its present form of 'inviting offers'. But there is nothing in the Bhabha Committee Report[25] as well as the legislative material preceding the enactment of the act to indicate that this was done

---

[23]   A.G. Guest (ed.), *Chitty on Contracts*, Vol. 1: *General Principles*, (27th edn, Sweet & Maxwell 1994), at p. 94. See also *National Textile Corporation (M.P.) Limited v. M.R. Jadhav*, (2008) 7 SCC 29; *Board of Trustees, Visakhapatnam Port Trust and Ors v. T.S.N. Raju and Anr*, (2006) 7 SCC 664; *Bank of India and Ors v. O.P. Swarnakar*, (2003) 2 SCC 721; *Vishal Builders (P) Limited v. Delhi Development Authority*, (1977) ILR 1 Del 724.

[24]   Sub-section (14) of section 2 of the Indian Companies Act, 1913.

[25]   Department of Economic Affairs, Ministry of Finance, Government of India, *Report of the Company Law Committee* (1952) (also called the 'Bhabha Committee Report'). The Government of India constituted the company law committee in 1950 to consider and report the amendments necessary in the Indian Companies Act, 1913. The report of this committee is commonly referred to as the 'Bhabha Committee Report' after the name of C.H. Bhabha, the chairman of the committee. The Bhabha Committee Report formed the basis for the enactment of the Companies Act, 1956.

to restrict the scope to invitation only, or that the contract law principles of invitation to treat and offer were intended to be strictly imported into the definition of a prospectus. On the contrary, the Bhabha Committee Report recommended broadening of the scope of the definition of a prospectus.[26] Further, several provisions of the Companies Act on prospectus also support the conclusion that a prospectus encompasses the contract law principle of 'invitation to treat' as well as 'offer'.[27]

'the public'

For the document to qualify as a prospectus, the offer of securities must have been made to the public. This is the most defining feature of a prospectus, and, juxtaposed with the capital requirement of companies for which the company engages with investors, it makes the prospectus an important document for a company intending to raise capital by issue of securities. If the document inviting subscription for securities is a prospectus, a wide gamut of statutory and regulatory provisions are attracted, non-compliance of which, whether intentional or accidental, can attract civil and criminal liabilities to a host of actors involved in the capital-raising programme. In *Sahara India Real Estate Corporation Limited and Ors v. Securities and Exchange Board of India and Anr*,[28] the Supreme Court of India directed the appellants to refund Rs 22,520 crore with interest to investors on the grounds that the appellants had offered the securities to the public without complying with the prospectus laws. The concept of public, therefore, is the cornerstone of primary market securities regulation.

To begin with, neither has the Companies Act defined 'public' nor is there a provision similar to section 67 of the Companies Act, 1956 designed to assist in determining whether an offer is to the public. It has also not been defined in the SCRA or the Securities and Exchange

[26] Department of Economic Affairs, Ministry of Finance, Government of India, *Report of the Company Law Committee* (1952), at p. 24.

[27] See sections 25, 28, 31, 32, 42, 71, and 388 of the Companies Act.

[28] (2013) 1 SCC 1. See also the order of the Supreme Court of India in *Sahara India Real Estate Exchange Corporation Limited and Anr v. Securities and Exchange Board of India*, (2013) 2 SCC 733.

Board of India Act, 1992 (or the SEBI Act) or the Depositories Act, 1996.[29] Instead, the SCRR defines 'public' to mean persons other than: (a) the promoter and promoter group; (b) subsidiaries and associates of the company.[30] The Companies Act, however, does not permit definitions in the SCRR to be incorporated by reference into it.[31] It is also not permitted because the context in which 'public' has been defined and used in the SCRR, which we examined earlier in this chapter, is different from the context in which it is used in the definition of prospectus, which we shall examine now.[32] Therefore, the meaning of 'public' will have to be determined in negative terms as provided under section 42 of the Companies Act on private placement. Private placement means any offer of securities or invitation to subscribe securities to a select group of persons by a company (other than by way of a public offer) through issue of private placement offer letter, and which satisfies the conditions specified in section 42.[33] The most important condition is:

---

[29] Clause (95) of section 2 of the Companies Act states that 'words and expressions used and not defined in this Act but defined in the Securities Contracts (Regulation) Act, 1956 (42 of 1956) or the Securities and Exchange Board of India Act, 1992 (15 of 1992) or the Depositories Act, 1996 (22 of 1996) shall have the meanings respectively assigned to them in those Acts'.

[30] Clause (d) of rule 2 of the SCRR defines public to mean 'persons other than—(i) the promoter and promoter group; (ii) subsidiaries and associates of the company. Explanation. – For the purpose of this clause the words "promoter" and "promoter group" shall have the same meaning as assigned to them under the Securities and Exchange Board of India (Issue of Capital and Disclosure Requirements) Regulations, 2009.'

[31] See clause (95) of section 2 of the Companies Act (n. 29).

[32] Section 2 of the Companies Act on 'Definitions' states 'In this Act, unless the context otherwise requires...'. This means that a definition has to be read in the context in which it is used and the purpose for which the legislation was enacted. If the context does not permit or where the context requires otherwise, the meaning assigned to the expression in the definition need not be applied. See also *Ichchpur Industrial Cooperative Society Ltd.* v. *Oil & Natural Gas Commission*, (1997) 2 SCC 42; *Youaraj Singh* v. *Chander Bahadur Karki*, (2007) 1 SCC 770; *Printers (Mysore) Ltd.* v. *CTO*, (1994) 2 SCC 434. For the context in which 'public' has been used in the SCRR, see the section 'Reasons to Go Public' in the earlier part of this chapter and 'Eligibility Criteria' in Chapter 5 of this volume.

[33] Clause (ii) of Explanation II of sub-section (2) of section 42 of the Companies Act.

[T]he offer of securities or the invitation to subscribe securities, shall be made to such number of persons not exceeding fifty or such higher number as may be prescribed [excluding qualified institutional buyers and employees of the company being offered securities under a scheme of employees stock option as per provisions of clause (b) of sub-section (1) of section 62], in a financial year and on such conditions (including the form and manner of private placement) as may be prescribed.[34]

Section 42 of the Companies Act, therefore, is pivotal to understanding the boundary between an offer to the public and a non-public offering (which is a private placement).[35] The effect of this provision is as follows:

1. The number of offerees in a financial year is the determining characteristic of a public offer. An offer of securities by a company to more than 50 persons (or such higher number as may be prescribed[36]) in the aggregate in a financial year is an offer to the public. Offers made to qualified institutional buyers and employees of the company under a scheme of employees' stock option as per the provisions of clause (b) of sub-section (1) of section 62 are excluded from the numerical limit. The intent seems to be that qualified institutional buyers,[37] being investors

---

[34] Sub-section (2) of section 42 of the Companies Act.

[35] The Companies (Amendment) Bill, 2016, introduced in the lower house of the Parliament on 16 March 2016, proposes to substitute section 42 with a new provision. However, the new provision is largely on the same line as section 42 and does not disturb its conceptual basis. It merely simplifies the sub-sections for better compliance, modifies the penalty provision for contravention of the section and restricts utilization of money raised through private placement unless securities are allotted and return of allotment is filed with the registrar of companies.

[36] Sub-rule (2) of rule 14 of the Companies (Prospectus and Allotment of Securities) Rules, 2014 prescribes 200 as the number.

[37] Qualified institutional buyers are institutional investors such as mutual funds, venture capital funds, alternative investment funds, public financial institutions, scheduled commercial banks, insurance companies, foreign portfolio investors, and foreign venture capital investors. See clause (i) of Explanation II of sub-section (2) of section 42 of the Companies Act and clause (zd) of sub-regulation (1) of regulation 2 of the ICDR Regulations.

sufficiently well informed of investment practices to be able to fend for themselves, do not need the protection of prospectus law. Employees of the company who have been offered securities under a scheme of employees' stock option have been excluded since such schemes are governed by a separate regulatory regime. It must be noted that the numerical limit rule would be reckoned individually for corporate security of each kind, that is, equity share, preference share, or debenture.[38]

2. A wide range of corporate actions in relation to persons, whose number exceeds the numerical limit, constitutes a public offer. If a company makes an offer to allot or invites subscription, or allots, or enters into an agreement to allot, securities to more than the prescribed number of persons, it is an offer to the public.[39] It is irrelevant that the other person was not capable of accepting the offer or rejected the offer, or that the allotment of securities did not take place or that the company did not intend to list the securities on any recognized stock exchange.

3. The legislative intent is clear that the number of offerees is the conclusive factor and not the class. Even if the offer is made to only a small circle of friends or relatives of the company's directors or promoters, to their business associates, or to select customers or suppliers of the company, it will be regarded as a public offer if the threshold of the prescribed number of persons is crossed. Marking a document 'for private circulation only' would not prevent an offer from being a public offer.

4. A corollary of points (2) and (3) above is that if a company offers shares for subscription to its shareholders on a rights basis and the number of shareholders is more than the prescribed number of persons, the rights issue is also a public offer. Even if the rights issue is to less than the prescribed number of persons, it may become a public offer if the rights issue includes a right exercisable by the equity shareholders to renounce the shares offered to them

---

[38] Explanation to clause (b) of sub-rule (2) of rule 14 of the Companies (Prospectus and Allotment of Securities) Rules, 2014.

[39] Explanation I to sub-section (2) of section 42 of the Companies Act.

in favour of any other persons.[40] This would be the case because of reasons stated in point (6) below. These conclusions are, however, not free from doubt, and are based on the strict wording of section 42, and the lack of adequate legislative guidance on such an important matter.[41] Nonetheless, the Companies Act exempts a rights issue from complying with some of the prospectus provisions. The prospectus need not state the information and set out the reports prescribed under sub-section (1) of section 26 of the Companies Act.[42] The rationale for this exemption is that preparing a prospectus with extensive prescribed disclosure is an expensive exercise and need not be undertaken in cases where the subscribers do not need the protection of mandatory disclosure. A member of a company is presumed to have knowledge of the company's financial position and its prospects. If the member renounces his right in favour of another member, the latter, who is already a shareholder, is presumed to be similarly acquainted. If, however, the member renounces his right in favour of a stranger, the latter may not have that advantage.[43] For similar reasons, the Companies Act extends the same relaxation 'to the issue of a prospectus or form of application relating to shares or debentures which are, or are to be, in all respects uniform with shares or debentures previously issued and for the time being dealt in or quoted on a recognized stock exchange.'[44] In reality, however, these relaxations are of not much benefit since SEBI's regulations on issue of shares and debentures contain no such relaxation.[45] This again is an indication of the incoherence that exists in our securities laws.

---

[40] See sub-clause (ii) of clause (a) of sub-section (1) of section 62 of the Companies Act.

[41] *Securities and Exchange Board of India v. Kunnamkulam Paper Mills Limited*, (2013) ILR 1 Ker 149.

[42] Clause (a) of sub-section (2) of section 26 of the Companies Act.

[43] Ministry of Finance, Government of India, *Report of the Companies Act Amendment Committee* (1957), at p. 37.

[44] Clause (b) of sub-section (2) of section 26 of the Companies Act.

[45] See the section 'Principal Legal Requirements of Prospectus' in the later part of this chapter.

5. Similarly, a bonus issue, and offer to allot or allotment of shares pursuant to a scheme of amalgamation or takeover to more than the prescribed number of persons too would constitute a public offer. However, there is no requirement to issue a prospectus in these cases as no cash consideration from the allottee is involved (and hence no subscription or purchase of shares).[46] It must be noted that rights issue and bonus issue to more than the prescribed number of persons is a public offer irrespective of the fact that section 23 of the Companies Act uses these methods in contradistinction with public offer. Section 23 uses these expressions to state the different methods of issue of corporate securities, but the issue of securities is still subject to other provisions of the Companies Act, notably section 42.

6. Mere compliance with the numerical limit is not sufficient. The offer of securities or invitation to subscribe securities must also comply with the other provisions of section 42, else it will be treated as a public offer.[47] Thus, the offer of securities must be through issue of a private placement offer letter to less than the prescribed number of persons in a manner that the offerees constitute a select group of persons. For this, the company must make offers only to such persons whose names it has recorded prior to the invitation to subscribe; such persons must have received the offer by name; and the company must have kept a complete record of such offers.[48] The restrictive nature of the group of persons is further ensured by the rule that the private placement offer letter must be accompanied by an application form serially numbered and addressed specifically to the person to whom the offer is made. It must be sent to them, either in writing or in electronic mode, within 30 days of recording the names of such persons.[49] No person other than the person so addressed in the

---

[46] See the analysis under the section "'for the subscription or purchase of any securities of a body corporate'" in the later part of this chapter.

[47] Sub-section (4) of section 42 of the Companies Act.

[48] Sub-section (7) of section 42 of the Companies Act.

[49] Clause (b) of sub-rule (1) of rule 14 of the Companies (Prospectus and Allotment of Securities) Rules, 2014.

application form is allowed to apply through such application form and the company must treat any application not conforming to this condition as invalid.[50] Thus renunciation of the offer, in part or full, by the addressee is not permitted.[51] The company is also prohibited from releasing any public advertisements or utilizing any media, marketing, or distribution channels or agents to inform the public at large about the private placement.[52]

7. Private placement is a method of issue of all corporate securities. For private placement of equity shares and securities convertible into or exchangeable with equity shares, company law uses a distinct expression, namely 'preferential offer' and prescribes some additional compliance.[53] Conceptually 'private placement' and 'preferential offer' are the same.[54] Unlike the Companies Act, 1956, the Companies Act, 2013 specifically defines 'private placement' and devotes a separate chapter of the act for it. Retention and continuance of the expression 'preferential offer' from the

---

[50] Proviso to clause (b) of sub-rule (1) of rule 14 of the Companies (Prospectus and Allotment of Securities) Rules, 2014.

[51] Section 42 of the Companies Act, in the form it is proposed to be substituted by the Companies (Amendment) Bill, 2016, introduced in the lower house of the Parliament on 16 March 2016, makes this position expressly clear.

[52] Sub-section (4) of section 42 of the Companies Act.

[53] The Explanation to sub-rule (1) of rule 13 of the Companies (Share Capital and Debentures) Rules, 2014 defines 'preferential offer' to mean 'an issue of shares or other securities, by a company to any select person or group of persons on a preferential basis and does not include shares or other securities offered through a public issue, rights issue, employee stock option scheme, employee stock purchase scheme or an issue of sweat equity shares or bonus shares or depository receipts issued in a country outside India or foreign securities'. The expression, 'shares or other securities' means 'equity shares, fully convertible debentures, partly convertible debentures or any other securities, which would be convertible into or exchanged with equity shares at a later date'.

[54] This is despite the fact that private placement is made to 'a select group of persons' and preferential offer is to 'any select person or group of persons'. The difference in defining the recipients of the offer is largely of semantic value and the legislative intention under section 42 is not to exclude from the ambit of private placement an offer of securities or invitation to subscribe securities to one select person.

rules framed under the Companies Act, 1956 was, therefore, unnecessary and will add to the incoherence.

Although section 42 of the Companies Act explains and clarifies what an offer to the public is, the absence of a statutory definition or specific provision that explains the meaning of 'public' is bound to create confusion. For example, the meaning of the expression 'the public at large' is unclear in the statutory provision prohibiting any company making a private placement from utilizing any media channel to inform the public at large.[55] It is a common business practice for public and private companies alike to inform potential investors about the proposed private placement before making the offer or inviting them to subscribe. Unless an investor is contacted and spoken to, it would be impossible to identify the prospective allottees whose names can be recorded and to whom the private placement offer letter can be sent. In such a scenario, does the expression 'the public at large' mean any section of the public selected at random as long as the number of persons informed about the private placement does not exceed the limit specified under sub-section (2) of section 42? If it does, then it defeats the investor protection objective of prospectus laws; if it does not, then the scope of 'the public at large' is unknown and it becomes challenging for any company to issue securities without making a public offer.

'for the subscription or purchase of any securities of a body corporate'

The prospectus must invite offers for the subscription or purchase of securities. Subscription is the acquisition of securities upon issue and allotment of unissued securities; purchase, on the other hand, is the acquisition of securities issued previously—in either case for cash payment.[56] As a result, when shares are issued to the public for non-cash consideration, the prospectus provisions do not apply.

[55] Sub-section (8) of section 42 of the Companies Act.

[56] *Khoday Distilleries Limited v. Commissioner of Income Tax*, [2008] 307 ITR 312 (SC); *Sri Gopal Jalan & Company v. Calcutta Stock Exchange Association Limited*, AIR 1964 SC 250; *Arnison v. Smith*, (1889) L.R. 41 Ch. D. 348; *In Re: VGM Holdings Limited*, [1942] 1 All ER 224; *Governments Stock and Other Securities Investment Co. Ltd. v. Christopher*, [1956] 1 All ER 490.

The subject matter of the subscription or purchase must be securities[57] of a body corporate, which are shares and debentures. Securities of other forms of business organizations such as collective investment schemes (CISs), mutual funds, etc.,[58] therefore, do not fall within the regulatory ambit of prospectus law under the Companies Act. It must be noted that the expression body corporate includes a company incorporated outside India.[59] Documents inviting offers from the public in India for the subscription or purchase of any securities of a company incorporated outside India would, thus, be a prospectus. However, Chapter III of the Companies Act on 'Prospectus and Allotment of Securities' applies only to companies incorporated under the Companies Act.[60] However, as we see later, Chapter XXII of the Companies Act on 'Companies Incorporated outside India' contains prospectus provisions in line with Chapter III of the Companies Act.[61]

'any document described or issued as a prospectus and...advertisement or other document'

The expression 'any document described or issued as a prospectus and includes a red herring prospectus referred to in section 32 or shelf prospectus referred to in section 31 or any notice, circular, advertisement or other document' refers to the form of the public offer. The form of the public offer must be a document with the possible exception of 'advertisement'. However, a *noscitur a sociis*[62] reading suggests that even

---

[57] For the meaning of 'securities', see the section 'Concept of Securities' in Chapter 1 of this volume.

[58] For these, see the section 'Concept of Securities' in Chapter 1 of this volume.

[59] Clause (11) of section 2 of the Companies Act.

[60] Section 23 of the Companies Act.

[61] See the section 'Prospectuses of Companies Incorporated Outside India' at the end of this chapter.

[62] *Noscitur a sociis* is a Latin maxim stating a linguistic canon of interpretation of statutes, which is that a statutory term is recognized by its associated words. The maxim states this contextual principle, whereby a word or phrase is not to be construed as if it stood alone but in the light of its surroundings. F.A.R. Bennion, *Bennion on Statutory Interpretation* (4th edn, LexisNexis 2002),

an advertisement must be in a documentary form. This inference is preferable since the use of the term 'prospectus' in various sections of the Companies Act supports it.[63] Red herring prospectus and shelf prospectus are types of prospectuses, the meanings of which will be explained in the section 'Types of Prospectuses' later in this chapter.

'Document' ordinarily refers to something tangible like paper on which words, symbols, or marks are recorded. This form is compatible with the traditional method of making public offers, which continues even today. The General Clauses Act, 1897 defines the term 'document' in wider terms and its scope extends to any matter expressed upon any substance by means of letters, figures, or marks for the purpose of recording the matter.[64] The form of the public offer would thus seem to extend to such recordings as well. However, pure oral communications, directly or through telephone, radio, and television, of a public offer would not be a prospectus. This is not to say that such communications are unregulated. As we shall see in Chapter 5, SEBI regulates these activities and restricts making of such public communications without preparing and registering a prospectus in terms of the Companies Act.[65]

---

at p. 1225. See also *Rohit Pulp and Paper Mills Limited* v. *Collector of Central Excise, Baroda*, AIR 1991 SC 754; *Prabhudas Damodar Kotecha* v. *Manhabala Jeram Damodar*, AIR 2013 SC 2959.

[63] This reading of the definition of a prospectus can be contradistinguished from the definition of a prospectus in other common law countries such as the US and the UK. Sub-clause (10) of clause (a) of section 2 of the [US] Securities Act of 1933 defines a prospectus to mean 'any prospectus, notice, circular, advertisement, letter, or communication, written or by radio or television, which offers any security for sale or confirms the sale of any security'

[64] Definitions contained in the General Clauses Act are applicable to all central acts unless there is anything repugnant in the subject or context. Sub-section (3) of section 18 of the General Clauses Act provides that, '[A document] shall include any matter written, expressed or described upon any substance by means of letters, figures or marks, or by more than one of those means which is intended to be used, or which may be used, for the purpose of recording that matter'.

[65] Regulation 60 of ICDR Regulations. See also the section 'Limitations on Publicity, Research Reports, and Financial Assistance' in Chapter 5 of this volume.

Principal Legal Requirements for a Prospectus

The principal legal requirements that a prospectus attracts are mandatory disclosure of prescribed information, vetting of the information prior to registration of the prospectus, and registration of the prospectus prior to its issuance. Every 'prospectus issued by or on behalf of a public company, either with reference to its formation or subsequently, or by or on behalf of any person who is or has been engaged or interested in the formation of a public company' must contain the prescribed information. The Companies Act and the regulations framed by SEBI for the issue of shares and debentures prescribe the information that the prospectus must contain.[66] The approach to disclosure of information is, therefore, broadly prescriptive or rule based. As Professor Solaiman puts it, prescriptive or rule based, and its converse, non-prescriptive or principles based, are the two systems of prospectus disclosure currently being followed worldwide.[67] The latter does not prescribe any specific prospectus contents. Rather, it provides guiding principles such as requiring the company to disclose all material information that may be of interest to potential investors. The responsibility of adequacy of disclosure is left with the company. Under the prescriptive approach, relevant legislation or the regulator determines the contents of a prospectus that has to be followed irrespective of whether it is material or not in

---

[66] Sub-section (1) of section 26 of the Companies Act, regulation 57 of the ICDR Regulations, regulations 5 of Securities and Exchange Board of India (Issue and Listing of Debt Securities) Regulations, 2008 (or the Debt Securities Regulations), and Securities and Exchange Board of India (Issue and Listing of Non-convertible Redeemable Preference Shares) Regulations, 2013 (or the Preference Shares Regulations). There are only two exceptions to the prescribed disclosure requirements under the Companies Act. The first is 'the issue to existing members or debenture-holders of a company, of a prospectus or form of application relating to shares in or debentures of the company'; and second, the 'issue of a prospectus or form of application relating to shares or debentures which are, or are to be, in all respects uniform with shares or debentures previously issued and for the time being dealt in or quoted on a recognised stock exchange'. See sub-section (2) of section 26 of the Companies Act.

[67] S.M. Solaiman, 'Disclosure Philosophy for Investor Protection in Securities Markets: Does one size fit all?' (2001) 28 (5) Company Lawyer 135, at p. 136.

relation to a particular company.[68] Though our securities law follows the prescriptive standard, it also adopts the non-prescriptive standard and mandates that 'the offer document shall contain all material disclosures which are true and adequate so as to enable the applicants to take an informed investment decision.'[69]

The next legal requirement is vetting and clearing of the draft prospectus by SEBI and the stock exchanges—an ex ante (before the event) enforcement mechanism where the company issuing the prospectus must obtain prior approval of it regardless of whether the prospectus violates any disclosure rule. However, reference to SEBI and stock exchanges in the same bracket is an overstatement. As Chapter 4 will show, the nature and extent of prospectus approval by them varies tremendously due to their differing legal mandate and the task environment. It must be clear that vetting and clearing the draft prospectus does not tantamount to assumption of responsibility for the prospectus. These authorities assume no responsibility for either the quality of information disclosed to the public through the prospectus or the public offer itself. The prospectus regime relies entirely on compliance with the disclosure requirements and provides remedies for non-compliance. Lastly, no prospectus must be issued by or on behalf of a company, or in relation to an intended company unless on or before the date of its publication a copy of the prospectus for registration has been delivered to the registrar of companies. The copy must be signed by every person who is named therein as a director or proposed director of the company or by his duly authorized attorney.[70]

To restate, once it is established that a document contains an offer to the public (and hence is a prospectus), it is critical that the document is not 'issued' unless on or before the date of its 'publication', the preceding legal requirements are complied with. What constitutes 'issued' was examined in *Nash v. Lynde*.[71] The question before the court was whether

---

[68] Solaiman (n. 67).

[69] Sub-regulation (1) of regulation 57 of the ICDR Regulations. See also regulation 5 of both Debt Securities Regulations and Preference Shares Regulations.

[70] Sub-section (4) of section 26 of the Companies Act.

[71] [1929] A.C. 158. See also *Rattan Singh v. Moga Transport Company*, AIR 1959 P&H 196.

a document, which the jury had found to be an offer to the public, had been 'issued'. Lord Hailsham L.C. held that for the prospectus to be 'issued', 'the prospectus in question should be proved to have been shown to any person as a member of the public and as an invitation to that person to take some of the shares referred to in the prospectus on the terms therein set out.'[72]

Functions of a Prospectus

A prospectus performs three functions—the first two being evident from the definition of a prospectus itself. First, a prospectus states a proposal that the company wishes to place before the public, and second, it provides the basis for the necessary contract to implement the proposal.[73] A prospectus is, therefore, not the contract but only the matter that induces the contract. The contract to take the securities is entered into by the acceptance of the application for the subscription or purchase of the securities. Where, on the contrary, the application incorporates by reference portions of the prospectus, reference to the prospectus would be necessary in determining the terms of the contract.[74] In a public issue of shares, the process, which begins with a company issuing a prospectus and culminates in the investors' names being entered as the beneficial owners in the records of a depository, produces two sets of contracts. The first contract is for the issue or sale of shares which is performed by the investor upon paying in full the share application money, and by the company (or by the selling shareholder) upon issuing the shares (or transferring the shares) and admitting the investor as a member of the company. After both parties have performed these obligations, this pre-liminary contract is discharged. The second contract comes into being by virtue of the articles of association of the company upon the investor (now a shareholder) becoming a member of the company.

The third function of a prospectus is to mandatorily disclose mate-rial information so as to enable the applicants to take an informed

[72] *Nash v. Lynde*, [1929] A.C. 158, at p. 164.

[73] New Zealand Securities Commission (now called the Financial Markets Authority of New Zealand), *Proposals for the Enactment of Regulations under the Securities Act, 1978* (20 March 1980), at p. 26.

[74] *Hindusthan Co-operative Insurance Society Limited v. Nathu Vinayak Wagh*, 1946 NLJ 128.

investment decision—a significant function performed by it in almost every jurisdiction. The prospectus functioning as a disclosure document is the manifestation of the disclosure philosophy that originated during the evolution of company law to prevent fraud and protect the public.[75] Even otherwise, it is axiomatic that the prospectus must contain the requisite information relating to the investment in securities given the very nature of securities. Company securities are intangible property and represent the rights of the holder of the securities *in* and/or *against* the company. The rights include the right to receive dividends and voting rights in case of shares and a fixed interest in case of debentures, and by virtue of securities being property, the right to transfer them for a gain. Due to the intangible character of securities and their nature, a person intending to subscribe or purchase them cannot ascertain their value and the proper price to be paid to acquire them, just by examining the securities. Instead, the investor would need to seek out information about the company. Therefore, for investment in securities, it is evident that sound investment decisions can only be made if an investor is put into possession of all material information relating to the investment.[76] Material information would generally include the history of the company and its business, its management and controlling shareholders, capital structure, and financial information including profits and losses, and assets and liabilities.

At least internationally, the last function of the prospectus has not been free from criticism and continues to be reexamined in changing business and economic conditions. For example, in the USA, several empirical studies have been conducted to assess its efficacy in terms of it leading to share price accuracy, efficient allocation of capital markets resources, and rectifying imperfections in market mechanisms, if a voluntary disclosure is made.[77] This has also been the case in the UK,

---

[75] See the section 'Disclosure Philosophy' in Chapter 2.

[76] J.P. Hambrook, 'The Obligation to Provide Offerees of Corporate Securities with Formal Disclosure Documents' (1975) 5(2) Adelaide Law Review 136.

[77] Some important writings in this regard are Frank H. Easterbrook and Daniel R. Fischel, 'Mandatory Disclosure and the Protection of Investors' (1984) 70 Virginia Law Review 669; John C. Coffee, 'Market failure and the Economic Case for a Mandatory Disclosure System' (1984) 70 Virginia Law Review 717;

New Zealand, and Australia.[78] However, in India, the justification for a mandatory prospectus disclosure that first emerged during the evolution of company law remains unchallenged and continues to dominate the outlook of the legislature and regulatory agencies.

Types of Prospectuses

The definition of a prospectus is wide enough to cover within its ambit all offering of securities to the public, irrespective of the terms and conditions of the offer. However, it is well accepted that commercial laws should facilitate business activities, especially laws on capital raising, so as to accelerate the expansion and growth of our economy.[79] Company law, therefore, recognizes and enables different types of prospectuses to be issued to suit the terms of offer and the extent of regulatory oversight. Three types of prospectuses are, thus, commonly issued for raising capital from the public—prospectus for fixed-price public issues, referred to simply as a 'prospectus'; prospectus for book-built public issues, referred to as a 'red herring prospectus'; and prospectus for subscription in one or more issues over a certain period issued by certain specified companies, referred to as a 'shelf prospectus'. A company makes a rights issue of shares by sending a 'letter of offer' to the equity shareholders.[80] If the rights issue also qualifies as a public offer, the letter of offer will become a type of prospectus.

Lawrence A. Cunningham, 'Capital Market Theory, Mandatory Disclosure, and Price Discovery' (1994) 51 Washington & Lee Law Review 843; and Merritt B. Fox, 'Retaining Mandatory Securities Disclosure: Why Issuer Choice is Not Investor Empowerment' (1999) 85 Virginia Law Review 1335.

[78] Eilís Ferran, *Principles of Corporate Finance Law* (Oxford University Press 2008), at p. 429; Iris Hse-Yu Chiu, 'Examining the Justifications for Mandatory Ongoing Disclosure in Securities Regulation' (2005) 26 (3) Company Lawyer 67; New Zealand Securities Commission (now called the Financial Markets Authority of New Zealand), *Proposals for the Enactment of Regulations under the Securities Act, 1978* (20 March 1980); Mark Blair, 'The Debate over Mandatory Corporate Disclosure Rules' (1992) 15 (1) University of New South Wales Law Journal 177.

[79] See the 'Statement of Objects and Reasons' to the Companies Act.

[80] Clause (a) of sub-section (1) of section 62 of the Companies Act.

Beginning with the 'prospectus' and the red herring prospectus, the need to choose between the two arises principally in a public issue of equity shares.[81] In a public issue of equity shares, the issuer company or the seller of the equity shares will normally not price them at the face value because, given the very innate characteristic of equity shares, its market price will be different from the face value. The market price, on the other hand, is time-sensitive and depends upon various qualitative and quantitative factors such as the business of the company and the industry in which it operates, etc. Thus, in many cases, it makes commercial sense to provide a price range for the offered equity shares and invite bids in that price range—a process referred to as 'book-building' that we examine in Chapter 5. A red herring prospectus is, therefore, a prospectus, which does not include complete particulars of the quantum or price of securities included therein and determines it through bids.[82] On the other hand, a 'prospectus' is an offer document that also includes the quantum and price of the securities. As a matter of practice, the number of red herring prospectuses far outweighs the number of fixed-price issue prospectuses.

Next, a shelf prospectus is 'a prospectus in respect of which the securities or class of securities included therein are issued for subscription in one or more issues over a certain period without the issue of a further prospectus.'[83] A shelf prospectus is generally issued for the public offer of debentures as it enables companies that frequently access the capital markets, such as finance companies, to raise money without undergoing the time-consuming process of filing a prospectus for every issue of debentures. The route of raising capital from the public through a shelf

---

[81] However, as we shall see in Chapter 5 of this volume, at times there is no choice available and the company is obligated to undertake the public issue of equity shares only by way of a red herring prospectus. See the section 'Eligibility Criteria' in Chapter 5.

[82] Explanation to section 32 of the Companies Act. A term often encountered in practice is 'draft red herring prospectus' which is simply a draft of the red herring prospectus which is required to be filed with SEBI for its vetting and approval before the red herring prospectus is issued to the public. See regulation 6 of ICDR Regulations.

[83] Explanation to section 31 of the Companies Act.

prospectus is available to only a small class of companies as specified by SEBI.[84]

Before concluding on the types of prospectuses, reference must be made to a 'statement in lieu of prospectus'. Under the Companies Act, 1956, a public company, which did not issue a prospectus on or with reference to its formation, or which had issued such a prospectus but had not proceeded to allot any of the shares offered to the public for subscription, was conditionally prohibited from allotting any of its shares or debentures.[85] The condition was that at least three days before the first allotment of shares or debentures, a statement in lieu of prospectus must have been delivered to the registrar of companies for registration. The statement in lieu of prospectus was required to be signed by every person who was named therein as a director or proposed director of the company or by their agent authorized in writing, and had to contain prescribed information and reports. An untrue statement in the statement in lieu of prospectus attracted criminal liability.[86] A statement in lieu of prospectus is, thus, a document registered by 'prospectus less' companies to give publicity about their affairs.[87] Its genesis lay in the regulation of a securities market practice during the earlier part of the twentieth century. The practice consisted of disposing of large blocks of a company's securities by means of 'placings' with private investors. Though the securities were initially allotted to investors privately, the securities in fact reached the public from the original allottee through

[84] Section 31 of the Companies Act. SEBI has prescribed, under regulation 6A of the Debt Securities Regulations, the class of companies who may file a shelf prospectus for the public issue of debt securities. Such companies include public financial institutions, companies making a public issue of tax-free secured bonds upon authorization by the Central Board of Direct Taxes, certain non-banking financial companies and housing finance companies, and certain listed companies.

[85] Section 70 of the Companies Act, 1956.

[86] Section 70 of the Companies Act, 1956. See also sections 44, 61, 76, and 149 of the Companies Act, 1956.

[87] Sir Francis Gore-Browne and Philip James Sykes, *Handbook on the Formation, Management and Winding up of Joint Stock Companies* (41st edn, Jordan & Sons Ltd. 1952), at pp. 112–13.

subsequent sale without any offer to the public and, therefore, without any obligation on the company to provide the public with prospectus information.[88] However, now the statement in lieu of prospectus has outlived its purpose. Sections 25 (document containing offer of securities for sale to be deemed prospectus) and 28 (offer of sale of shares by certain members of company) of the Companies Act, discussed later in this chapter, require prospectus-type information to be given in the kind of case referred to above. The need to register a statement in lieu of prospectus, therefore, has rightly been done away with under the Companies Act.

Listing of Securities and Types of Public Offering

Listing means the admission of securities of a company to trading privileges on a stock exchange. The principal objective of listing is to provide ready marketability and impart liquidity to the securities. A public limited company has no obligation to have its securities listed on a recognized stock exchange. However, if the company intends to offer its securities to the public, it must, before making such offer, make an application to one or more recognized stock exchange or exchanges and obtain permission for the securities to be dealt with in such stock exchange or exchanges.[89] It must be noted that the permission must be for not just the securities that have been offered to the public, but for all the issued securities belonging to that class of securities. The stock exchange grants the permission to list the securities upon fulfilment of the prescribed legal conditions. Listing of securities is, thus, a necessary corollary to the public offering of securities and an obligation after allotment; failure to list the securities defeats the public offering.[90] However, the reverse is not true, and every listing of securities need not be preceded by a public offering of the securities. This can be understood in two ways: initial

---

[88] Board of Trade, Government of the UK, *Report of the Company Law Committee* (June 1962), at para 247.

[89] Sub-section (1) of section 40 of the Companies Act and clause (a) of sub-rule (4) of rule 19 of the SCRR.

[90] See *Sahara India Real Estate Corporation Limited*, (2013) 1 SCC 1; *Raymond Synthetics Limited and Ors v. Union of India and Ors*, (1992) 2 SCC 255.

listing of a class or kind of securities, and listing of securities belonging to a class or kind of securities that is already listed on the stock exchange.

For initial listing of equity shares or debentures convertible into equity shares, the general rule is that at least 25 per cent (or less than 25 per cent subject to satisfaction of certain conditions) of those securities must have been allotted by way of a public offer.[91] SEBI has carved out a few exceptions to this general rule.[92] Thus, a company whose equity shares are not listed on a stock exchange (an unlisted company) may get its equity shares listed without making a public offer if, among other things, the equity shares sought to be listed have been allotted by the unlisted company to the holders of equity shares of a listed company pursuant to a scheme of reconstruction or amalgamation sanctioned by a high court under the Companies Act. Similarly, a company whose equity shares are already listed may get its warrants listed without making a public offer. For securities other than equity shares or debentures convertible into equity shares, there is no legal requirement that the listing of such securities must be preceded by a public offering of a certain percentage of securities belonging to that class or kind of securities. Once securities of a class or kind are listed on the stock exchange, all further issues of securities belonging to that class or kind can be listed on the stock exchange, irrespective of the manner of such further issue.[93] Thus, a company whose equity shares are listed on a stock exchange can and must get subsequent allotment of equity shares also listed, whether the allotment is by way of a public offer, private placement, rights issue, or bonus issue.

Based on the legal requirement of listing of securities upon making a public offer, offer of equity shares can be categorized into IPO, and further public offer (FPO). An IPO is a company's first public offer of equity shares; the company is, therefore, an unlisted company at the time of making the public offer. Subsequent public offer of equity shares by the listed company is called an FPO. Though the legal requirement of listing

---

[91]   Clause (b) of sub-rule (2) of rule 19 of the SCRR.

[92]   See SEBI Circular No. CIR/CFD/DIL/5/2013 dated 4 February 2013; SEBI Circular No. CIR/CFD/DIL/8/2013 dated 21 May 2013; and SEBI Circular No. CIR/CFD/CMD/16/2015 dated 30 November 2015.

[93]   Clause (b) of sub-rule (4) of rule 19 of the SCRR.

upon making a public offer is applicable to all securities, IPO and FPO are used to describe offerings of equity shares, and not of preference shares or debentures. This is because preference shares and debentures are redeemable instruments unlike equity shares, which is permanent capital.

Proponents of Public Offer and Offer for Sale

Persons who initiate a public offer programme may be classified into three categories—promoters, issuer companies, and holders of existing securities. All of them have an important role and function in a public offering programme due to their distinct commercial interests and legal obligations.

A company is the creation of the Companies Act—an artificial legal entity. Such entities do not come into being on their own. Their formation is the result of someone else's planning and operation, namely the promoter. A promoter of a company is, therefore, 'one who undertakes to form a company with reference to a given project and to set it going, and who takes the necessary steps to accomplish this purpose'.[94] Once formed, the company is under the control and management of the shareholders and the board of directors, respectively. Historically, an important role played by the promoters was the issue of a prospectus to raise capital for the proposed business. Promoters issued prospectuses inviting the public to make applications for shares in companies to be formed and, if there was sufficient interest, the promoters then proceeded to form the company.[95] This process now rarely takes place in India though the Companies Act continues to provide for it.[96] The Companies Act

---

[94] *Twycross v. Grant*, (1877) 2 C.P.D. 469, 541 as referred to and relied upon by the Madras High Court in G. *Thiruvenkatachariar v. A.T. Velu Mudaliar and Anr*, AIR 1938 Mad 154. See also *Ritesh Agarwal v. Securities and Exchange Board of India*, (2008) 8 SCC 205; *Probir Kumar Misra v. Ramani Ramaswamy*, [2010] 154 Comp Cas 658 (Mad); *Murari Ganguly v. Kanailal Garai*, AIR 2003 Cal 105; *The Weavers Mills Limited v. Balkis Ammal*, AIR 1969 Mad 462.

[95] New Zealand Securities Commission (now called the Financial Markets Authority of New Zealand), *Proposals for the Enactment of Regulations under the Securities Act, 1978* (20 March 1980), at pp. 31–2.

[96] See sub-sections (1), (3), and (4) of section 26 of the Companies Act.

has now also defined the meaning of 'promoter' to reduce the difficulty in identifying them.[97] However, as we shall discuss in Chapter 7, the definition is unsuited for identifying the promoters of an unborn company, and is conceptually unsound for identifying the promoters of an incorporated company that is a going concern.[98] The next category, the issuer company, is the most common proponent of a prospectus to raise capital in return for allotment of its securities. Most of the provisions of the Companies Act and other securities laws are worded with the issuer company as the principal. The last category comprises the holders of existing securities who offer to sell them to the public through a public offering programme commonly called 'offer for sale'. An 'offer for sale' is therefore also a public offer similar to an initial public offer and a further public offer.[99] In this category, two situations are distinguishable—covered by section 25 and section 28 of the Companies Act. In both these situations, though securities holders are the initiators of the public offer, it is the company that is burdened with being the proponent by virtue of a statutory fiction.

Section 25 of the Companies Act provides that 'where a company allots or agrees to allot any securities of the company with a view to all or any of those securities being offered for sale to the public,[100] any document by which the offer for sale to the public is made shall, for all purposes, be deemed to be a prospectus issued by the company'. It must be noted that section 25 does not assume that the document by which the offer for sale to the public is made would not otherwise be a prospectus. This is because the definition of a prospectus applies to purchase of any securities of a body corporate. However, the real effect of section 25 is to create a statutory fiction, for reasons that we examine a little later, and deem the offer document to be a prospectus *issued by the* company. Thus, all enactments and rules of law as to the contents of a prospectus

---

[97] See clause (69) of section 2 of the Companies Act.

[98] See the section 'Compensation under Companies Act for Misstatements in Prospectus' in Chapter 7 of this volume.

[99] Explanation to section 23 of the Companies Act.

[100] Sub-section (2) of section 25 of the Companies Act lays down the conditions under which a statutory presumption will be raised that an allotment of, or an agreement to allot, securities was made with a view to the securities being offered for sale to the public.

and as to liability in respect of misstatements relating to the prospectus apply, subject to a few modifications, as if the securities had been offered to the public for subscription and as if persons accepting the offer in respect of any securities were subscribers for those securities.[101]

Section 28 of the Companies Act, on the other hand, provides a mechanism for members of a company to offer their shares to the public. This provision too deems any document by which the offer for sale to the public is made to be a prospectus issued by the company. All laws and rules relating to the contents of the prospectus and as to liability in respect of misstatements relating to the prospectus apply as if the offer document is a prospectus issued by the company.[102] Similar to section 25, the effect of section 28 is to deem the offer document to be a prospectus *issued by the* company. It must be noted that an offer for sale under section 28 is limited to shares only and not all corporate securities as it is under section 25. At first glance, section 28 appears to be an enabling provision providing an option to the holder of shares to opt for the prospectus route. However, section 33 of the Companies Act provides that no form of application for the purchase of any corporate securities offered to the public will be issued unless an abridged prospectus accompanies such form.[103] An offer for sale of securities to the public through application forms without adopting the prospectus route is thus impliedly prohibited. The position that emerges is, despite the enabling character of section 28, it is mandatory to follow the prospectus provisions for an offer for sale of shares to the public through application forms.

Given the importance of offers for sale, these two cases warrant some further consideration. During the early stage of prospectus law, an offer for sale did not attract the requirement of a prospectus. This led to

---

[101]   Section 25 of the Companies Act.

[102]   Rule 8 of the Companies (Prospectus and Allotment of Securities) Rules, 2014 relaxes some of the legal requirements in respect of a prospectus such as provisions relating to minimum subscription, minimum application value, provisions requiring any statement to be made by the board of directors in respect of the utilization of money, and any other provision or information which cannot be compiled or gathered by the offeror, with detailed justifications for not being able to comply with such provisions.

[103]   An abridged prospectus is a document containing prescribed salient features of a prospectus. Clause (1) of section 2 of the Companies Act.

the unscrupulous practice of subscribing shares from the company in contemplation of a subsequent offer for sale to the public. The purpose was to evade prospectus law requirements. On the recommendation of a company law committee, a statutory provision was introduced in British company law on the lines of section 25 of the Companies Act.[104] However, offer for sale of the kind envisaged under section 28 of the Companies Act was left outside the ambit of the prospectus legal regime—the reason being that there was no complicity of the company to evade prospectus requirements and the independent shareholder had made the offer for sale for realizing his investment.[105] Imposing requirement of a prospectus would also have been very onerous because it may have been impossible for the shareholder to obtain from the company the necessary information to comply with the law relating to prospectuses. There was also no justification for placing the company under any liability in such cases.[106]

Thus, under the Companies Act, 1948 (UK), it was well established that such offers for sale did not attract prospectus law requirement.[107] The prospectus provisions of the Companies Act, 1956, being based on the corresponding provisions of the Companies Act, 1948 (UK), also governed offers for sale in the foregoing terms. Prospectus provisions needed to be complied with only with respect to a prospectus issued (a) by or on behalf of a company, and (b) by or on behalf of any person who is or has been engaged or interested in the formation of a company—the former being an act of an existing company and the latter being an act of a promoter in relation to an intended company.[108] A

---

[104] Board of Trade, Government of U.K., *Report of the Company Law Amendment Committee, 1925–26* (8 May 1926), at p. 17.

[105] Company Law Amendment Committee, 1925–26 (n. 104).

[106] Company Law Amendment Committee, 1925–26 (n. 104).

[107] See, K.W. Mackinnon and R. Buchanan-Dunlop (eds), *Palmer's Company Precedents, Part I* (17th edn, Stevens & Sons Limited 1956), at p. 109; J.P. Hambrook, 'Prospectuses and Offers of Securities for Purchase: A Reply to Professor Ford' (1978) 6 (2) Adelaide Law Review 318, at p. 320.

[108] See sub-section (1) of section 56 and sub-section (1) of section 60 of the Companies Act, 1956 and *in pari materia* sub-sections (1) and (4) of section 26 of the Companies Act, 2013.

prospectus issued for an offer for sale was covered only under section 64 of Companies Act, 1956 (now section 25 of Companies Act, 2013).[109] From 2000 onwards, Indian capital markets witnessed a stream of offers for sale through prospectuses by the Government of India as part of its disinvestment programme. During this period, a market practice of ensuring that such prospectuses were in compliance with the prospectus provisions of the Companies Act, 1956, developed. This practice found its way into guidelines and regulations issued by SEBI regulating the issue of capital to the public. Finally, the Companies Act gave statutory recognition to this practice under section 28.

Offer for Sale without a Prospectus

Existing shareholders can also make an offer for sale of shares to the public without issuing or circulating application forms, and, therefore, without issuing a prospectus. The facility for such an offer for sale of shares is available on BSE Limited and the National Stock Exchange of India Limited, and is governed by the enabling SEBI circular.[110] The permitted sellers are promoters (and their related entities) of such companies that are eligible for trading, and are required to increase public shareholding to meet the minimum public shareholding requirements. The promoters (and their related entities), and any non-promoter

---

[109] An argument can be made that sub-section (1) of section 33 of the Companies Act means that prospectuses issued for an offer for sale always impose an obligation to publish a formal prospectus irrespective of section 25 of the Companies Act. Professor Gower has taken this view. See L.C. Gower and J.B. Cronin, *Gower's Principles of Modern Company Law* (4th edn, Stevens & Sons 1979), at p. 357. However, it is submitted that sub-section (1) of section 33 of the Companies Act cannot be read in isolation to reach this conclusion. It must be read along with and subject to sub-sections (1) and (4) of section 26 of the Companies Act. This approach is also supported by the legislative history of these statutory provisions as discussed in the preceding paragraph. See also Hambrook (n. 107), at p. 320.

[110] Circular No. CIR/MRD/DP/18/2012 dated 18 July 2012 issued by SEBI. SEBI revises this circular from time to time to streamline the process and ensure greater participation by investors.

shareholder holding at least ten per cent of the share capital of the top 200 companies based on their market capitalization are also eligible to adopt this route.[111] Naturally such offers for sale would not attract the legal requirements in respect of a prospectus since neither the selling shareholder nor the company issues any document in the nature of a prospectus.

Prospectuses of Companies Incorporated Outside India

Attention must be drawn to Chapter XXII of the Companies Act, which includes sections 387–91 dealing with issuance, circulation, or distribution in India of any prospectus offering securities for subscription of a company incorporated or to be incorporated outside India. These provisions are broadly in line with prospectus provisions for companies incorporated under Indian company law.

Public offering of securities in India of a company incorporated outside India is rare, if not altogether absent. The only such offering was made in May 2010 by Standard Chartered PLC, a public limited company incorporated in the UK. Standard Chartered PLC had made a public offering of Indian Depository Receipts (IDRs)—an instrument in the form of a depository receipt created by a domestic depository in India and authorized by a company incorporated outside India making an issue of such depository receipts.[112] Both the Companies Act and ICDR Regulations contain special provisions for the issuance of IDRs in section 390 and Chapter X respectively.

---

[111] Circular No. CIR/MRD/DP/24/2014 dated 8 August 2014 issued by SEBI.

[112] Clause (48) of section 2 of the Companies Act.

4. Regulatory Agencies

By now, it is fairly clear that an offer of securities to the public and issue of a prospectus is an intricate process. Before we examine the process in detail and its legal setting, we look at the regulatory agencies that administer and enforce securities laws on public offerings. We examined in Chapter 2 that securities markets were, at the beginning, self-regulating with little or no state intervention. With time, regulation by stock exchanges grew stronger and state intervention through the Controller of Capital Issues (CCI) and registrar of companies emerged. This regime witnessed a paradigmatic shift with the enactment of the Securities and Exchange Board of India Act, 1992 (or the SEBI Act). Today, the regulatory agencies that primarily administer and enforce securities laws on public offerings are the Securities and Exchange Board of India (SEBI) and stock exchanges. The registrar of companies, though strictly not a regulatory agency, also exercises some powers and functions.

This chapter begins with examining in general the manner and style of enforcement of laws by regulatory agencies. With this as the background, we then look at SEBI, the registrar of companies, and stock exchanges. We also examine the regulatory role of Reserve Bank of India (RBI) in a public offering programme.

Regulatory Enforcement Styles

SEBI, registrar of companies, and stock exchanges operate at different levels and differ in their style of enforcing securities laws on public offerings. SEBI is far more intense in its enforcement style than the registrar of companies and the stock exchanges. An understanding of the differing regulatory enforcement styles is, therefore, key to understanding the regulatory agencies themselves. In this regard, one can take the aid of the conceptual framework on regulatory enforcement styles developed by Robert Kagan.[1]

Kagan posits three sets of explanatory factors to understand regulatory enforcement styles: the regulatory agency's political environment, regulatory legal design, and regulatory task environment.[2] The regulatory agency's political environment means the level of insulation of the regulatory agency from the political executive and interest groups. Next, regulatory legal design means the manner in which the authorizing legislation defines the agency's goal; the power the legislature grants to the agency; and the specificity with which the law prescribes the standards, procedures, and remedies to be employed in case-by-case administration.[3] Generally the power that the legislature can grant to a regulatory agency, besides the standard ex post (after the event) enforcement mechanism, is ex ante (before the event) review of the regulated conduct. Ex ante review is one in which the regulatory agency is 'authorized to review, and must provide prior approval for, all regulated conduct within a designated category, regardless of whether the conduct violates any rule.'[4]

---

[1] Robert A. Kagan, 'Editor's Introduction: Understanding Regulatory Enforcement' (1989) 11 Law and Policy 89.

[2] Kagan (n. 1), at p. 95.

[3] Kagan (n. 1), at p. 95.

[4] Ashutosh Bhagwat, 'Modes of Regulatory Enforcement and the Problem of Administrative Discretion' (1999) 50 Hastings Law Journal 1275, at p. 1282.

This approach must be understood in contradistinction with the ex post enforcement mechanism in which the regulatory agency is 'expected to identify and investigate conduct by regulated parties who have already violated the substantive rules being enforced, and then to bring a judicial action to punish the conduct.'[5] However, an ex ante mechanism should not be understood to mean that the potential violation will never occur. Such mechanisms are framed and implemented within the bounds of practicality. Finally, regulatory task environment means the frequency of interaction between the regulatory agency and the regulated entities.[6]

Securities and Exchange Board of India

SEBI has been constituted as a body corporate having perpetual succession under the SEBI Act.[7] As a statutory regulatory body for the securities market, SEBI is akin to a typical American regulatory agency—largely independent of the executive, derives full law-making power directly from the legislature, and has an adjudicative as well as enforcement function.[8] But SEBI is not completely autonomous. The general superintendence, direction, and management of the affairs of SEBI are vested in a board of members, which the central government appoints. The central government also has the power to give directions to SEBI on questions of policy and the power to completely supersede the board.[9] However, the effect of these provisions need not be

---

[5] Bhagwat (n. 4).

[6] Kagan (n. 1), at p. 101.

[7] In its formative years, SEBI was established as an interim administrative body pending enactment of a comprehensive legislation for setting up a statutory apex board to promote orderly and healthy growth of the securities market and for investor protection. See Ministry of Finance, Government of India, Notification No. 1(44) SE/86 dated 12 April 1988. Subsequently, the president of India promulgated an ordinance on 30 January 1992 establishing SEBI as a statutory authority, and thereafter, assented to the SEBI Act on 4 April 1992. The SEBI Act was deemed to have come into force on 30 January 1992.

[8] Anthony Ogus, *Regulation Legal Form and Economic Theory* (Hart Publishing 2004), at p. 104.

[9] Sections 16 and 17 of the SEBI Act. The circumstances in which the central government can supersede the board is:

overstated. The former is a function that, indisputably, the government must perform. The latter is a power granted to the central government to be exercised in extraordinary circumstances, the occasion for which has rarely arisen. Thus, other than the limited control exercised by the political executive, SEBI is not only autonomous and insulated from the political environment including pressures from interest groups, but also purportedly functions as such.

The regulatory legal design of SEBI is its most defining feature. The SEBI Act sets out SEBI's goal and mission in an ambitious and far-reaching manner: 'to protect the interests of investors in securities and to promote the development of, and to regulate the securities market'.[10] This statutory objective has tremendously influenced SEBI's functioning and enforcement actions, especially in the context of the public offering of securities where both investors and the securities market are at risk. For example, SEBI had unearthed massive irregularities relating to the initial public offerings (IPOs) of many companies during the years 2005 and 2006. It set up a committee under the chairmanship of former justice D.P. Wadhwa to advise and recommend on the procedure of identification of persons who might have been deprived on account of such IPO irregularities and the manner in which reallocation of shares to such persons should take place. Based on the recommendations of the committee,[11] SEBI reallocated the illegally acquired securities among the

---

(i) [if] on account of grave emergency, the Board is unable to discharge the functions and duties imposed on it by or under the provisions of this Act; (ii) [the] Board has persistently made default in complying with any direction issued by the Central Government under this Act or in the discharge of the functions and duties imposed on it by or under the provisions of this Act and as a result of such default the financial position of the Board or the administration of the Board has deteriorated; and (iii) that circumstances exist which render it necessary in the public interest so to do.

In these circumstances the central government may, by notification, supersede the board for such period, not exceeding six months, as may be specified in the notification.

[10] Preamble and sub-section (1) of section 11 of the SEBI Act.

[11] Securities and Exchange Board of India, *Report of the Committee on Reallocation of Shares in the Matter of IPO Irregularities* (29 December 2009).

genuinely deprived investors and initiated penalty proceedings against the offenders. Under its ordinary enforcement actions, SEBI frequently passes orders against companies and their directors for violating prospectus laws so as to debar them from collecting fresh money and refund to the investors the money already collected along with interest. SEBI also issues caution notices to investors informing them not to subscribe to issues or schemes floated by companies against whom SEBI has taken action.

Other than setting a zealous goal for SEBI, the legislature has conferred on SEBI immense powers and functions under Chapter IV of the SEBI Act. These powers are in addition to SEBI's powers under other legislation such as the Companies Act and the Securities Contracts (Regulation) Act, 1956 (or the SCRA). It is needless to describe these powers and functions, since Chapter IV of the SEBI Act is self-explanatory in this regard. Nonetheless the important powers and functions of SEBI are to regulate the business in stock exchanges and any other securities market; register and regulate securities market intermediaries; prohibit fraudulent and unfair trade practices relating to the securities markets, and insider trading in securities; regulate substantial acquisition of shares and takeover of companies; and such other matters. SEBI also registers and regulates two classes of investors, namely pooled investment vehicles and foreign institutional investors.[12]

To make these powers effective in practice, SEBI has the power to call for information, undertake inspection, and conduct enquiries and search operations; and the power to levy fees and other charges. In respect of certain matters,[13] it also has some of the powers as are vested in a civil

---

[12] Foreign institutional investors have now been reclassified as foreign portfolio investors. SEBI regulates them under the Securities and Exchange Board of India (Foreign Portfolio Investors) Regulations, 2014 upon having repealed the Securities and Exchange Board of India (Foreign Institutional Investors) Regulations, 1995. The SEBI Act is however yet to be amended to reflect this change.

[13] These matters are (a) 'calling for information from, undertaking inspection, conducting inquiries and audits of the stock exchanges, mutual funds, other persons associated with the securities market, intermediaries and self-regulatory organisations in the securities market'; (b) 'calling for information and records from any person including any bank or any other authority or

court such as summoning and enforcing the attendance of persons and examining them on oath. It can appoint an investigating authority to carry out detailed investigations into the affairs of persons associated with the securities market, and otherwise, can pass, under certain circumstances,[14] an order requiring a person to cease and desist from committing or causing violations of the SEBI Act or any rules and regulations made thereunder. SEBI also has the power to, in the interests of investors or the securities market, issue directions to all regulated entities and any person associated with the securities market, and the power to take certain specified measures such as restraining persons from accessing the securities market and prohibiting any person associated with the securities market to buy, sell, or deal in securities, and impound and retain the proceeds or securities in respect of any transaction that is under investigation. The Supreme Court of India summarized the nature of these powers in *Clariant International Limited and Anr v. Securities and Exchange Board of India*,[15] where it held that SEBI 'exercises its legislative power by making regulations, executive power by administering the regulations framed by it and taking action against any entity violating these regulations and judicial power by adjudicating disputes in the implementation thereof. The only check upon exercise of such wide ranging power is that it must comply with the Constitution and the Act'.[16]

---

board or corporation established or constituted by or under any Central or State Act which, in the opinion of the Board, shall be relevant to any investigation or inquiry by the Board in respect of any transaction in securities'; and (c) 'inspection of any book, or register, or other document or record of any listed public company or a public company (not being intermediaries referred to in section 12) which intends to get its securities listed on any recognised stock exchange where the Board has reasonable grounds to believe that such company has been indulging in insider trading or fraudulent and unfair trade practices relating to securities market'. See sub-section (3) of section 11 of the SEBI Act.

[14] The circumstances are if SEBI 'finds, after causing an inquiry to be made, that any person has violated, or is likely to violate, any provisions of this Act, or any rules or regulations made thereunder'. See section 11D of the SEBI Act.

[15] (2004) 8 SCC 524.

[16] (2004) 8 SCC 524, at p. 550.

The SEBI Act has also conferred express powers on SEBI to regulate public offering of corporate securities. SEBI, thus, has the power to regulate or prohibit issue of a prospectus, or advertisement soliciting money for the issue of securities.[17] No other law including the Companies Act creates a fetter on the power of SEBI under the SEBI Act. The Companies Act, in fact, supplements it. Thus, SEBI is empowered to administer the provisions contained in Chapter III of the Companies Act on 'Prospectus and Allotment of Securities', insofar that they relate to issue and transfer of securities, and non-payment of dividend, by listed companies or those companies which intend to get their securities listed on any recognized stock exchange in India. In this regard, the Supreme Court of India in *Sahara India Real Estate Corporation Limited and Ors v. Securities and Exchange Board of India and Anr*[18] noted that both the SEBI Act and the Companies Act have to be interpreted and made to work in tandem, in the interest of investors, especially when public money is raised by the issue of securities from the people at large.[19] Under the SEBI Act, SEBI's powers to regulate public offers and issue of prospectuses are couched in general terms. These empower SEBI to not only lay down detailed and precise rules by framing regulations on matters relating to issue of capital, but also vest in SEBI the power to pass general or special orders prohibiting any company from issuing a prospectus, any offer document, or advertisement soliciting money from the public for the issue of securities.

In exercise of its statutory power, SEBI has framed the Securities and Exchange Board of India (Issue and Listing of Debt Securities) Regulations, 2008 (or the Debt Securities Regulations); the Securities and Exchange Board of India (Issue of Capital and Disclosure Requirements) Regulations, 2009 (or the ICDR Regulations); and the Securities and Exchange Board of India (Issue and Listing of Non-Convertible Redeemable Preference Shares) Regulations, 2013 (or the Preference Shares Regulations) for regulating the public issue of non-convertible debt securities; equity shares and convertible securities; and non-convertible redeemable preference shares, respectively. These

[17] Section 11A of the SEBI Act.

[18] (2013) 1 SCC 1.

[19] *Sahara India Real Estate Corporation Limited and Ors v. Securities and Exchange Board of India and Anr*, (2013) 1 SCC 1, at p. 57.

regulations set out substantive rules governing almost every aspect of a public offering of corporate securities, and prescribe the matters that companies must disclose to the public through the prospectus. Some of their important aspects must be noted.

First, the approach of these regulations towards regulation of the public offering of corporate securities is primarily disclosure based. This approach is similar to that of the Companies Act and is expected to complement it. But, over the years, the scope of disclosure of has kept increasing and far outweighs the disclosure requirements under the Companies Act.[20] However, to a limited extent, the regulations also follow the merit-based approach and prohibit entities that SEBI has debarred from accessing the capital markets from making public offerings.

Second, as is evident from the foregoing, the standard of disclosure is prescriptive. However, the regulations also lay down principle-based guidance and provide that the offer document must contain all material disclosures, which are necessary for the applicants to take an informed investment decision.

Third, these regulations implement the substantive regulatory regime of disclosure requirement through ex ante preapproval or preclearance. The ex ante enforcement is most stringent under the ICDR Regulations under which companies are prohibited from making a public issue of equity shares and convertible securities unless their draft prospectuses have been filed with and cleared by SEBI. SEBI vets the draft prospectuses to ensure not just the disclosure of the prescribed information, but also compliance with the substantive norms. This process of vetting is a time-consuming process. Under the Debt Securities Regulations and Preference Shares Regulations, ex ante enforcement is less stringent. SEBI does not vet the draft prospectuses; instead, these are required to be filed with the designated stock exchange. But under all the regulations, the draft prospectus is required to be made public for comments for a specified number of days.

Fourth, SEBI is assisted by a host of market intermediaries, the chief being the merchant banker, to ensure effective compliance with the ex

---

[20] In fact, the Companies (Amendment) Bill, 2016, introduced in the lower house of the Parliament on 16 March 2016, seeks to do away with the prescribed disclosure under the Companies Act. Instead, disclosure shall be as prescribed by SEBI and as prescribed by the Central Government under the Companies (Prospectus and Allotment of Securities) Rules, 2014.

ante as well as ex post mechanisms of these regulations. These intermediaries are appointed by the company and are regulated by SEBI in accordance with regulations for intermediaries.

SEBI's wide and general powers under the SEBI Act, and SEBI's detailed regulations including the ex ante character of some of them, do make SEBI a supreme regulatory agency in the area of regulation of public offering of corporate securities. Issuer companies must wait for SEBI's approval to act, or approach the Securities Appellate Tribunal or the writ courts to obtain relief. However, given SEBI's regulatory task environment, concerns regarding delay tend to get mitigated. A public offering programme involves periodic interaction of the company and the intermediaries with SEBI. The intermediaries are repeat players, and the expectation is that they establish a reputation of good faith and reliability with SEBI, leading to cooperation in achieving regulatory goals.

Registrar of Companies

The Companies Act confers on the central government a wide variety of powers and functions for the effective regulation and supervision of companies. The central government, that is, the Ministry of Corporate Affairs (MCA), Government of India exercises its powers and functions through a multi-tiered organizational structure consisting of regional directors, the registrar of companies, official liquidators, and registrar of companies-cum-official liquidators. From among these, the registrar of companies principally administers the provisions of the Companies Act on prospectus and allotment of securities.

The registrar of companies is a registration office headed by registrars at different hierarchical levels and established by the central government at such places as it thinks fit.[21] It is not an autonomous body and the central government exercises administrative control over these offices through the respective regional directors. In terms of its legal design, being a mere administrative authority, its primary goal is to serve as an office of record.[22] Thus, every application, financial statement,

---

[21] Section 396 of the Companies Act.

[22] *S.K. Bhattacharya and Anr v. Union of India and Ors*, [1998] 91 Comp Cas 37 (Del).

prospectus, return, declaration, memorandum of association, particulars of charges, or any other document or intimation required to be filed or delivered under the Companies Act must be filed or delivered to the registrar of companies.[23] Any person may inspect such records and obtain its copies or extracts upon payment of prescribed fees.[24]

The registrar of companies exercises the powers and discharges the functions specifically conferred on it by the Companies Act or the rules made thereunder, or delegated to it by the central government.[25] In the context of the public offering of securities, the primary power and function of the registrar of companies is the registration of prospectuses. This registration requirement is enforced through ex ante and ex post mechanisms. Thus, no prospectus must be issued by or on behalf of a company or in relation to an intended company unless on or before the date of its publication, there has been delivered to the registrar of companies for registration, a copy thereof signed by every person who is named therein as a director or proposed director of the company or by their duly authorized attorney.[26] The registration of a prospectus is not a matter of right and the registrar of companies is under a duty to not register a prospectus unless the requirements of section 26 of the Companies Act, with respect to its registration, are complied with and the prospectus is accompanied by the consent in writing of all the persons named in the prospectus.[27] The registered prospectus has a shelf life and it is not valid if it is issued more than 90 days after the date on which a copy thereof was delivered to the registrar of companies.[28] Non-compliance with these requirements attracts fine and imprisonment. Though the Companies Act provides for an ex ante scrutiny of the prospectus, such a process differs from its counterpart under the ICDR Regulations. First, the prospectus must be vetted and cleared under the ICDR Regulations prior to its registration with the registrar of companies. In fact, as a matter of practice, the registrar of companies refuses

---

[23] Section 398 of the Companies Act and rule 7 of the Companies (Registration Offices and Fees) Rules, 2014.

[24] Section 399 of the Companies Act.

[25] See rule 5 of the Companies (Registration Offices and Fees) Rules, 2014.

[26] Sub-section (4) of section 26 of the Companies Act.

[27] Sub-section (7) of section 26 of the Companies Act.

[28] Sub-section (8) of section 26 of the Companies Act.

to register a prospectus unless acknowledgement from SEBI indicating completion of SEBI's review process is produced before them. Second, SEBI's prospectus review process is far more extensive, detailed, and time-consuming than that of the registrar of companies.

Stock Exchanges

The terming of stock exchanges as regulators of public offering of corporate securities is, strictly speaking, a misnomer. Stock exchanges are primarily concerned with listing and trading in securities after the public offering, and not with the public offering itself. However, the regulatory character of certain functions that stock exchanges generally perform does have a bearing on the public offering of corporate securities. These functions are: setting up and implementing listing norms, self-regulation of stockbrokers who are intermediaries in a public offer programme, and certain ancillary functions such as approving the basis of allotment of securities in a public issue. Additionally, stock exchanges also provide non-regulatory services such as system of online offer of securities in book-built public issues through a red herring prospectus.

As regulators of public offering of corporate securities, stock exchanges occupy a unique position by virtue of also being the object of regulation. Setting up of stock exchanges requires recognition under the SCRA as it prohibits the existence of stock exchanges other than recognized stock exchanges. Power to grant recognition vests with SEBI and is subject to fulfilment of the prescribed conditions under the SCRA, the Securities Contracts (Regulation) Rules, 1957 (or the SCRR), and the Securities Contracts (Regulation) (Stock Exchanges and Clearing Corporations) Regulations, 2012. Entry conditions under these laws are designed to ensure that only corporatized and demutualized persons that are fit and proper such as those having adequate net worth and financial capacity, necessary expertise and infrastructure, dispute redressal mechanisms, and good governance structure are granted recognition. Once recognized, stock exchanges operate as any other company carrying on business and operations, but under the regulatory oversight of SEBI and the central government. Being companies, stock exchanges are owned and controlled by their respective shareholders. Consequently, political interference is possible only if the government is a significant shareholder. Fundamentally, the legal design of the stock exchanges for regulating the public offering of securities is based on the same regulatory powers that stock exchanges have been exercising since inception, namely setting up and implementing listing norms, and self-regulation of the stockbrokers who act as intermediaries in the public offering process. At inception, both these powers had their basis in contract. Now, they also have statutory recognition. In addition, stock exchanges also regulate the public offering of securities by virtue of their power to supervise and approve the basis of allotment of securities.

One may recall the discussion in Chapter 3 that listing of securities is a necessary corollary to the public offering of securities.[29] Thus, every company making a public offer must, before making such offer, make an application to one or more recognized stock exchange or exchanges and obtain permission for the securities to be dealt with in such stock exchange or exchanges.[30] For an IPO of equity shares and convertible securities, there is an additional condition: The application for listing of the securities must be made to at least one recognized stock exchange having nationwide trading terminals.[31] Though application for listing is required to be made before making the public offer, approval for listing is granted in two stages: one, before making the public offer called the in-principle approval, and the other, after completion of the public offering programme called the final listing and trading approval.[32] However, receipt of the listing approval from a stock exchange(s) of one's choice is not a matter of right. A stock exchange grants permission to list the securities upon fulfilment of the prescribed legal conditions and the power to grant the in-principle listing approval involves ex ante review of the regulated conduct. These intricacies of listing of securities are entirely within the domain of the stock exchange.[33]

[29] See the section 'Listing of Securities and Types of Public Offering' in Chapter 3 of this volume.

[30] Sub-section (1) of section 40 of the Companies Act.

[31] Clause (d) of sub-regulation (2) of regulation 4 of ICDR Regulations. Currently, there are 6 recognized stock exchanges (excluding commodity stock exchanges) in India. Out of these, only three have nationwide trading terminals namely BSE Limited, Metropolitan Stock Exchange Limited and National Stock Exchanges of India Limited.

[32] See regulations 107 and 108 of the ICDR Regulations.

[33] *Pentamedia Graphics Limited v. The Bombay Stock Exchange*, [2008] 145 Comp Cas 327 (Mad).

Stock exchanges lay down the prerequisites for listing under their regulations and bye-laws, and the listing agreement—an agreement that a company enters into with the stock exchange at the stage of initial listing of any of the securities.[34] Its characterization as an agreement is misleading, for it is much more than a mere contract. A listing agreement is a non-negotiable agreement between the company and the stock exchange containing the terms and conditions subject to which the securities shall qualify for listing and continue to remain listed. The agreement, by applying Securities and Exchange Board of India (Listing Obligations and Disclosure Requirements) Regulations, 2015 (or the LODR Regulations), covers several matters such as further issue of capital, distribution of dividend, publicity through the stock exchange of any unpublished price-sensitive information, corporate governance, and disclosure of quarterly financial results. Stock exchanges monitor compliance with the listing agreement and submit reports to SEBI in respect thereof.[35] Consequences of non-compliance with the listing agreement or other applicable securities laws include levy of fines and penalties, suspension of the securities from the trading list, and eventually 'delisting' of the securities.[36] Securities can also be delisted voluntarily subject to compliance with the specified conditions.[37] Listing of securities is, thus, not an irreversible process.

Other than through the process of listing of securities, stock exchanges indirectly regulate the public offering of securities by regulating the conduct of stockbrokers who are members of recognized stock exchanges and are registered with SEBI under the Securities and Exchange Board of India (Stock-brokers and Sub-brokers) Regulations, 1992. As we shall see later, in a public offering programme, stockbrokers accept

---

[34] See section 21 of the SCRA; regulation 109 of the LODR Regulations and regulation 109 of the ICDR Regulations.

[35] Regulation 97 of the LODR Regulations.

[36] Sections 21A, 23A, and 23E of the SCRA; rule 21 of the SCRR; and regulation 98 of the the LODR Regulations. See also SEBI Circular No. CIR/CFD/CMD/12/2015 dated 30 November 2015 on the 'Standard Operating Procedure for Suspension and Revocation of Trading of Specified Securities'.

[37] Rule 21 of the SCRR. For delisting of equity shares, see also the Securities and Exchange Board of India (Delisting of Equity Shares) Regulations, 2009.

applications for the securities on behalf of the company. Stock exchanges generally supervise and regulate the conduct of the stockbrokers. Finally, stock exchanges also regulate the public offering of securities by supervising the basis of allotment of securities. Given that investors belonging to different categories make applications for securities during a period consisting of a few days, and that there is possibility of oversubscription or under-subscription in different categories, SEBI has prescribed the procedure that the issuer company must follow for making allotment of securities. It is the task of the stock exchange to ensure that the basis of allotment is finalized in a fair and proper manner in accordance with the prescribed allotment procedure.

The regulatory task environment of the stock exchanges provides them a great opportunity to achieve their regulatory goals. Stock exchanges interact quite frequently with and are accessible to the regulated entities. The large size and sophistication of the regulated entities also makes the task of regulation much easier. In the past, however, stock exchanges poorly executed their regulatory responsibilities. As an International Monetary Fund Working Paper notes with regard to BSE Limited, one of the largest stock exchanges in India:

> [I]ts failure to maintain adequate regulatory standards (a direct result of member self-interest) and under funding of its regulatory functions has led to a lack of regulation[,] culminating in a number of market manipulation scandals which have caused market volatility and serious losses to investors, and which have undermined the Indian capital markets as a whole.... [S]imilar challenges apply to [regulation of listed companies]— there is risk of underfunding and the tension between attracting listings from public companies and enforcing listing standards against those same companies.[38]

With corporatization and demutualization of stock exchanges, and increased oversight by SEBI, the situation is expected to have improved. Benefits of demutualization have already been noted earlier. Pursuant

---

[38] Jennifer Elliott, 'Demutualization of Securities Exchanges: A Regulatory Perspective' (2002) IMF Working Paper WP/02/119 <http://www.imf.org/external/pubs/ft/wp/2002/wp02119.pdf> accessed on 5 May 2014, at p. 7.

to SEBI's intervention, stock exchanges are now required to segregate their regulatory departments from other departments. Regulatory departments consist of surveillance, listing, compliance, inspection, enforcement, etc., and these must be sufficiently staffed.

Reserve Bank of India

Recall the discussion on money market instruments in Chapter 1 and their transactions falling within the regulatory jurisdiction of RBI.[39] Corporate securities (barring the overlap that we discussed in Chapter 1)[40] are not money market instruments and RBI, therefore, does not directly regulate the public offering of corporate securities under the Reserve Bank of India Act, 1934. However, public offering of corporate securities in India inevitably involves subscription or purchase of securities by persons resident outside India, thereby attracting the applicability of the Foreign Exchange Management Act, 1999 (or the FEMA). This legislation is administered by the RBI through an overwhelming number of regulations, circulars, directions, etc., one of them being the Foreign Exchange Management (Transfer or Issue of Security by a Person Resident outside India) Regulations, 2000. Therefore, RBI regulates aspects of public offering of corporate securities that touch upon foreign exchange matters and investment by persons resident outside India. If the investment pertains to matters reserved for the consideration of the central government under the foreign exchange laws, permission of the Foreign Investment Promotion Board (an inter-ministerial body under the Department of Economic Affairs, Ministry of Finance, Government of India) may also be required.[41] These are not securities laws and

[39] See sections 'Concept of Securities' and 'Securities Market' in Chapter 1 of this volume. See also Chapter IIID of the Reserve Bank of India Act, 1934.

[40] The Companies (Amendment) Bill, 2016, introduced in the lower house of Parliament on 16 March 2016, seeks to remove the overlap by amending the definition of debenture in the Companies Act. Instruments referred to in Chapter IIID of the Reserve Bank of India Act, 1934 shall not be treated as debenture.

[41] See regulation 5 of Foreign Exchange Management (Transfer or Issue of Security by a Person Resident outside India) Regulations, 2000 read with

therefore we would not examine them in detail. However, familiarity with some of these foreign exchange laws is necessary for actually undertaking a public offering of corporate securities involving subscription or purchase of securities by persons resident outside India.

Schedule I to it. See also the consolidated foreign direct investment policy circular of 2015 dated 12 May 2015 issued by the Department of Industrial Policy & Promotion, Ministry of Commerce & Industry, Government of India.

5. Public Offering Programme: General

Once a decision has been made to take a company public, there are several pre-offering matters that must be addressed before the draft prospectus can be presented for clearance to the regulatory authority and then issued to the public. The extent and complexity of these matters depend largely on the type of security being offered to the public. Public offering of equity shares is a far more detailed process than that of preference shares or debentures. This chapter, therefore, describes and examines the stage of the public offering programme before the clearance of the draft prospectus. Nevertheless, we must distinguish this stage with measures that the company takes, from a commercial viewpoint, to ready it for a public offering in general, and initial public offering (IPO) in particular. These commercial measures are aimed to ensure that the company has the necessary elements to make it a viable candidate for primary market investors—elements such as a good financial condition and recent operating results, an experienced management team, and a sustainable business model. To strengthen itself on these lines in order to get a good value for the offered shares, a company may be required to take several measures before it takes a formal decision to go public. The valuation of the offered shares also depends on the market conditions. Thus, even companies with sound financial condition and good prospects would have to look out for the periods when the primary market is receptive to public issues. After the company has taken measures to address these internal and external factors, the stage is set for the pre-offering matters.

In this chapter, we examine the pre-offering matters—choice of trading segment, eligibility criteria, appointment of intermediaries and participants other than intermediaries, initial considerations such as pricing, etc., preparation of the prospectus, and limitations on publicity, 'research reports', and financial assistance. The expression 'equity shares' in this chapter, unless otherwise specified, will mean equity shares and corporate securities convertible into equity shares since the Securities and Exchange Board of India (SEBI) regulates public issue of equity shares and convertible securities through a common regulation, which is the Securities and Exchange Board of India (Issue of Capital and Disclosure Requirements) Regulations, 2009 (or the ICDR Regulations).

Choice of Trading Segment

For different securities, stock exchanges provide different trading segments—segments into which the securities admitted for dealings on the exchange are classified for trading. Trading segments of the stock exchange may include segments for equity shares, debt securities, government securities, different kinds of derivative contracts, and other securities, as may be decided by the stock exchange from time to time. For the introduction of any new trading segment, stock exchanges are required to obtain the prior approval of SEBI. Each trading segment is governed by its own set of rules on listing such as conditions precedent for listing, administrative procedure, terms of listing agreement, and listing fees; on trading such as trading units, form of contracts, brokerage, and market-lots; and on clearing and settlement.

Traditionally, stock exchanges had a single trading segment for equity shares. Over time, it was felt that the eligibility conditions for listing on the equity trading segment and compliance with the equity listing agreement were onerous for companies classified as small and medium enterprises (SMEs). And several studies had concluded that SMEs play a significant role in the economic growth of developing countries, both in terms of contribution to the GDP and creation of employment.[1] However, they suffered from poor access to capital market finance. Resultantly, a separate trading segment was introduced in 2011 in the form of the SME Exchange—a trading platform of a recognized stock exchange having nationwide trading terminals permitted by SEBI to list equity shares (and convertible securities) issued in accordance with the ICDR Regulations.[2] Currently, the National Stock Exchange of India Limited (NSE) and BSE Limited operate SME Exchanges in India. The eligibility conditions to list on the SME Exchange pursuant to an IPO and the listing agreement have both been customized to facilitate listing by SMEs. Thus, a company having a post-public-issue face value capital not exceeding Rs 10 crore may list its equity shares on the SME Exchange. A company whose post-public-issue face value capital is more than Rs 10 crore and up to Rs 25 crore has the option of listing their equity shares on both the SME Exchange and the traditional equity trading segment of the stock exchange (which is called the Main Board when used in contradistinction with the SME Exchange).[3]

In addition to the Main Board and SME Exchange, we have a third category called the institutional trading platform (ITP). This trading platform has its genesis in the growth of start-up companies in India which have innovative business models and a valuation methodology not generally understood by common investors. To facilitate their growth, since 2015, ITP offers an alternate capital raising and trading platform where these new-age companies can list their securities

---

[1] See Shigehiro Shinozaki, 'Capital Market Financing for SMEs: A Growing Need for Emerging Asia' (2014) Asian Development Bank Working Paper Series on Regional Economic Integration <http://www.adb.org/publications/capital-market-financing-smes-growing-need-emerging-asia> accessed on 11 June 2014; Securities and Exchange Board of India, 'Discussion Paper on Developing a Market for Small and Medium Enterprises in India' (2008) <http://www.sebi.gov.in/sebiweb/home/list/4/38/35/0/Reports-for-Public-Comments> accessed on 11 June 2014.

[2] See chapter XB of the ICDR Regulations.

[3] Regulation 106M of the ICDR Regulations.

with or without making a public issue.[4] Given the higher risk involved in investing in these companies, only institutional and high net-worth investors are permitted to trade on the ITP. Both NSE and BSE Limited offer the services of an ITP. Thus, a company 'which is intensive in the use of technology, information technology, intellectual property, data analytics, bio-technology or nano-technology to provide products, services or business platforms with substantial value addition and at least twenty five per cent of its pre-issue capital is held by qualified institutional buyers', or a company 'in which at least fifty per cent of the pre-issue capital is held by qualified institutional buyers' can seek listing of their securities on the ITP.[5] Thus, Main Board, SME Exchange, and ITP, each perform the essential function of providing a platform for the buying and selling of equity shares but can be distinguished on the basis of the different size of companies and business models that they cater to.

Eligibility Criteria

Companies are prohibited from making a public offer of corporate securities if they do not meet the eligibility criteria specified under the ICDR Regulations, Securities and Exchange Board of India (Issue and Listing of Debt Securities) Regulations, 2008 (or the Debt Securities Regulations), and Securities and Exchange Board of India (Issue and Listing of Non-Convertible Redeemable Preference Shares) Regulations, 2013 (or the Preference Shares Regulations). Eligibility criteria are designed broadly to ensure that honest entities access the capital markets, and securities are dematerialized and application has been made for listing the securities on the stock exchange.[6] For an IPO of equity shares, another noticeable eligibility condition is sound financial state and profitability track record as per prescribed norms. If the company is unable to meet these norms, then the public issue can only be made

[4] See chapter XC of the ICDR Regulations.
[5] Regulation 106Y of the ICDR Regulations.
[6] See regulation 4 of each: the ICDR Regulations, Debt Securities Regulations, Preference Shares Regulations, the Securities and Exchange Board of India (Prohibition on Raising Further Capital from Public and Transfer of Securities of Suspended Companies) Order, 2015.

through the 'book-building process' and the company must allot, at least 75 per cent of the offered securities to qualified institutional buyers, a class of sophisticated investors.[7] The rationale behind the alternative rule is that qualified institutional buyers are better equipped to analyse the credentials and financials of such companies. If the IPO of equity shares is by way of an offer for sale, the selling shareholders must have held the equity shares for a period of at least one year prior to the filing of the draft prospectus with SEBI for vetting.[8] Similarly, for public offers of debentures and preference shares, another noticeable eligibility condition is to obtain a credit rating from at least one credit rating agency registered with SEBI.

In addition to imposing eligibility criteria on a company for making a public offer, securities laws also prescribe conditions that make securities eligible for initial listing on the stock exchange, a reference to which was made in Chapter 3. A prominent condition in this regard for listing of equity shares and debentures convertible into equity shares is that at least 25 per cent of each class or kind of such securities issued by the company was offered and allotted to the public in terms of an offer document.[9] If the post-public-issue capital of the company calculated at offer price is more than Rs 1,600 crore, the initial listing percentage is relaxed to less than 25 per cent, subject to a minimum of 10 per cent. However, companies adopting the latter route are required to increase the public

---

[7] See sub-regulations (1) and (2) of regulation 26 of the ICDR Regulations. This is applicable only for listing on the Main Board and is not applicable for listing on the SME Exchange and ITP. On sound financial conditions, it must be noted that stock exchanges too have prescribed norms such as minimum paid-up capital and track record of operation.

[8] There are a few exceptions to this rule such as offer for sale of equity shares of infrastructure sector government companies, etc. Sub-regulation (6) of regulation 26 of the ICDR Regulations.

[9] Here 'public' must be understood in contradistinction with 'promoters', namely persons in control of the company. Clause (d) of rule 2 of the SCRR defines public to mean 'persons other than– (i) the promoter and promoter group; (ii) subsidiaries and associates of the company. Explanation.– For the purpose of this clause the words "promoter" and "promoter group" shall have the same meaning as assigned to them under the Securities and Exchange Board of India (Issue of Capital and Disclosure Requirements) Regulations, 2009.'

shareholding to at least 25 per cent within a period of three years from the date of listing of the securities in a manner specified by SEBI.[10] As discussed in detail in Chapter 3, the justification for the minimum public shareholding rule is that distributing a large number of shares among many shareholders provides greater liquidity to the investors and helps discover fair prices. The larger the number of shares and the number of shareholders, that is, the larger the public float, the less is the scope for price manipulation.

Thus, companies intending to make a public offer must ensure that the company is eligible to access the capital markets in terms of the ICDR Regulations, the Debt Securities Regulations, and the Preference Shares Regulations, any general order passed by SEBI, and norms laid

---

[10] Clause (b) of sub-rule (2) of rule 19 of the Securities Contracts (Regulation) Rules, 1957 or the SCRR, which is the following:

The minimum offer and allotment to public in terms of an offer document shall be –

   (i) at least twenty five per cent of each class or kind of equity shares or debenture convertible into equity shares issued by the company, if the post issue capital of the company calculated at offer price is less than or equal to one thousand six hundred crore rupees;

  (ii) at least such percentage of each class or kind of equity shares or debentures convertible into equity shares issued by the company equivalent to the value of four hundred crore rupees, if the post issue capital of the company calculated at offer price is more than one thousand six hundred crore rupees but less than or equal to four thousand crore rupees;

 (iii) at least ten per cent of each class or kind of equity shares or debentures convertible into equity shares issued by the company, if the post issue capital of the company calculated at offer price is above four thousand crore rupees:

Provided that the company referred to in sub-clause (ii) or sub-clause (iii), shall increase its public shareholding to at least twenty five per cent within a period of three years from the date of listing of the securities, in the manner specified by the Securities and Exchange Board of India:

Provided further that this clause shall not apply to a company whose draft offer document is pending with the Securities and Exchange Board of India on or before the commencement of the Securities Contracts (Regulation) Third Amendment Rules, 2014, if it satisfies the conditions prescribed in clause (b) of sub-rule (2) of rule 19 of the Securities Contracts (Regulation) Rules, 1956 [sic] as existed prior to the date of such commencement.

down by the stock exchanges; and that the securities that must be listed are otherwise eligible for listing on the stock exchanges.

Appointment of Intermediaries

In a public offer of corporate securities and its subscription or purchase by the investors, both the company and the investors are serviced by a host of intermediaries. Intermediaries are entities between the seller and buyer of securities and provide services that benefit them directly or indirectly. Intermediaries servicing the issuer company include merchant bankers, underwriters, registrar to the issue, and bankers to the issue; those servicing the investors include research analysts. It must be noted that SEBI regulates all securities market intermediaries, and no merchant banker, underwriter, registrar to an issue, banker to an issue, stockbroker, sub-broker, portfolio manager, depository, participant, credit rating agency, etc., must buy, sell, or deal in securities except under, and in accordance with, the conditions of a certificate of registration obtained from SEBI. SEBI grants the certificates in accordance with the regulations made under the Securities and Exchange Board of India Act, 1992 (or the SEBI Act). As a result, even though these intermediaries may have contracted to service the issuer company, they must act in accordance with SEBI regulations that impose on them the obligation to, among other things, protect the interest of investors. In protecting the interest of investors, intermediaries also gain. Investors, for example, are known to show more willingness to pay for securities of an issuer associated with particular intermediaries, such as high-reputation merchant bankers, who are known to work in the best interest of investors. The issuer company may then pay a correspondingly higher fee to such intermediaries.[11]

We now examine these intermediaries and the role played by them in a public offering programme in detail.

Merchant Banker

A merchant banker is a person who is engaged in the business of managing the public issue, which consists of preparation of the prospectus;

---

[11] Stephen J. Choi, 'A Framework for the Regulation of Securities Market Intermediaries' (2004) 1 Berkeley Business Law Journal 45, at p. 48.

making arrangements regarding selling, buying, or subscribing to securities; acting as manager, consultant, adviser; or rendering corporate advisory service. Merchant bankers are regulated by SEBI through the Securities and Exchange Board of India (Merchant Bankers) Regulations, 1992.

Although engaging merchant bankers is an obvious necessity, it has been made mandatory for an issuer company to appoint one or more merchant bankers to manage a public issue of corporate securities. Among the appointed merchant bankers, at least one is designated as the lead merchant banker. The role of lead merchant bankers (and correspondingly the fee payable) in managing the public issue is much larger than the non-lead merchant bankers. The general practice is to appoint all the merchant bankers as lead merchant bankers. The ICDR Regulations, the Preference Shares Regulations, and the Debt Securities Regulations impose specific obligations on lead merchant bankers. These include advising the issuer company on appointment of other intermediaries upon independently assessing their capability, undertaking the book-building process in book-built public issues, exercising due diligence about all aspects of the public issue including adequacy of disclosure in the prospectus, filing the draft prospectus with SEBI for vetting and being involved in the vetting process, and undertaking minimum underwriting obligations. In a public issue of equity shares that is managed by more than one merchant banker, the rights, obligations, and responsibilities of each merchant banker are required to be predetermined and disclosed in the prospectus.

Underwriter

An underwriter is a person who engages in the business of underwriting. Generally speaking, underwriting means assuming a risk over something. In the context of public offering of corporate securities, it means agreeing to subscribe to the securities of a company when the public does not subscribe to the securities offered to them. Underwriters thus assume the risk that the public will not take up all of the securities on offer. For assuming the risk of the shortfall, they receive a commission. As a result, if the public issue is successful, underwriters receive their commission without having to take up any of the securities, but if it is a failure, underwriters, who have been on standby, must take up the non-subscribed portion of the offering.[12] This traditional meaning of underwriting is also contained in the Securities and Exchange Board of India (Underwriters) Regulations, 1993 (or the SEBI Underwriters Regulations)—a set of regulations framed by SEBI in exercise of its powers to regulate underwriters in the Indian securities market. These define underwriting to mean 'an agreement with or without conditions to subscribe to the securities of a body corporate when the existing shareholders of such body corporate or the public do not subscribe to the securities offered to them.'[13]

The need for underwriting arises because the issuer company would invariably want to insure against the risk that the securities offered to the public may not be taken up. Special circumstances, too, warrant that the public issue be underwritten. For instance, a company cannot proceed to allot shares offered to the public, unless the issue of shares raises the amount specified in the prospectus as the minimum subscription.[14] A person intending to act as an underwriter must be registered with SEBI. However, a merchant banker and a stockbroker can also act as an underwriter without obtaining a separate certificate of registration under the SEBI Underwriters Regulations.

Underwriting must be distinguished from 'firm commitment underwriting' and 'best efforts underwriting'—arrangements loosely referred to as underwriting but strictly not so in the context of the public offering of securities in India. Similarly, underwriting must also be distinguished from 'market making'.

---

[12] *Commissioner of Income Tax v. UP State Industrial Development Corporation*, [1997] 225 ITR 703 (SC); *Dena Bank v. K. Motiram Vakil*, AIR 1989 Bom 264; *Syndicate Bank v. Commissioner of Income Tax*, [1988] 172 ITR 561 (Kar). See also judgment of the Privy Council in *Australian Investment Trust Limited v. Strand and Pitt Street Properties Limited*, [1932] AC 735. See also FB Palmer and Geoffrey Morse, *Palmer's Company Law* (25th edn, Sweet & Maxwell 1994), at para 5.209.

[13] Clause (fa) of regulation 2 of the SEBI Underwriters Regulations.

[14] Section 39 of the Companies Act, 2013 and rule 11 of the Companies (Prospectus and Allotment of Securities) Rules, 2014. See also *Naina Gopal Lahiri v. State of Uttar Pradesh*, [1965] 35 Comp Cas 30 (SC).

In firm commitment underwriting, which is common in the US, the issuer company sells the entire securities issue to underwriters, who in turn offer and sell the securities to the public for an expected profit. A firm commitment underwriter, thus, assumes the risk of the entire securities offering.[15] Contradistinguished with traditional underwriting, the objective of the underwriter is not to purchase the unsold portion of a public offering (although in rare instances it may be required to do so) but to offer the securities to the public investors.[16] In India, such an arrangement would not constitute underwriting; instead, section 25 of the Companies Act, 2013 would get attracted. The document by which the offer of securities to the public, made by the 'underwriter', will, for all purposes, be deemed to be a prospectus issued by the company; and the 'underwriter' would be deemed to be named in the prospectus as a director of the company.[17]

In best efforts underwriting, the underwriter does not assume any risk if the issue is under-subscribed nor does the underwriter give a firm commitment to take securities. Instead the underwriter undertakes to use its best endeavours to sell the securities for the issuer company as its agent.[18] Many have questioned whether best efforts underwriting is actually even a type of underwriting; they instead have called

[15] Lori Anne Czepiel, 'Best Efforts Underwriting: Does Glass Steagall Allow it?' (1988) 7 Annual Review of Banking Law 557, at p. 564.

[16] Simon Gleeson and Harold S. Bloomenthal, 'The Public Offer of Securities in the United Kingdom' (1999) 27 Denver Journal of International Law and Policy 359, at p. 362. See also Charles J. Johnson and Joseph McLaughlin, *Corporate Finance and the Securities Laws* (4th edn, Aspen Publishers 2006). Johnson and McLaughlin note that the traditional form of underwriting was commonly used in the US in the latter part of the nineteenth century. However, by the turn of the twentieth century, as the banking houses gained prestige, it became common for them to purchase securities issues and to be responsible for their sale, rather than merely agreeing to purchase the securities should the company not succeed in marketing them itself.

[17] See section 25 of the Companies Act, 2013 and its analysis in the section 'Proponents of Public Offer and Offer for Sale' in Chapter 3 of this volume.

[18] *Aberfoyle Limited v. Western Metal Limited*, (1998) 28 Australian Corporations and Securities Reports 187.

it merchandising.[19] In India, it is unlikely that such an arrangement would qualify as underwriting since the central element of underwriting—assumption of risk to subscribe for securities in the event of a shortfall—is absent.

Market making, as the name implies, means creating a liquid market for trading in shares. The need for market making arises in a securities market where increase in trading volume on the stock exchange is limited to fewer listed securities. The remaining securities are not actively or frequently traded although many of them have some fundamental strength and intrinsic value. To infuse liquidity in these securities, members of the stock exchange carry out market making. SEBI has laid down detailed guidelines on market making such as the methods of increasing the market for the shares, commitment to buy and sell shares up to a certain quantity on a continuous basis, criteria for selecting the securities eligible for market making, and qualifications for a registered market maker.[20] Underwriting does not include market making because the risk inherent in underwriting is that the public will not take up all of an offer of securities.

In a public issue of debentures and preference shares, underwriting is optional. This is also the case in a public issue of equity shares, other than through the book building process—if the issuer company desires to have the issue underwritten, it can appoint underwriters in accordance with the SEBI Underwriters Regulations. However, underwriting is mandatory in a public issue of equity shares through the book building process.[21] Underwriting is also mandatory if the equity shares pursuant to the public issue are proposed to be listed on the SME Exchange.[22]

Owing to the increase in the monetary size of public issues, issuer companies often appoint more than one underwriter to spread the risk of loss. To reduce the risk further, it is common for underwriters to get the public issue sub-underwritten. A sub-underwriter enters into a contract with the underwriter assuming some or all of the obligations of the

---

[19] *Aberfoyle Limited v. Western Metal Limited*, (1998) 28 Australian Corporations and Securities Reports 187; Czepiel (n. 15).

[20] See Securities and Exchange Board of India, *Master Circular for Stock Exchanges* (26 May 2015).

[21] Regulation 13 of the ICDR Regulations.

[22] Regulation 106P of the ICDR Regulations.

underwriter for a commission. The obligation of the sub-underwriter is, therefore, to the underwriter and the sub-underwriter is not contractually bound to the issuer company, although it will usually subscribe for shares directly from the company.[23] It is unclear whether sub-underwriting is permissible in terms of the SEBI Underwriters Regulations since underwriting has been defined to mean an act of subscribing to the securities of a body corporate, and not to nominate other persons to subscribe for the shortfall. In fact, the report of a committee constituted by SEBI to review the SEBI Underwriters Regulations had recommended that the definition of underwriting be extended to include procuring subscription in addition to subscribing, and that sub-underwriting be included in underwriting.[24] Conceptually, at least one judicial decision has recognized sub-underwriting to be part of underwriting.[25]

An underwriter is prohibited from deriving any benefit, direct or indirect, from underwriting the public issue, other than the commission or brokerage payable under the underwriting agreement.[26] Further, given that such commission relates to subscription of a company's securities, the Companies Act regulates the power of a company to pay commission to underwriters. Sub-section (6) of section 40 of the Companies Act read with rule 13 of the Companies (Prospectus and Allotment of Securities) Rules, 2014 makes it lawful for a company to pay commission to any person in connection with the subscription or procurement of subscription to its securities, whether absolute or conditional, subject to the following conditions:

1. The payment of the commission must be authorized in the company's articles of association. The rate of the commission paid or agreed to be paid must not exceed, in case of shares, 5 per cent of the price at which shares are issued or a rate authorized by the

---

[23] Australian Securities & Investment Commission, *Underwriting: Application for Exemptions, Regulatory Guide 61* (1993).

[24] Securities and Exchange Board of India, *Report of the Review Committee on SEBI (Underwriters) Rules and Regulations, 1993 [sic]* (October 2002).

[25] See *Dena Bank v K. Motiram Vakil*, AIR 1989 Bom 264.

[26] Sub-regulation (1) of regulation 15 of the SEBI Underwriters Regulations. See also sub-regulation (5) of regulation 13 and sub-regulation (5) of regulation 106P of the ICDR Regulations.

articles of association, whichever is less; in case of debentures, must not exceed 2.5 per cent of the price at which the debentures are issued, or as specified in the company's articles of association, whichever is less.

2. The commission may be paid out of the proceeds of the issue or the profit of the company or both. Further, the commission may be satisfied by the payment of cash or the allotment of fully or partly paid shares, or partly in the one way and partly in the other.[27]

3. The prospectus of the company must disclose the name of the underwriters, the rate and amount of commission payable to the underwriters, and the number of securities which are to be underwritten or subscribed by the underwriters absolutely or conditionally.

4. A company must not pay any commission to any underwriter on securities which are not offered to the public for subscription.

5. A copy of the contract for payment of commission must be delivered to the registrar of companies at the time of delivery of the prospectus for registration.

Bankers to an Issue, Syndicate, and Stockbroker

In Chapter 3, we discussed that a prospectus contains the matter that induces investors to enter into a contract of subscription or sale of securities. The contract proper, however, is to be found in the application form issued and distributed by the issuer company and its nominated agents. An important exercise in a public offering programme, therefore, is the distribution and collection of application forms and the accompanying application money. Traditionally, bankers to an issue have performed this task.

Bankers to an issue are scheduled banks[28] carrying out the activity of accepting applications and application money, and registered with SEBI

---

[27] See regulation 5 of the 'Articles of Association of a Company Limited by Shares' contained in Table F of Schedule I to the Companies Act.

[28] Scheduled bank means a bank included in the Second Schedule of the Reserve Bank of India Act, 1934.

under the Securities and Exchange Board of India (Bankers to an Issue) Regulations, 1994.[29] An investor intending to subscribe or purchase the securities would, directly or indirectly through nominated agents of the issuer company, approach the collection centre of one of the enlisted bankers to an issue, complete and submit the application form along with the application money through a prescribed payment instrument such as a demand draft or cheque. In a public issue of equity shares through the book-building method, the process is rather different, because such public issues involve 'building a book', a process that we shall examine later in this chapter. An investor makes a bid as well as an application through a single document. Consequently, the issuer company appoints syndicate members by entering into a syndicate agreement for collecting bids from investors.[30] Underwriters, merchant bankers, and stockbrokers are eligible to act as syndicate members. Syndicate members in turn appoint stockbrokers to increase their reach and coverage. Thus, the merchant bankers, syndicate members, and stockbrokers accept the 'bid-cum-application form', build the book, and hand over the form along with the payment instrument to the enlisted bankers to the issue for realizing the application money.

With advancement in technology, and desire of the government and the regulator to increase participation in and efficiency of public issues, the process of collecting application forms and application money has evolved. In July 2008, SEBI introduced 'Application Supported by Blocked Amount' (ASBA) as a supplementary process for applying in public issue of equity shares. ASBA is an application for subscribing to an issue, containing an authorization to block the application money in a bank account. The ASBA facility is provided by Self Certified Syndicate Banks (SCSBs), which are SEBI-registered bankers to an issue that have submitted to SEBI a self-certification. Once included in the notified list, an SCSB is deemed to have entered into an agreement with an issuer

[29] Sub-regulation (aa) of regulation 2 of the Securities and Exchange Board of India (Bankers to an Issue) Regulations, 1994.

[30] In book-built public issues, the syndicate members and the merchant bankers also procure bids and applications for subscription in the public issue for which the issuer company pays them a commission. The syndicate agreement covers this aspect as well.

company and is obligated to offer the ASBA facility to all its account holders for public issues.

The ASBA process works in the following manner: An investor who is eligible to apply through the ASBA process submits, physically or electronically through the internet banking facility, an ASBA form to the SCSB with whom the bank account to be blocked is maintained. Investors can also submit the physical ASBA form through merchant bankers and syndicate members. The SCSB then, based on the authorization in the ASBA, blocks the application money in the bank account. The application money remains blocked in the bank account till the finalization of the basis of allotment, or till withdrawal or failure of the public issue, or till withdrawal or rejection of the application form. In book-built public issues, the SCSB uploads the bid and application data on the electronic bidding system through a web-enabled system that stock exchanges provide, thereby 'building the book'. Upon finalization of the basis of allotment, the registrar to the issue sends a request to the SCSB for unblocking the application money and transferring it to the issuer company's bank account.

The process of collecting application forms was further simplified. SEBI, in October 2012, permitted all stockbrokers, who may not be syndicate members or appointed by the syndicate members, to accept application forms. From 1 January 2016, even registrars to an issue and depository participants have been permitted to accept application forms in public issue of equity shares.[31] To aid the process, stock exchanges also provide application forms that can be downloaded from their website. With effect from 1 January 2016, only ASBA facility can be used for bids and applications in public issue of equity shares.[32] In a public issue of debentures, the ASBA facility exists alongside the traditional application method. Investors also have an additional method of direct application by using the stock exchange's online interface with an online payment facility.[33]

---

[31] SEBI circular no. CIR/CFD/POLICYCELL/11/2015 dated 10 November 2015.

[32] Sub-regulation (5) of regulation 58 of the ICDR Regulations.

[33] SEBI circular no. CIR/IMD/DF-1/20/2012 dated 27 July 2012.

Registrar to an Issue

Merchant bankers, syndicate members, bankers to the issue including the SCSBs, stockbrokers, and stock exchanges collect application forms in some way or the other depending upon the type of public issue. These application forms are processed by the registrar to the issue—an entity registered with SEBI under the Securities and Exchange Board of India (Registrars to an Issue and Share Transfer Agents) Regulations, 1993. The issuer company appoints a registrar to the issue to process the application forms, assist the issuer company in determining the basis of allotment of securities, and finalize the list of persons entitled to allotment of securities. The registrar to the issue is also responsible for issuing instructions for transfer of application money to the bank account of the issuer company, and dispatching allotment letters, refund orders, and other related documents in respect of a public issue.

Depository

Every company making a public offer must issue the securities in dematerialized form in compliance with the provisions of the Depositories Act, 1996 (or the Depositories Act).[34] Depositories provide the service of dematerialization of securities, a process that we examined in Chapter 1. The issuer company, therefore, must enter into an agreement with a depository for dematerialization of corporate securities already issued and proposed to be issued by way of public issue. Depositories perform another function in a public offering programme: To receive securities in a dematerialized form, investors are required to provide details of their beneficial ownership account maintained with a depository through the depository participant. The beneficial ownership account contains the personal details of an investor such as address, investor status, permanent account number under the Income-tax Act, 1961, and bank account details. The registrar to the issue matches the depository account details mentioned in the application form with those maintained by the depository for validating an application form. The registrar to the issue also obtains the personal details from the depository

---

[34] Section 29 of the Companies Act.

for performing public-issue-related functions such as giving refunds and other correspondence with the investor.

Credit Rating Agency

A credit rating is an opinion on the creditworthiness or the relative degree of risk of timely payment of interest and principal on fixed income securities like debt securities and preference shares.[35] It is an assessment of the probability of default of the rated instrument and, therefore, provides a benchmark for measuring and pricing credit risk.[36] But it neither provides guidance on other aspects essential for investment decisions such as price nor is it a recommendation to purchase, sell, or hold any security.[37] The rating is generally expressed in letters or alphanumeric symbols.

Credit rating of equity shares is a misnomer and credit rating agencies do not typically rate equity shares. Instead, credit rating agencies grade IPOs of equity shares to provide additional information to investors for their investment decision. IPO grading is an assessment of the 'fundamentals' of the issuer company on a relative five-point grading scale—'fundamentals' meaning the prospects of the industry in which the issuer company operates, the company's competitive strengths and financial position, its operating performance, management capability, corporate governance practices, and such other parameters. IPO grading is not an assessment of the price of the offered equity shares or the likely returns and it is a one-time assessment prior to the IPO without any on-going grading. Thus, an issuer company making an IPO of equity shares may obtain grading for such offer from one or more credit rating agencies registered with SEBI.[38] Given its value, the business of rating

---

[35] Ministry of Finance, Government of India, *Report of the Committee on Comprehensive Regulation for Credit Rating Agencies* (December 2009).

[36] Credit Rating Agencies Report (n. 35), at p. 17.

[37] Jonathan Katz and others, 'Credit Rating Agencies: No Easy Regulatory Solutions' (October 2009) <http://siteresources.worldbank.org/EXTFINANCIALSECTOR/Resources/282884-1303327122200/Note8.pdf> accessed on 10 July 2014.

[38] SEBI introduced IPO grading in April 2006 on an optional basis and made it mandatory in April 2007. However, SEBI subsequently realized that

has grown and expanded to products other than securities such as bank deposits and loans, and rating of industry sectors such as finance, infrastructure, and insurance.

Credit rating and IPO grading are of value to not just the investors, but also to the issuer company and the regulator. Better rating and grading allows the company to access a wider investor base and price the securities competitively. SEBI uses them as a tool to protect the securities market from excessively risky securities. Thus, obtaining credit rating is a precondition for issuing debt securities and preference shares, and in case of a public issue of preference shares, the rating must not be less than 'AA–'.[39] In turn, SEBI regulates the rating agencies. Thus, any person proposing to engage in the business of rating of securities offered by way of public issue or rights issue must be registered, and act in accordance with SEBI under the Securities and Exchange Board of India (Credit Rating Agencies) Regulations, 1999.

Debenture Trustee

On the basis of security, debentures could be unsecured or secured. Security for the debentures is generally in the form of a charge or mortgage on the properties of the issuer company.[40] As a form of security, a corporate mortgage is no different from a mortgage that an individual borrower gives on his home. The individual borrower gives the mortgage directly to the lending bank. But when a company issues debentures to members of the public, it would not be convenient or practicable to divide the mortgage among them individually. This necessitates the intervention of a trustee, properly called the debenture trustee, who is

---

IPO grading had not fully served its intended purpose. IPOs with grade four had yielded high losses and retail investors, for whose benefit IPO grading was primarily introduced, were not taking any cues from the grading. However, there did exist a correlation between the grades and the valuation multiples. Accordingly, SEBI made IPO grading a voluntary exercise. See sub-regulation (7) of regulation 26 of the ICDR Regulations.

[39] Regulation 4 of the Debt Securities Regulations and the Preference Shares Regulations.

[40] Rule 18 of the Companies (Share Capital and Debentures) Rules, 2014.

constituted under a deed of trust, to hold the mortgage in the interests of all the debenture holders.[41]

Though the foregoing is the foundational basis for the appointment of a debenture trustee, the functions performed by them have evolved over the years. A debenture trustee is now required to do all that is necessary to protect the interests of the debenture holders such as ensuring timely dispatch of debenture certificates, ensuring that the company complies with the debt listing agreement, monitoring utilization of the funds raised for the issue, and investor grievance redressal. Thus, even for a public issue of unsecured debentures, the issuer company must appoint one or more debenture trustees. They are appointed in accordance with the provisions of the Companies Act and the Securities and Exchange Board of India (Debenture Trustees) Regulations, 1993 (or the Debenture Trustees Regulations)—a regulation for the registration of debenture trustees, containing the terms and conditions subject to which they must act. The issuer company must appoint the debenture trustee before filing the draft prospectus for review with the regulatory authorities, although the trust deed for securing the issue of secured debentures is executed after the issue of debentures. The Debenture Trustees Regulations prohibit a debenture trustee from being appointed in that capacity in respect of the issue of debentures if it is an associate of the issuer company, it has lent and the loan is not yet fully repaid, or is proposing to lend money to the issuer company.[42] Other than acting as a trustee for the benefit of the debenture holders, the debenture trustee also acts as a liaison with SEBI on an ongoing basis. It has the duty to inform SEBI of any breach of the trust deed, and as and when required by SEBI, submit information and documents in relation to its functions.[43]

Participants Other than Intermediaries

A public offering programme necessitates the involvement of participants other than securities market intermediaries, the chief among them

[41] William H. Walker, *Corporation Finance: Modern Business*, vol. II (Alexander Hamilton Institute 1918), at p. 116.

[42] Regulation 13A of the Debenture Trustees Regulations.

[43] Clause (l) of sub-regulation (1) of regulation 15 and regulation 18 of the Debenture Trustees Regulations.

being the company's auditor, 'experts', monitoring agencies, legal advisers, and advertising agencies. They are not regulated by SEBI; some of them are appointed or get involved depending upon the size and needs of the public offering programme.

Beginning with the auditor, a company must set out in the prospectus, prescribed reports by its auditors on its profits and losses, assets and liabilities, and other financial information. To perform this task, the company engages the statutory auditor. Additionally, the statutory auditor may also be engaged to deliver to the merchant bankers, at different stages of the public offering programme, a 'comfort letter' on the financial condition of the issuer company. A comfort letter must be understood in the backdrop of auditors' reports that are set out in the prospectus. Securities laws mandate these reports to be up to a date not earlier than six months of the date of issue of the prospectus.[44] For this six-month period, there is no report by the auditors in the prospectus on the financial statements of the company. Merchant bankers, on account of their due diligence obligation, seek to find out whether any material adverse development in the financial health of the company has occurred during the six-month period. Therefore, in addition to examining the company's internal financial statements, they contractually obligate the company to obtain a 'comfort letter' from the auditor. A comfort letter is thus a letter by the auditors of the company addressed to the merchant bankers wherein they confirm that they have reviewed the financial data of the company (and other entities such as material subsidiaries) for a period between the date up to which reports have been set out in the prospectus and the date of the issue of the prospectus. This is followed by a statement of negative assurance wherein they confirm that they are not aware of any materially adverse development in the position of the issuer company during this period. The letter is not disclosed in the prospectus and is retained by the merchant bankers. The purpose of a comfort letter is thus to meet the due diligence obligation of the merchant bankers and therefore it is not inconceivable for it to also become a source of liability for the auditors.

Next, sometimes the nature of the issuer company's business requires disclosure of highly technical information in the prospectus

---

[44] Rule 4 of the Companies (Prospectus and Allotment of Securities) Rules, 2014.

and it may be appropriate, though not mandatory, to involve an expert to provide it. For example, if landholding is central to a company's business, it may be prudent to get it measured and certified by an expert. Similarly, a company engaged in the business of exploration and production of oil and natural gas may require certification of the estimates of its crude oil and natural gas reserves. An expert's profession gives authority to a statement made by him, and thus, such certifications add credibility to the technical information. Resultantly, the Companies Act regulates disclosure of an expert's statement in the prospectus. It defines an expert to include an engineer, a valuer, a chartered accountant, a company secretary, a cost accountant, and any other person who has the power or authority to issue a certificate in pursuance of any law for the time being in force.[45] To ensure the independence of the expert, the prospectus must not include a statement purporting to be made by an expert, unless the expert is a person who is not, and has not been, engaged or interested in the formation or promotion or management of the company. He must have also given his written consent to the issue of the prospectus and should not have withdrawn such consent before the delivery of a copy of the prospectus to the registrar of companies for registration. The prospectus must include a statement to this effect.[46] Considering the special value of an expert's statement, the Companies Act imposes civil liability for its misstatement in the prospectus.[47]

In public issue of equity shares of a size exceeding Rs 500 crore, the issuer company must make arrangements for the use of the proceeds to be monitored by a public financial institution or by one of the enlisted bankers to the issue.[48] The purpose of appointing a monitoring agency is investor protection, and the monitoring agency is required to submit a report to the issuer company on a half-yearly basis, till the proceeds of the

---

[45] Clause (38) of section 2 of the Companies Act.

[46] Sub-section (5) of section 26 of the Companies Act.

[47] Section 35 of the Companies Act.

[48] For obvious reasons, a monitoring agency is not required to be appointed in a public offer consisting only of an offer for sale. They are also not required to be appointed in a public issue by a bank or public financial institution or an insurance company. See regulation 16 of the ICDR Regulations.

issue have been fully utilized.[49] The report is expected to cover matters such as progress of the project for which capital was raised, methods of utilization of surplus capital, and cost and time overruns. The company must submit the report or any comments from the monitoring agency to the stock exchange(s).[50]

Generally, both the company and merchant bankers appoint legal advisers to assist them in preparing the prospectus and transactional agreements such as the issue agreement and underwriting agreement, and provide legal advice on securities law matters. The legal advisers are also required to provide a customary legal opinion to the underwriters on the prospectus and the public offering programme. Finally, during a public offering programme, the company and intermediaries associated with the public issue are subject to regulatory restrictions on public communications and advertisements. Further, the company has to make certain prescribed advertisements at different stages of the public offering programme. The company appoints an advertising agency to carry out these tasks.

Initial Considerations

After ensuring compliance with the eligibility conditions, choosing a trading segment, and appointing the early set of intermediaries, the company must decide on the method of pricing the securities to be offered. To this is linked several pre-offering matters such as allocation of securities among the different classes of investors and preparing the prospectus. Other important activities before making the public offer include enhancing the company's corporate governance, investment by promoters, and tidying up the company's memorandum of association and articles of association.

Pricing

From what has been already discussed in Chapter 1, corporate securities are essentially rights in and against the company and have no intrinsic

---

[49] Sub-regulation (2) of regulation 16 of the ICDR Regulations.

[50] Sub-regulation (6) of regulation 32 of the Securities and Exchange Board of India (Listing Obligations and Disclosure Requirements) Regulations, 2015 (or the LODR Regulations).

value; their value is dependent upon the value attached to the rights. A debenture, being a borrowing, carries with it the right to receive the principal and interest amount. The issue price of a debenture is, therefore, generally the amount being borrowed, which is also its nominal value. To make the debentures attractive for subscription by the public, the company offers a competitive rate of interest as a return on investment, and offers security on its assets to secure the return of the principal and interest. Shares, on the other hand, pose a challenge in terms of pricing especially equity shares since preference shares somewhat follow the pricing methodology of debentures. They are subject to rules restricting dealing in share capital, and in return, carry the right to receive declared dividend and voting while the company is a going concern. But, unlike the right to receive a fixed income in the case of debentures, it is difficult to assess the monetary value of the rights associated with shares. It must be clear that the nominal value of shares provides no measure of their real value.

Among the multiple factors that influence determination of the real value of shares, Pennington lists four factors that account for any difference between the value of a company's shares and those of any other similarly placed company: capital cover, yield, earnings, and marketability.[51] Capital cover is the extent to which the company can repay the paid-up share capital from the assets after meeting its debts and liabilities. If the capital cover is insufficient, shares will tend to be worth less than their paid-up value, though the company can make up the reduced value by a higher than average earning capacity.[52] Yield is the proportion which the dividends paid in respect of shares bear to the price at which they can be bought. Earnings are the profit that the company earns using the capital employed in the business. Higher yield and earning increases the value of the shares. Marketability is the ease with which the shares can be sold which depends on factors such as whether the shares are listed on a stock exchange, whether a single person or group of persons who are likely to act in concert hold large blocks of shares or whether share ownership is widely dispersed.[53] Listed shares which are dispersed

[51]   Robert R. Pennington, *Company Law* (8th edn, Oxford University Press 2001), at p. 164.

[52]   Pennington (n. 51).

[53]   Pennington (n. 51).

among a large class of shareholders command a better price since voting rights attached to such shares can be meaningfully exercised. Thus, depending on these and several other factors, the real price of shares will quite often be more than the nominal value, and will command a premium. The issue price of shares will thus comprise two components: nominal value of the shares and the premium. Theoretically, debentures too can be issued at a premium, though for reasons stated earlier, it is unusual for a company to do so.

Though the foregoing factors are important for the company to consider while pricing securities being offered to the public, the Companies Act does not prescribe a method for determining the public issue price. Under the Companies Act, the board of directors of the company is guided by its general fiduciary and statutory duty to act in the best interests of the company and the shareholders while determining the issue price; provided that shares are not issued at a discount to the nominal value.[54] Until 1992, the Capital Issues (Control) Act, 1947 (or the Capital Issues Control Act), orders and rules framed thereunder, and guidelines issued by the Ministry of Finance (MoF) controlled and regulated the volume of securities to be offered to the public, the issue price, and the timing of the public issue. The market practice was to determine and obtain approval of the issue price before commencement

---

[54] Section 53 of the Companies Act. As discussed in the section 'Raising Capital by Issue of Securities' in Chapter 1 of this volume, it may be possible to apply clause (c) of sub-section (1) of section 62 of the Companies Act to a public issue of shares and conclude that the issue price must be determined by the valuation report of a registered valuer (and should not be less than the price so determined). But this conclusion is not free from doubt for sub-rule (1) of rule 13 of the Companies (Share Capital and Debentures) Rules, 2014 seems to suggest that this requirement is applicable to a 'preferential offer' only. 'Preferential offer' means an issue of shares or other securities, by a company to any select person or group of persons on a preferential basis and does not include shares or other securities offered through a public issue, rights issue, employee stock option scheme, employee stock purchase scheme or an issue of sweat equity shares or bonus shares or depository receipts issued in a country outside India or foreign securities. For a discussion on 'preferential offer', see the section 'Raising Capital by Issue of Securities' in Chapter 1 and the section 'Prospectus' in Chapter 3 of this volume.

of the issue period and disclose it in the prospectus. Upon repeal of the Capital Issues Control Act and setting up of SEBI, companies could issue securities to the public without the prior consent of the central government and price such securities freely. The practice of fixed price public issues continued, meaning that the company would determine the issue price and the volume of securities being offered, state it in the prospectus, register the prospectus with the registrar of companies, and issue the prospectus to the public.

This method, however, met with difficulties owing to the newly established SEBI, which, unlike the registrar of companies, began vetting draft prospectuses as part of its statutory duty. Initially, issue price had to be determined at the time of filing of the draft prospectus with SEBI for vetting. As considerable time often elapsed between the stage of the submission of the draft prospectus with SEBI for vetting, and the opening of the public issue, early pricing often led to the issue price being not always aligned to market conditions close to the issue period. To enable pricing public issues closer to the issue period, SEBI allowed the company to indicate a price band in the draft prospectus submitted to it, instead of specifying the issue price. Issue price could be specified in the prospectus registered with the registrar of companies.[55] This practice evolved into an additional method of pricing securities in public issues called 'book building'. Before we examine the book-building method under Indian securities laws, we look at its origin, for this method presents considerable conceptual challenges in its present form and practice.

Book building originated in the US where the standard method of undertaking an IPO of securities is through a syndicate of investment banking firms or underwriters. These entities engage in a marketing and 'book building' process and then agree, on a firm commitment basis, to subscribe to the securities from the issuer company and offer to sell them to the public.[56] How it works is that the company files the

---

[55] Securities and Exchange Board of India, *Annual Report* (1993–94).

[56] Johnson and McLaughlin (n. 16), at p. 55. In India, this method of undertaking the public issue would fall under section 25 of the Companies Act. For 'underwriting' and 'firm commitment basis', see the section 'Underwriting' of this chapter.

prospectus with the securities regulator with an initial estimated price range. During the period between the filing of the prospectus and the prospectus becoming effective (meaning that the securities regulator has approved the prospectus, which can be then used as the basis for selling securities to the public), underwriters carry out the 'book building' process. This means that the underwriters gather and assess potential investor demand for the offering of securities and seek information as to the size and pricing of an issue.[57] They do so by conducting 'road shows' to market the offering to potential investors, generally institutional investors.[58] The road shows provide investors, the issuer, and underwriters the opportunity to gather important information from each other.[59] Investors seek information about the company, its management, and its prospects, and underwriters seek information from investors that will assist them in determining particular investors' interest in the company, assessing demand for the offering, and improving pricing accuracy for the offering.[60] However, no written offers are made to the investors. By aggregating information obtained during this period from investors with other information, the underwriters and the issuer agree on the size and pricing of the offering, and the underwriters decide how to allocate the IPO shares to purchasers.[61]

It must be noted that no prospectus is issued to the public for book building, for no effective prospectus exists. Further, no uniform process exists for book building—it may even be carried out at informal face-to-face meetings with institutional investors. The process continues for many days until a few days before the shares are priced and the

[57] United States Securities and Exchange Commission, *Commission Guidance Regarding Prohibited Conduct in Connection with IPO Allocations* (April 2005), at p. 10.

[58] The [US] Securities Act, rule 433(h)(4) defines a 'road show' to mean, to the extent it is relevant, 'an offer (other than a statutory prospectus or a portion of a statutory prospectus filed as part of a registration statement) that contains a presentation regarding an offering by one or more members of the issuer's management...and includes discussion of one or more of the issuer, such management, and the securities being offered'.

[59] Commission Guidance (n. 57).

[60] Commission Guidance (n. 57), at p. 11.

[61] Commission Guidance (n. 57), at p. 11.

prospectus registration becomes effective.[62] Lastly, book building is not just a method of determining the issue price but also of allocating the securities—securities are ordinarily offered to the investors that would have shown an interest during the book building process. A price discovered through book building is thus a price that the market can bear and may not necessarily relate to the real value of the equity shares. If there is great enthusiasm for the securities during the bidding period, the public offering price will increase. This phenomenon particularly benefits companies in pricing unlisted equity shares for which no public market exists and whose market demand is difficult to assess. Book building, therefore, is the preferred pricing method in large-size IPOs of equity shares.

This is what was sought to be imported in India at the stage outlined earlier when SEBI began allowing companies to indicate a price range in the draft prospectus. However, both in form and practice, it differed from the American practice owing to muddled statutory provisions that sought to codify it.[63] Presently, securities laws on undertaking book building for public issue of equity shares can be summarized as follows, although undertaking a book building is a far more complicated process than this description.[64]

A company registers with the registrar of companies a red herring prospectus—a prospectus that does not include complete particulars of the quantum or price of equity shares and carries the same obligations as are applicable to an ordinary prospectus. A red herring prospectus, like an ordinary prospectus, must state dates of opening and closing of the public issue, meaning the period during which the company issues the document to the public and invites participation in the public issue. The red herring prospectus may disclose a price band—a price range containing a floor price and a cap price such that the cap on the price

[62] Christine Hurt, 'Moral Hazard and the Initial Public Offering' (2005) 26 Cardozo Law Review 711, at p. 733.

[63] See section 60B of the Companies Act, 1956.

[64] As per section 28 of the Companies Act, a company can issue a red herring prospectus and undertake book building for public issues of preference shares and debentures also. However, unlike for equity shares under the ICDR Regulations, SEBI has not prescribed a procedure for undertaking book building under the Debt Securities Regulations and the Preference Shares Regulations.

band is less than or equal to 120 per cent of the floor price. Or the price band may be disclosed separately by way of a public announcement at least five working days before the opening of the public issue. The company and the merchant bankers determine the price band based on their assessment of the value of the equity shares.

Prior to the opening of the public issue, the company puts in place the necessary facilities for undertaking book building such as appointing one or all of the merchant bankers with the task of 'running the book', agreement with one or more of the stock exchanges which have the system of online offer of securities, and appointment of relevant intermediaries for accepting bids and applications, which intermediaries are deemed as bidding and collection centres. The company then issues the red herring prospectus to the public. During the public issue period, the company invites 'bids' from investors on the 'bidding form'. Bids are stated to be indications by investors of their offer to subscribe a certain number of equity shares at a price within the price band by submitting the bidding form and paying the bid amount. In reality, bids are nothing but applications to subscribe securities at different price levels, and thus, the bidding form is called the 'bid-cum-application form'. Details from the bid-cum-application forms are electronically uploaded on the platform of the stock exchange on a regular basis and the book gets 'built up' at various price levels.

Upon closure of the public issue, the company and relevant intermediaries process the built-up book to discover the price. Price discovery is essentially a function of demand at various price levels, and the highest price at which the company is able to issue the desired number of equity shares becomes the issue price. All applications at and above the issue price are considered successful and eligible for allotment of equity shares. Applications below the issue price are rejected. Ready with the quantum of equity shares and the issue price, the company completes the missing particulars of the red herring prospectus and files the prospectus with the registrar of companies and SEBI.

A significant difference between the Indian book-building method and its American counterpart is that book building in India is not carried out prior to the public issue at road shows, etc., but during the public issue period itself. During the public issue, the red herring prospectus and applications are the bases for carrying out book building as well as for subscribing or purchasing the securities. The red herring prospectus performs functions that a prospectus should perform. The final prospectus instead performs the functions of a record book containing details of the issue price and volume of securities and is filed with the registrar of companies and SEBI. It is not issued to the public, as issue of prospectus is understood in law, though the Companies Act seems to require it to be so issued.[65] An important fallout of this disorderly method is that in a public issue of equity shares through the book building method, the underwriting agreement is entered into after the public issue is over, thereby nullifying the very purpose of an underwriting agreement.

In book building, though bids are solicited at different price levels within the price band, the issue price is uniform for all successful bidders. Successful bidders who had bid above the issue price are entitled to refund of the excess bid amount. To secure this excess amount as well to benefit issuer companies, SEBI introduced an additional method of pricing equity shares, namely 'alternate method of book building', also known as the auction method.[66] This method is akin to the book-building method except as follows. Instead of a price band, the company announces a single floor price to the investors. Applications are solicited from the investors at any price above the floor price. The applicant who applies at the highest price is allotted the number of equity shares that he has applied for, and then the applicant who has applied at the second highest price, and so on, until all the equity shares on offer are exhausted. The issue price is not uniform and varies from one applicant to the other. The alternate method of book building can be opted for only in case of a further public offer (FPO) and not an IPO, and thus is aimed at benefiting the union or the state governments who undertake FPOs for disinvestment. The Companies Act, however, does not expressly recognize this method of pricing equity shares.

Of the three methods of pricing corporate securities in public issues, SEBI regulations permit fixed price and book building for all corporate securities, and alternate method of book building only in an FPO of

---

[65] Sub-section (1) of section 32 of the Companies Act states that: 'A company proposing to make an offer of securities may issue a red herring prospectus prior to the issue of a prospectus.'

[66] Clause (d) of regulation 29 of the ICDR Regulations.

equity shares. The market practice is to resort to the fixed price method for pricing debentures and small size equity offerings typically to be listed on the SME exchange. For large-size public offerings of equity shares, book building is the common method. In a public offering of equity shares, the ICDR Regulations permit the company to provide a small discount on the issue price to certain small investors and employees participating in the public issue.[67] The Indian market is yet to see a public offering of preference shares in accordance with the Preference Shares Regulations, and the alternate method of book building has been resorted to only once, namely in the FPO of equity shares of the Rural Electrification Corporation Limited in January 2010.

Whatever be the method of pricing, if the company invites offers from 'person(s) resident outside India'[68] to subscribe or purchase the securities or if the public issue consists of an offer for sale of securities by a 'person resident outside India', the price of the securities must be in comformity with the Foreign Exchange Management Act, 1999 (or FEMA) and the regulations framed thereunder, particularly the Foreign Exchange Management (Transfer or Issue of Security by a Person Resident outside India) Regulations, 2000; Foreign Exchange Management (Borrowing or Lending in Foreign Exchange) Regulations, 2000; and Foreign Exchange Management (Borrowing and Lending in Rupees) Regulations, 2000. These laws do not dictate the actual price to be arrived at but lay down pricing guidelines such as adherence to SEBI regulations and guidelines; and restrict companies from issuing securities to residents outside India at a price, which is less than the price at which securities are issued to residents in India.

Managing Risk Relating to Issue Price

The foregoing methods of pricing equity shares in a public issue increase the prospects of an optimum issue price. However, given the risks inherent in pricing equity shares and external factors such as aggressive price setting to maximize the company's or selling shareholders' gains, the possibility of the price of the equity shares becoming volatile upon listing

[67] Regulation 29 of the ICDR Regulations.

[68] Clause (w) read with clause (v) of section 2 of FEMA defines 'person resident outside India'.

and trading is not unusual. Likelihood of price volatility is even higher in IPOs because no prior public market exists for the equity shares. In fact, past experience suggests that this is the norm.[69] While price volatility is generally detrimental for a sustainable trade in the company's equity shares as it may lead to panic among traders, it also adversely affects the investors' decision, particularly of small investors, to invest their savings in the securities market.

To manage these risks, securities laws permit two mechanisms—green shoe option and safety net arrangement—each of which is optional. Though both these mechanisms are put into action upon the completion of the public issue, they form part of the initial considerations since a decision on whether to adopt them must be made at the earliest and before filing of the draft prospectus with SEBI for review. One benefit of an express provision in the securities laws for the green shoe option and safety net arrangement is that these are considered as legitimate methods for managing the price of equity shares in the secondary market. They do not thus carry the risk of amounting to market manipulation under the Securities and Exchange Board of India (Prohibition of Fraudulent and Unfair Trade Practices Relating to Securities Market) Regulations, 2003 (or the PFUTP Regulations).

Green shoe option is a mechanism for stabilizing the post-listing price of equity shares.[70] In this option, the company appoints one of the merchant bankers as a stabilizing agent to be responsible for the price stabilization process. The stabilizing agent enters into an agreement with certain existing shareholders for borrowing equity shares with the objective of selling these along with the public issue. The prospectus carries detailed disclosure of the green shoe option and the borrowed

---

[69] A SEBI discussion paper notes that in the analysis of price performance of the different equity shares or scrips listed during 2008–11, it was observed that out of 117 scrips, 72 (around 62 per cent issues) were trading below the issue price after six months of their listing. Out of those 72 scrips that witnessed a fall in price, in 55 scrips the fall was more than 20 per cent of the issue price. See Securities and Exchange Board of India, *Discussion Paper on Mandatory Safety Net Mechanism* (September 2012).

[70] Regulation 45 of the ICDR Regulations. The colourful name is based on the offering of shares of the Green Shoe Manufacturing Company in the US in 1963 and this offering is credited to have first used this mechanism.

equity shares are treated, for all practical purposes, as part of the public issue. Depending upon the extent of demand for the equity shares in the public issue, the stabilizing agent sells the borrowed equity shares to the public and credits the money in a special account. During a period not exceeding 30 days from the date on which stock exchanges grant the trading permission, the stabilizing agent carries out the stabilization process. If the price of the equity shares starts falling below the issue price, the stabilizing agent begins purchasing them using the money lying in the special account. These purchases serve to support and stabilize the price of the equity shares in the secondary market. The stabilizing agent determines the relevant aspects of stabilization including the timing, quantity, and the price at which the equity shares must be bought. After the completion of the stabilization period, the stabilizing agent returns the purchased equity shares to the entity that had lent them initially. If there is a shortfall, the company issues and allots equity shares to that entity in consideration of the money lying in the special account.

Safety net arrangement, on the other hand, is a mechanism for boosting the confidence of small investors to participate in a public issue.[71] Under this arrangement, the company arranges for a person who offers to purchase a certain number of equity shares at the issue price from the small investors (now shareholders). The safety net provider must offer to purchase the shares within a period of six months from the last date of credit of dematerialized shares into the account of the small investors. This arrangement provides an assurance to small investors that in the event the share price falls below the issue price upon listing and trading, they have a 'safety net' for a certain number of equity shares.

Single and Multiple Offers

An important pre-offering matter that the company and merchant bankers must consider is whether to undertake the public offer of corporate securities as a single offer on the basis of an ordinary prospectus or multiple offers on the basis of a shelf prospectus—a type of prospectus whose meaning and function we examined in Chapter 3.[72] The latter route is, however, available to only a small class of companies that SEBI

---

[71] Regulation 44 of the ICDR Regulations.

[72] See the section 'Types of Prospectuses' in Chapter 3 of this volume.

may specify.[73] These companies may file a shelf prospectus with the registrar of companies at the stage of the first offer of securities included therein. The shelf prospectus is valid for a period of one year that commences from the date of opening of the first offer of securities under that prospectus. In respect of a second or subsequent offer of securities issued during the period of validity of the shelf prospectus, no new prospectus is required.[74] Instead, the company must file an information memorandum with the registrar of companies.[75] An information memorandum states the material developments after the first offer of securities or the previous offer of securities like new charges created and changes in the financial position of the company.[76] Where an information memorandum is filed, every time an offer of securities is made, the information memorandum together with the shelf prospectus is deemed to be a prospectus.[77]

Classes of Investors and Apportioning of Offered Securities

A common perception is to view members of the investing public as a single homogenous class. To a limited extent this is true. Members of the public invest in public offerings with the common objective of seeking a profitable return on their investment. However, beyond this

---

[73] For the public issue of debentures, SEBI has specified under regulation 6A of the Debt Securities Regulations, public financial institutions, companies authorized by the notification of the Central Board of Direct Taxes (CBDT) to make public issue of tax free secured bonds, non-banking financial companies and housing finance companies meeting prescribed norms, and companies whose equity shares or debentures are listed on a recognized exchange and who meet prescribed norms to use the shelf prospectus route. SEBI has made no such provision for public issues of preference shares and equity shares, though the ICDR Regulations implicitly recognize the shelf prospectus route for equity shares. However, unlike for debentures, there has not been a public issue of equity shares through a shelf prospectus.

[74] Sub-section (1) of section 31 of the Companies Act.

[75] Sub-section (2) of section 31 of the Companies Act and rule 10 of the Companies (Prospectus and Allotment of Securities) Rules.

[76] Sub-section (2) of section 31 of the Companies Act.

[77] Sub-section (3) of section 31 of the Companies Act.

commonality investors can be categorized into classes founded on different bases. SEBI has classified the investing public into three classes on certain bases to achieve the statutory objective of protecting the interests of investors in securities and to promote the development of the securities market. The classification exists in relation to investors of equity shares, and not of debentures and preference shares given the unique nature of investment in equity shares discussed earlier.[78]

For the public issue of equity shares, SEBI has classified the investing public into three classes, namely retail individual investors, qualified institutional buyers, and non-institutional investors. Retail individual investors are investors who apply or bid for equity shares for a value not more than two lakh rupees. The ceiling of two lakh rupees is not sacrosanct, and SEBI increases it based on the rate of inflation and higher investing capacity. Whatever be the ceiling, the objective is to create a class of the 'average small investors' who possess varying levels of knowledge, aptitude, and experience, generally bordering on inexperience in obtaining and understanding investment-related information. SEBI's approach towards retail individual investors is generally very protective. Thus, SEBI permits companies to offer equity shares to retail individual investors at a discount of not more than 10 per cent on the issue price. In book-built public issues, retail individual investors have the option to participate in the public issue without actually making a bid.

If retail individual investors were to be at one end of the spectrum of the investing public, then at the other end of the spectrum would fall qualified institutional buyers. Qualified institutional buyers are institutional investors such as mutual funds, provident funds, pension funds, venture capital funds (VCFs), alternative investment funds (AIFs), foreign portfolio investors (FPIs), public financial institutions, and scheduled commercial banks (SCBs).[79] They are a permanent feature of

---

[78] See the section 'Corporate Securities' in Chapter 1 of this volume.

[79] Clause (zd) of sub-regulation (1) of regulation 2 of the ICDR Regulations defines 'qualified institutional investor' to mean

(i) a mutual fund, venture capital fund, Alternative Investment Fund and foreign venture capital investor registered with the Board; (ii) a foreign portfolio investor other than Category III foreign portfolio investor, registered with the Board; (iii) a public financial institution as defined in section 4A of the Companies Act, 1956; (iv) a scheduled commercial bank; (v) a multilateral

any capital market and their market function is to provide large blocks of capital to equity markets, in addition to large trading in other securities in the primary and secondary market. Indeed as examined in Chapter 1, some institutional investors such as mutual funds are conduits by which the average small investors participate in the capital market.[80] Given the large investible amount they possess, these institutional investors are proximate to the securities market, and are able to accumulate on their own and act on current information relevant for investment in the public offering of securities. Resultantly, qualified institutional buyers play a dominant role in bidding (and influencing the decision of other investors to bid) in book-built public issues.

Lastly, non-institutional investors are investors other than a retail individual investor and qualified institutional buyer. They are an amorphous class of investors participating in substantial investment activities.

The ICDR Regulations mandate that equity shares offered in a public issue must be apportioned or allocated among the three classes of investors in a specified ratio and applications must be invited accordingly.[81] Thus in book-built public issues, the company must allocate not less than 35 per cent and 15 per cent of the offered shares to retail individual investors and non-institutional investors, respectively. For qualified institutional buyers, the company must allocate not more than 50 per cent of the offered shares, 5 per cent of which must be allocated to mutual funds.[82] Mutual funds are also eligible to participate in the

---

and bilateral development financial institution; (vi) a state industrial development corporation; (vii) an insurance company registered with the Insurance Regulatory and Development Authority; (viii) a provident fund with minimum corpus of twenty five crore rupees; (ix) a pension fund with minimum corpus of twenty five crore rupees; (x) National Investment Fund set up by resolution no. F. No. 2/3/2005-DDII dated November 23, 2005 of the Government of India published in the Gazette of India; (xi) insurance funds set up and managed by army, navy or air force of the Union of India; and (xii) insurance funds set up and managed by the Department of Posts, India.

[80] Ralph K. Winter, 'Protecting the Ordinary Investor' (1988) 63 Washington Law Review 881, at p. 887. See also the section '"(ib) units or any other instrument"' and '"(id) units or any other such instrument"' in Chapter 1 of this volume.

[81] Regulation 43 of the ICDR Regulations.

[82] Sub-regulation (2) of regulation 43 of the ICDR Regulations.

balance portion allocated to qualified institutional buyers. The allocation percentage is different for book-built public issues that do not meet the eligibility condition of sound financial state and profitability track record as per prescribed norms. In such a situation, securities laws seek to reduce the exposure limit for retail individual investors and increase it for qualified institutional investors who are better equipped to analyse the credentials and financials of such companies. Accordingly, the company must allocate not more than 10 per cent and 15 per cent of the offered shares to retail individual investors and non-institutional investors, respectively, and not less than 75 per cent to qualified institutional buyers.[83] In fixed price public issues, a minimum of 50 per cent must be allocated to retail individual investors and the remaining to other investors.[84] Evidently, allocation serves the purpose of providing an opportunity to different classes of investors to participate in a public issue and manage their exposure limit.

Allocation does not mean allotment of the equity shares. In case, the number of equity shares applied for in a particular category exceeds or is less than the number of allocated equity shares, allotment is done on a proportionate basis or by allotting to investors of other categories, respectively. There are two exceptions to this general rule. First, in public issues where book building is mandatory due to the company not fulfilling the financial conditions for eligibility, not less than 75 per cent of the equity shares must not only be allocated but also be allotted to qualified institutional buyers.[85] Else, the public issue fails and the company must refund the subscription money of all investors. The rationale seems to be that investment in such companies carries high risk and if enough qualified institutional buyers, being experienced and well-informed investors do not view it as a viable investment target, other investors must be precluded from investing in it. On a similar rationale is based the second exception. In all book-built public issues, the unsubscribed portion in the qualified institutional category must not be allotted to any other class of investor.[86]

---

[83] Sub-regulation (2A) of regulation 43 of the ICDR Regulations.
[84] Sub-regulation (4) of regulation 43 of the ICDR Regulations.
[85] Sub-regulation (2) of regulation 26 of the ICDR Regulations.
[86] Paragraph 15 of schedule XI to the ICDR Regulations.

Allocation must also be distinguished from 'reservation'. The ICDR Regulations permit companies to reserve a small percentage of offered equity shares for certain types of employees, shareholders, depositors, bondholders, and customers. The terms of reservation differ depending upon the type of public offering and the pricing methodology.[87] Due to the preferential treatment of the beneficiaries of reservation, the ICDR Regulations exclude them from forming part of the 'public' for the purpose of meeting initial listing norms under the Securities Contracts (Regulation) Rules, 1957 (or the SCRR).[88]

Corporate Governance

Public issue of equity shares, and its listing and trading in the secondary market substantially increases the number of shareholders of the company. This necessitates better corporate governance of the company. Corporate governance may be understood by examining the two primary organs of the company—the board of directors and shareholders. In a company, shareholders provide the capital for the business and the board of directors manages it. The return on shareholders' investment is generally dependent on how well the company is managed and functions. Indeed this division is one of the core features of a company as a form of business organization. But this feature gives rise to the problem that the directors may not act in the interest of the shareholders as a class; instead they may act in their own interest. This problem may seem artificial in private companies and unlisted public companies with only a small body of shareholders, since, in such cases, shareholders are inevitably the directors of the company. In any event, standard statutory provisions manage whatever little of the problem arises in such companies.[89] However, in listed companies, the division between the

---

[87]   Regulation 42 of the ICDR Regulations.

[88]   Clause (u) of sub-regulation (1) of regulation 2, and regulation 41 of the ICDR Regulations.

[89]   The Companies Act sets out provisions such as shareholders' control over the company's memorandum of association and articles of association that contain the regulations for the management of the company, power with the shareholders to decide important matters like further issue of share capital to non-shareholders, right of the shareholders to appoint and remove the directors,

board of directors and shareholders is stark, with the former exercising extensive powers of management. Due to a large body of shareholders in listed companies, they face another problem: The majority or controlling shareholders, quite often the promoters of the company, will behave opportunistically toward the non-controlling shareholders. In India, the latter problem is acute due to the majority shareholding structure following a common pattern of being in the hands of members of a family, and the members of the investing public forming the fragmented minority.

Due to the twin problems of directors acting against the interest of shareholders as a class, and controlling shareholders acting opportunistically toward the non-controlling shareholders, special corporate governance rules are needed for listed companies. Sometimes corporate governance rules are also designed to protect non-shareholder constituencies such as employees, creditors, and prospective investors. SEBI provided the rules in 2000 by amending the equity listing agreement.[90] Corporate governance has evolved since then and now also exists under the Companies Act.[91] The bulk of the corporate governance rules have, however, been framed by SEBI and currently exist under Securities and Exchange Board of India (Listing Obligations and Disclosure Requirements) Regulations, 2015 (or the LODR Regulations).[92] Given the nature of the problems that corporate governance rules seek to address, these rules under the LODR Regulations are largely applicable to companies that have listed their equity shares.

Though corporate governance rules are very detailed, they focus primarily on the composition of the board of directors and constitution of specialized committees of directors. Thus, the board of directors must have an optimum combination of executive and non-executive directors

---

consent of the shareholders for exercise of certain powers by the board of directors, regulation of acts of the board of directors to prevent misuse of power, and imposing duties on directors to act for the benefit of the members as a whole.

[90] See SEBI circular no. SMDRP/POLICY/CIR-10/2000 dated 21 February 2000.

[91] See clause (p) of sub-section (3) of section 134, clause (e) of sub-section (5) of section 134, clause (4) of section 149, section 151, section 177, and section 178 of the Companies Act.

[92] See sub-regulation (2) of regulation 4, regulations 17 to 27 of, and para C to E of Schedule V to the LODR Regulations.

(not less than half of the number of directors being non-executive directors) with at least one woman director.[93] Executive directors are the ones that possess intimate knowledge of the business of the company and are responsible for its day-to-day management; non-executive directors are directors from the outside who bring a broader view to the company's activities and provide a check on the acts of the executive directors. One of the directors acts as the chairman of the board, and is primarily responsible for the working of the board and ensures that it acts as a unitary body. To ensure effectiveness of non-executive directors, corporate governance rules mandate that at least half (or, in certain cases, one-third) of the board of directors should comprise independent directors.[94] An independent director is a non-executive director, other than a nominee director, who meets the prescribed requirements of possessing the capability of exercising an independent judgment such as being independent of the promoter(s) and free from any business or other such relationship with the company.[95]

Corporate governance rules also require setting up of several committees of directors, consisting largely of independent directors, to whom certain special tasks can be delegated for meticulous functioning. A key committee is the audit committee whose task is to address financial aspects of corporate governance such as oversight of the company's financial reporting process to ensure that its financial statements are correct, sufficient, and credible.[96]

Corporate governance rules are applicable to the company upon listing of its securities. However, a company intending to make a public offer of its equity shares must comply with these prior to listing, and must make a disclosure to this effect in the prospectus.[97] Accordingly,

---

[93] Clause (a) of sub-regulation (1) of regulation 17 of the LODR Regulations.

[94] Clause (b) of sub-regulation (1) of regulation 17 of the LODR Regulations.

[95] Clause (b) of sub-regulation (1) of regulation 16 of the LODR Regulations.

[96] Section 177 of the Companies Act and regulation 18 of the LODR Regulations.

[97] Sub-clause (7) of clause (E) of sub-paragraph (VIII) of paragraph (2) of Part A of Schedule VIII to the ICDR Regulations.

the company may be required to significantly alter the composition of its board of directors by identifying and appointing the requisite number of non-executive directors and independent directors, and constitute the various committees of directors. Preferably this should be done much in advance and not on the eve of the public offering. This is due to the fact that every director is exposed to civil and criminal liability for mis-statements in the prospectus, and thus, would need adequate time to familiarize oneself with the company and the public offering programme.

Promoters' Investment and Lock-in

We examined in Chapter 3 who promoters are and their role in issuing a prospectus.[98] Ordinarily, some or all of the promoters are the control-ling shareholders and in public offerings of equity shares part with some control in return for investors' money. On pragmatic grounds, securi-ties laws obligate the promoters to continue to remain associated with the company. Thus, in an IPO of equity shares, the promoters' share in the post-issue share capital must not be less than 20 per cent. This is commonly referred to as promoters' contribution.[99] Any one or more of the promoters can satisfy the promoters' contribution requirement. For existing share capital of the promoters to qualify for the promot-ers' contribution, it must meet the prescribed eligibility conditions.[100] If enough share capital of the promoters is not eligible, promoters must subscribe for the requisite number of equity shares along with the public

[98] See the section 'Proponents of Public Offer and Offer for Sale' in Chapter 3 of this volume.

[99] In case the post-issue shareholding of the promoters is less than 20 per cent, alternative investment funds may contribute for the purpose of meeting the shortfall subject to a maximum of 10 per cent of the post-issue capital. In case of an FPO of equity shares, required promoters' contribution is either to the extent of 20 per cent of the proposed issue size or 20 per cent of the post-issue share capital. Sub-regulation (1) of regulation 32 of the ICDR Regulations. Promoters' contribution is not required in a few prescribed cases under regula-tion 34 of the ICDR Regulations such as rights issue, in case of an issuer which does not have an identifiable promoter, and for an FPO by companies whose equity shares are frequently traded.

[100] See regulation 33 of the ICDR Regulations

issue, and cash consideration for the same must be brought in at least one day prior to the date of opening of the public issue.[101]

To make promoters' contribution effective, the ICDR Regulations restrict promoters from transferring the contributed share capital for a period of three years generally from the date of allotment of equity shares in the public issue; the restriction is commonly called 'lock-in'.[102] In addition to the lock-in of the minimum promoters' contribution, the remaining pre-public issue share capital must be locked-in for a period of one year from the date of allotment of equity shares in the public issue.[103] This latter lock-in serves the purpose of providing some assurance to the public investors that there will be a market for their equity shares free from additional supply of pre-public issue equity shares.

Memorandum and Articles of Association

The company's memorandum of association may need to be altered to increase the authorized share capital to accommodate the further issue of capital by way of the public offer. For a public issue of preference shares, the articles of association must contain an authorization for the issue of the shares.[104] The articles of association must also provide for matters specified under the listing agreement and the SCRR (a) that the company shall use a common form of transfer, and (b) that the fully paid shares will be free from all lien.[105]

The articles of association may also require amendment to remove regulations that SEBI generally considers to be undesirable in companies intending to list equity shares. Such regulations typically grant preferential rights in and against the company and the shareholders to one shareholder or a small class of shareholders. The preferential rights

[101] Sub-regulation (4) of regulation 32 of the ICDR Regulations.

[102] Regulations 35 and 36 of the ICDR Regulations.

[103] Regulations 36 and 37 of the ICDR Regulations. An exemption from such lock-in, subject to specified conditions, is provided for equity shares allotted to employees under a scheme prior to the public offer, and equity shares held by a VCF or AIF of category I or a foreign venture capital investor (FVCI).

[104] Sub-rule (1) of rule 9 of the Companies (Share Capital and Debentures) Rules, 2014.

[105] Clause (a) of sub-rule (2) of rule 19 of the SCRR.

may deal with the preemptive right to purchase or subscribe and sell equity shares, unconventional quorums, and special voting rights on important corporate matters.

Miscellaneous Matters

A company must also take care of a few other principal pre-offering matters. The board of directors must pass a resolution at a meeting of the board authorizing the public issue of all corporate securities.[106] For the public issue of equity shares and preference shares, members of the company too must authorize the issue by way of special resolution.[107] At times, third-party consents may also be required. The company may be under a contractual obligation to its lenders or investor shareholders to obtain their consent for making the public offer. Consent may also be required for some actions in connection with the public offer such as naming a customer in the prospectus or disclosing in the prospectus agreements containing confidentiality clauses.

Sometimes changes to the company's capital structure may be necessary, since a company is prohibited from making an IPO of equity shares if there are any outstanding convertible securities or any other right which would entitle any person with an option to receive equity shares.[108] Such outstanding convertible securities must be made fully paid-up and converted on or before the date of filing the red herring prospectus or the prospectus, as the case may be.

---

[106] Clause (c) of sub-section (3) of section 179 of the Companies Act.

[107] Clause (c) of sub-section (1) of section 62 of the Companies Act and sub-rule (1) of rule 9 of Companies (Share Capital and Debentures) Rules, 2014.

[108] Such a prohibition is not applicable to a public issue made during the currency of convertible debt instruments which were issued through an earlier IPO, if the conversion price of such convertible debt instruments was determined and disclosed in the prospectus of the earlier issue of convertible debt instruments. Similarly the prohibition is not applicable to outstanding options granted to employees pursuant to an employee stock option scheme framed in accordance with the relevant guidance note or accounting standards, if any, issued by the Institute of Chartered Accountants of India. Sub-regulation (5) of regulation 26 of the ICDR Regulations.

Preparing the Prospectus

Chapter 3 discussed the various facets of a prospectus to show how it occupies a pivotal position in a public offering of corporate securities. Preparing the prospectus is, therefore, a key pre-offering matter, and can be best understood by examining the participants involved in its preparation, and its form and contents.

The company issues the prospectus for carrying out three functions—to state the proposal for investing in its securities that the company wishes to place before the public; to provide the basis for the necessary contract to implement the proposal; and to disclose the legally prescribed information and reports.[109] Therefore, it is the company that prepares the prospectus and is the maker of statements contained in it.[110] To the extent the company includes any statement in the prospectus made or purported to be made by an expert, the latter is also the maker of the statement. There is another category of persons that is involved in the preparation of the prospectus. This category consists of merchant bankers on whom securities laws impose a positive obligation to ensure that the prospectus is free from misstatements or material omissions.

Generally merchant bankers play a dominant role in the preparation of the prospectus due to their regulatory responsibility of exercising 'due diligence'. Due diligence is a process of ensuring that disclosures in the prospectus are true, fair, and adequate to enable the investors to make a well-informed decision as to the investment.[111] To this effect,

[109] See the section 'Functions of a Prospectus' in Chapter 3 of this volume.

[110] If the prospectus is issued in relation to an intended company, the promoter is the maker of the statement. However, as examined in the section titled 'Proponents of Public Offer and Offer for Sale' in Chapter 3 of this volume, such instances are rare. The common practice is for the promoters to form the company, which in turn makes the public offer and issues the prospectus.

[111] This is not to say that due diligence is limited to prospectus disclosure. It extends to various public-issue-related activities such as ensuring that the proponents of the public issue fulfil their legal obligations, and issue and allotment of securities are made in accordance with securities laws. See *Doogar and Associates Limited* v. *Securities and Exchange Board of India*, SAT Order dated 25 May 2001; *Securities and Exchange Board of India* v. *Keynote Corporate Securities Limited and Maha Chemicals Limited*, SEBI order dated 26 September 2009; *Securities and Exchange Board of India* v. *Imperial Corporate Finance and Services Private Limited*, SEBI Order dated 10 April 2003.

merchant bankers are required to submit due diligence certificates to SEBI in public offerings of corporate securities.[112] The standard of due diligence is the traditional negligence standard which is of a reasonable and prudent man under the particular facts and circumstances. Thus, as long as the merchant bankers have undertaken reasonable investigation and reasonable care to ensure accuracy and completeness of statements made in the prospectus, they would have discharged their responsibility of due diligence.[113] The exercise need not be absolute and perfect, just reasonable under the facts and circumstances. Resultantly, due diligence procedures vary depending on the nature of the issuer company, securities being offered, and statements being made in the prospectus.

There are certain basic due diligence procedures that merchant bankers often follow. These include discussions with and questionnaires to the management and officers of the company, and its major customers and suppliers; review of the industry in which the company operates; visits to principal facilities and bases of operation; review of material corporate documents such as memorandum of association, articles of association, and minutes of meetings of the board of directors and shareholders; review of the company's financial statements and discussions with the statutory auditor; review of material contracts that the company has entered into; obtaining independent third party reports

---

[112] See clause (c) of sub-regulation (1) of regulation 8, clause (a) of sub-regulation (3) of regulation 10, sub-regulation (2) of regulation 106O, and sub-regulation (5) of regulation 91E of the ICDR Regulations read with Schedule VI to the ICDR Regulations; sub-regulation (7) of regulation 6 of the Debt Securities Regulations read with Schedule II to the Debt Securities Regulations; and sub-regulation (7) of regulation 6 of the Preference Shares Regulations read with Schedule II to the Preference Shares Regulations.

[113] *Keynote Corporate Securities Limited* v. *Securities and Exchange Board of India*, SAT order dated 19 February 2014 in Appeal No. 84 of 2012; *HSBC Securities and Capital Markets (India) Private Limited* v. *Securities and Exchange Board of India*, SAT order dated 20 February 2008 in Appeal No. 99 of 2007; *Worldlink Finance Limited* v. *Securities and Exchange Board of India*, SAT Order dated 24 April 2007 in Appeal No. 36 of 2007; *JM Mutual Fund and JM Capital Management Private Limited* v. *Securities and Exchange Board of India*, SAT order dated 22 November 2004 in Appeal No. 39 and 39A of 2004; *Imperial Corporate Finance and Services Private Limited* v. *Securities and Exchange Board of India*, SAT order dated 30 July 2004 in Appeal No. 56 of 2003.

to verify major claims of the company; obtaining opinion from legal counsel and comfort letter from the auditor; maintaining a documentary record of the due diligence exercise; and a thorough review of the draft prospectus. In practice, the prospectus is drafted and exercise of due diligence is carried out in parallel.

Form and Content of the Prospectus

A prospectus is prepared in the form of a single document and is issued to the public in both digital and paper form. Given the voluminous size of the prospectus, it is issued as an abridged prospectus along with the application form. An abridged prospectus is a memorandum containing the salient features of the prospectus. For public issues of equity shares and debentures, SEBI has prescribed the form and features of the abridged prospectus and it is essentially a reproduction of selective portions of the prospectus.[114] The abridged prospectus must not contain any matter extraneous to the prospectus and a copy of the prospectus must, on a request being made by any person before the closing of the subscription list and the offer, be furnished to him.[115]

In a public issue of equity shares, to further ensure that investors are not overloaded with information, contents of the abridged prospectus which are of a generic nature and not specific to the issuer company must be prepared and issued to the public in the form of a separate document called general information document.[116] The general information document contains matters such as categories of investors eligible to participate in the issue, manner of making applications in the public issue, issue and allotment procedure, and interest and refunds. These provide general guidance to investors and must be supplied to the investor as and when requested.[117]

---

[114] For equity shares, see sub-regulation (1) of regulation 58 of the ICDR Regulations read with Part D of Schedule VIII to the ICDR Regulations; and for debentures see SEBI circular no. CIR/IMD/DF-1/19/2012 dated 25 July 2012.

[115] Sub-section (2) of section 33 of the Companies Act.

[116] Sub-regulation (1) of regulation 58 of the ICDR Regulations read with Part D of Schedule VIII to the ICDR Regulations.

[117] See SEBI circular no. CIR/CFD/DIL/12/2013 dated 23 October 2013 on the form and content of a general information document.

As noted in Chapter 3, the prospectus must contain the information specified in sub-section (1) of section 26 of the Companies Act read with rules 3 to 6 of the Companies (Prospectus and Allotment of Securities) Rules, 2014.[118] The Companies Act prescribed disclosure is not applicable to (a) 'the issue to existing members or debenture-holders of a company, of a prospectus or form of application relating to shares in or debentures of the company, whether an applicant has a right to renounce the shares or not under sub-clause (ii) of clause (a) of sub-section (1) of section 62 [of the Companies Act] in favour of any other person'; and (b) 'to the issue of a prospectus or form of application relating to shares or debentures which are, or are to be, in all respects uniform with shares or debentures previously issued and for the time being dealt in or quoted on a recognized stock exchange'.[119] In addition to the disclosure prescribed under the Companies Act, a prospectus for equity shares must also contain the information specified in Part A of Schedule VIII to the ICDR Regulations subject to the provisions of Parts B and C thereof. For a letter of offer for rights issue of equity shares, prescribed information is contained in Part E of Schedule VIII to the ICDR Regulations. Similarly, a prospectus for debentures and preference shares must contain the information specified in Schedule I to the Debt Securities Regulations and Schedule I to the Preference Shares Regulations, respectively.

Although the Companies Act and SEBI regulations are two separate laws that prescribe the information to be mandatorily disclosed in a prospectus, the information prescribed under each substantially overlaps with the other, and the latter prescribes the bulk of the prescribed information. The prescribed information is very detailed and specific and persons preparing the prospectus must disclose it even if some of it may not be material for investing in the public issue at hand. Also, an overriding requirement under each of the foregoing SEBI regulations is

[118] See the section 'Principal Legal Requirements of a Prospectus' in Chapter 3 of this volume. The Companies (Amendment) Bill, 2016, introduced in the lower house of the Parliament on 16 March 2016, seeks to do away with the prescribed disclosure under the Companies Act. Instead, disclosure shall be as prescribed by SEBI and as prescribed by the central government under the Companies (Prospectus and Allotment of Securities) Rules, 2014.

[119] Sub-section (2) of section 26 of the Companies Act.

that the prospectus must contain all material disclosures that are necessary to enable the applicants to take an informed decision.[120]

Before proceeding to examine the principal items that must be included in a prospectus, a few comments are in order on the content of a prospectus. Since 1992, the content of the prospectus is largely confined to factual information, meaning statements concerning objectively verifiable present or historical events or situations, and distinguished from opinions, forecasts, or subjective evaluations. Examples of the latter class are statements about the integrity or competence of the directors and promoters of the company, projections relating to the financial performance of the company, and statements with words such as 'excellent' which are hyperbolic and for which there are no generally accepted standards of measurement in most contexts.[121]

There are three principal reasons for this approach. First, securities laws have evolved with the objective of providing reliable information and easily establishing accountability for misstatement; and thus largely cover present and historical facts. Little room is available for other kinds of information. Second, merchant bankers, while exercising due diligence, would ordinarily ask the persons preparing the prospectus to remove non-factual information since such information is difficult to verify. Third, the makers of the statements, as a self-protective mechanism, avoid non-factual information since, as we shall see in Chapter 7, the likelihood of statutory and common law liability arising out of such information is higher. This is not to say that a prospectus contains no opinions, forecasts, or subjective evaluation. Quite often securities laws themselves expressly require such statements to be made when they deem such information to be of value to investors. For example, securities laws mandate disclosure of the manner and schedule in which the

---

[120] Sub-regulation (1) of regulation 57 of the ICDR Regulations, and sub-regulation (1) of regulation 5 of each of the Preference Shares Regulations and the Debt Securities Regulations.

[121] Carl W. Schneider, 'Nits, Grits and Soft Information in SEC Filings' (1972) 121 University of Pennsylvania Law Review 254. In this article, Schneider considers several categories of soft information traditionally excluded from filings with the US Securities and Exchange Commission and examines its policy implications. Schneider's identification of soft information is to a great degree relevant to disclosures made in Indian prospectuses.

company intends to use the proceeds of the public issue. Similarly, the company must disclose risks associated with investment in its securities, which are essentially negative inferences, based on subjective evaluation. Sometimes opinions are inevitable. For example, the report by the auditors of the company with respect to its profits and losses, and assets and liabilities is expressed in the form of an opinion. At times, the company may itself choose to disclose opinions and forward-looking statements—statements disclosed in the form of projections, forecasts, plans, objectives, or estimates—provided it substantiates and has a reasonable basis for such statements.[122]

Principal Contents of a Prospectus for Equity Shares

For reasons discussed earlier in this chapter, investors need much greater information in their hands for investment in equity shares than for preference shares and debentures. Though the information prescribed under the Companies Act and SEBI regulations is self-explanatory, an overview of matters that a prospectus for equity shares must contain is as follows:

Risk Factors

The perception of the company's board of directors about the material risks that the company faces or factors that may cause investment in the equity shares to be risky must be disclosed as 'risk factors'. Each individual risk must be determined on the basis of its materiality and disclosed separately. The risks must be classified as those that are specific to the company's projects and operations, and those that are external and beyond the control of the company. Risks must be stated as envisaged by the board of directors and the proposals, if any, to address them. The proposals must not contain any speculative statement. Wherever risks

---

[122] See clause (e) of paragraph (1) of Part A of Schedule VIII to the ICDR Regulations. The only exception to this rule is that no forecasts or projections relating to the financial performance of the company must be made in the prospectus. Though this rule on forward-looking statements is expressly stated in the ICDR Regulations, it is practiced and is applicable to prospectuses for preference shares and debentures as well.

about material impact are stated, the financial and other implications must be quantified.[123]

The ICDR Regulations contain a standard list of risks that prospectuses must, to the extent applicable, contain. These include criminal charges and violations of securities laws by the issuer company, seasonality of the company's business or its business being dependent upon a single customer or a few customers, stock exchanges having refused to list the company's securities in the past, inexperience of the promoters in the activities for which capital is being raised, and pending legal proceedings and disputed tax demands.[124] Given the significance of risk factors, the prospectus must state them at the outset.

Introductory Information

By way of introduction, the prospectus must contain a summary of the business of the company and the industry in which it operates; brief details of the public issue; and a summary of the financial statements.[125] General information about the company, its directors, company secretary, auditor, compliance officer, and legal adviser; and securities market intermediaries involved in the public issue must also be stated.[126]

A principal component of the introductory information is the capital structure of the company. The capital structure section of the prospectus must contain the size of the public issue along with details of reservation, if any; detailed information about each allotment of the company's shares; particulars of major shareholders of the company and employees' stock option scheme or employees' stock purchase scheme; shareholding pattern of the promoters and promoter group entities; transactions in shares of the company by the directors and promoter group entities; and details of

---

[123] Clauses (C), (D), (E), and (G) of sub-paragraph (IV) of paragraph (2) of Part A of Schedule VIII to the ICDR Regulations.

[124] Clause (H) of sub-paragraph (IV) of paragraph (2) of Part A of Schedule VIII to the ICDR Regulations.

[125] Clause (A) of sub-paragraph (VI) of paragraph (2) of Part A of Schedule VIII to the ICDR Regulations.

[126] Sub-rule (1) of rule 3 of the Companies (Prospectus and Allotment of Securities) Rules; and clause (B) of sub-paragraph (VI) of paragraph (2) of Part A of Schedule VIII to the ICDR Regulations.

promoters' contribution and lock-in of shares.[127] These must be followed by a statement that the company, its directors, or the lead merchant bankers have not entered into any buy-back arrangements for purchase of the equity shares of the company, other than the arrangements, if any, entered into for safety net facility as permitted in the ICDR Regulations.[128]

Particulars of the Public Issue

The prospectus must state the purpose(s) for which capital is being raised, which is known as the objects of the issue.[129] If one of the objects is investment in a joint venture or a subsidiary or an acquisition, the form of the investment, that is, equity, debt, or any other instrument, and its details must be provided. If one of the objects of the issue is the grant of a loan to any entity, the prospectus must state the details of the loan agreement, including the rate of interest, whether secured or unsecured, duration, nature of security, terms of repayment, subordination, etc., and the nature of benefit expected to accrue to the issuer as a result of the investment. If, as is generally the case, capital is being raised to undertake projects of the company, details of the project cost, appraisal of the project, schedule of implementation of the project, funds deployed, as well as prospective deployment of funds must be disclosed.[130] For funding the project, the company must confirm in the prospectus firm arrangements of finance towards 75 per cent of the cost of the project, excluding the amount to be raised through the proposed issue and existing identifiable internal accruals.[131] This is a significant confirmation and is also one of the regulatory preconditions for making a public issue.[132]

---

[127] Sub-rule (2) of rule 3 of the Companies (Prospectus and Allotment of Securities) Rules; and clause (D) of sub-paragraph (VI) of paragraph (2) of Part A of Schedule VIII to the ICDR Regulations.

[128] Item (k) of sub-clause (2) of clause (D) of sub-paragraph (VI) of paragraph (2) of Part A of Schedule VIII to the ICDR Regulations.

[129] Sub-rule (3) of rule 3 of the Companies (Prospectus and Allotment of Securities) Rules, 2014.

[130] Clauses (A) to (F) of sub-paragraph (VII) of paragraph (2) of Part A of Schedule VIII to the ICDR Regulations.

[131] Clause (C) of sub-paragraph (VII) of paragraph (2) of Part A of Schedule VIII to the ICDR Regulations.

[132] Clause (g) of sub-regulation (2) of regulation 4 of the ICDR Regulations.

Statements made on the objects of the issue have a binding effect on the company. A company is prohibited from varying the objects for which the prospectus was issued, except subject to an authority given by the members of the company in general meeting by way of a special resolution.[133] The dissenting shareholders being those shareholders who have not agreed to vary the objects referred to in the prospectus must be given an exit offer by the promoters or controlling shareholders at an exit price specified by SEBI.[134]

Whether the proceeds of the public issue are being utilized for the objects stated in the prospectus is also subject to monitoring by the monitoring agency.[135] The company must prepare an annual statement of funds utilized for purposes other than those stated in the prospectus, and place it before the audit committee.[136] Further, the company must furnish to the stock exchanges on a quarterly basis, a statement indicating material deviations, if any, in the use of the proceeds from the objects stated in the prospectus.[137]

The other major component of the particulars of the public issue is the basis for the issue price. The prospectus must state the basis for the issue price, floor price, or price band, as the case may be, and justify it on the basis of accounting ratios such as earnings per share, price–earnings ratio, average return on net worth in the last three years, and net asset value.[138] Determination of accounting ratios is decisive and the company must not proceed with the public issue in case the accounting ratios do not justify the issue price.[139]

---

[133] Sub-section (8) of section 13 and sub-section (1) of section 27 of the Companies Act read with rule 7 of Companies (Prospectus and Allotment of Securities) Rules, 2014.

[134] Sub-section (8) of section 13 and sub-section (1) of section 27 of the Companies Act. Chapter VI-A of the ICDR Regulations specifies the conditions and manner of providing exit opportunity to dissenting shareholders.

[135] See the section titled 'Participants Other than Intermediaries' of this chapter.

[136] Sub-regulation (5) of regulation 32 of the LODR Regulations.

[137] Clause (a) of sub-regulation (1) of regulation 32 of the LODR Regulations.

[138] Clause (K) of sub-paragraph (VII) of paragraph (2) of Part A of Schedule VIII to the ICDR Regulations.

[139] Sub-clause (2) of clause (K) of sub-paragraph (VII) of paragraph (2) of Part A of Schedule VIII to the ICDR Regulations.

Information about the Company

The bulk of the prospectus, for obvious reasons, contains the prescribed information about the company. The prospectus, therefore, must contain an overview of the industry in which the company operates and a comprehensive description of the company's business.[140] The latter must specifically include the location of the company's projects; plant, machinery, technology, and processes; business collaborators; infrastructure facilities for raw materials and utilities like water and electricity; and the company's products or services.[141] The prospectus must also contain a statement about the company's business strategy and future prospects. However, no forecast or projections relating to the financial performance of the company should be given in the prospectus.[142] Information about the assets of the company such as land and intellectual property rights must also be disclosed.[143] An important segment of information in this section is particulars of any property that the company has purchased or proposes to purchase, for which the price is to be paid wholly or partly out of the proceeds of the public issue, or if the purchase of this property has not been completed at the date of issue of the prospectus.[144]

The next set of information about the company that the prospectus must contain is the company's history and its corporate structure. Important events since the incorporation of the company such as change of name and registered office; changes to the memorandum of association; setting up of factories and plants; and negative features like

---

[140] Clauses (A) and (B) of sub-paragraph (VIII) of paragraph (2) of Part A of Schedule VIII to the ICDR Regulations.

[141] Sub-clause (1) of clause (B) of sub-paragraph (VIII) of paragraph (2) of Part A of Schedule VIII to the ICDR Regulations.

[142] Sub-clause (2) of clause (B) of sub-paragraph (VIII) of paragraph (2) of Part A of Schedule VIII to the ICDR Regulations.

[143] Sub-clauses (4) and (6) of clause (B) of sub-paragraph (VIII) of paragraph (2) of Part A of Schedule VIII to the ICDR Regulations.

[144] This disclosure rule is not applicable to any contract for the purchase of property that was entered into in the ordinary course of the company's business and property in respect of which the amount of purchase money is not material. Sub-clause (5) of clause (B) of sub-paragraph (VIII) of paragraph (2) of Part A of Schedule VIII to the ICDR Regulations.

time and cost overruns in setting up projects, defaults, and lock-outs and strikes at its plants, must be disclosed. As part of the company's corporate structure, the prospectus must contain complete details regarding its subsidiaries and holding company.[145] The prospectus must also contain details of shareholders' agreements, and every other material contract, not being a contract entered into in the ordinary course of business carried on or intended to be carried on by the company or a contract entered into more than two years before the date of the prospectus.[146]

The other significant set of information about the company that the prospectus must contain is about the board of directors, key management personnel, and the promoters. The prospectus must state the name, age, experience, and other details of each of the directors of the company; nature of any family relationship between any of the directors; arrangement or understanding with major shareholders, customers, suppliers, or others, pursuant to which any of the directors was selected; details of contracts appointing or fixing the remuneration of directors or manager, or contracts with directors providing for benefits upon termination of employment; and particulars of the interest of directors in promoting the company and in any property that the company proposes to acquire or has acquired in the two years preceding the date of the prospectus.[147] An important set of information about the directors that the prospectus must contain is the details of current and past directorship in listed companies whose shares have been or were suspended from being traded or delisted from the stock exchanges.[148] This must be followed by a statement that the company has complied with the requirements of corporate governance contained in the equity listing agreement, particularly those

---

[145] Sub-clauses (1) to (3) of clause (D) of sub-paragraph (VIII) of paragraph (2) of Part A of Schedule VIII to the ICDR Regulations.

[146] Sub-clauses (4) and (5) of clause (D) of sub-paragraph (VIII) of paragraph (2) of Part A of Schedule VIII to the ICDR Regulations.

[147] Sub-rule (5) of rule 3 of the Companies (Prospectus and Allotment of Securities) Rules; Sub-clauses (1) to (3) of clause (E) of sub-paragraph (VIII) of paragraph (2) of Part A of Schedule VIII to the ICDR Regulations.

[148] Items (a)(i) and (a)(ii) of sub-clause (1) of clause (E) of sub-paragraph (VIII) of paragraph (2) of Part A of Schedule VIII to the ICDR Regulations.

relating to the composition of the board of directors and constitution of the committees of directors.[149]

Information about the management must not be limited to the board of directors and must also include information about key management personnel—officers of the company vested with executive powers, officers of the company at the level immediately below the board of directors of the company, and any other persons whom the company may declare as key management personnel.[150]

The prospectus must also contain information about the company's promoters. Present and historical information about the promoters, whether individuals or companies, must be stated along with particulars of group companies—companies, firms, ventures, etc., promoted by the promoters.[151]

Financial Information

One of the most challenging tasks in the preparation of the prospectus is the preparation of financial information, which principally consists of the financial statement of the company, and the management's discussion and analysis (MD&A) of the financial condition and results of operations as reflected in the financial statements.[152] The auditor is required to prepare the former in the form of a report, generally prepared on a

---

[149] Sub-clause (7) of clause (E) of sub-paragraph (VIII) of paragraph (2) of Part A of Schedule VIII to the ICDR Regulations.

[150] Clause (s) of sub-regulation (1) of regulation 2 read with sub-clause (8) of clause (E) of sub-paragraph (VIII) of paragraph (2) of Part A of Schedule VIII to the ICDR Regulations.

[151] Clause (F) of sub-paragraph (VIII) of paragraph (2) of Part A of Schedule VIII to the ICDR Regulations.

[152] Other than the financial statement of the company, financial information of other entities, in the prescribed form, too, may be required to be stated under certain circumstances. Such circumstances include proposed utilization of the proceeds of the issue to purchase a business or acquire a company that is significant, or material acquisition or divestment made by the company after the end of the latest disclosed financial results in the prospectus. See sub-clauses (4), (5), and (23) of clause (B) of sub-paragraph (IX) of paragraph (2) of Part A of Schedule VIII to the ICDR Regulations.

standalone as well as on a consolidated basis, on the company's profits and losses, assets and liabilities, and other prescribed matters.[153] The report must be made upon profits and losses of the company for each of the five financial years immediately preceding the issue of the prospectus and assets and liabilities on the last date to which the accounts of the business were made up, being a date not more than 180 days before the issue of the prospectus.[154] The statutory objective behind the prescribed period is that investors must have financial information for a full business cycle to evaluate how the management performed. An important element of the report is that the financial statement on which the report is based must be prepared after making certain prescribed adjustments such as adjustments and rectification for all incorrect accounting practices or change in accounting policies.[155]

In the MD&A section, the management discusses the company's financial results for the past three years on prescribed lines such as major items of income and expenditure, and unorthodox procedure for recording sales and revenues. In addition, the management compares the results of the recent financial year with those of the previous financial years on the major heads of the profit and loss statement, and on other prescribed matters.[156] These must be followed by a statement by the directors whether in their opinion any circumstances have arisen since the date of the last financial statements disclosed in the prospectus which materially and adversely affect, or are likely to affect, the trading or profitability of the company, or the value of its assets,

---

[153] Note 1 to sub-paragraph (IX) of paragraph (2) of Part A of Schedule VIII to the ICDR Regulations mandates that only such auditors must prepare the report who have subjected themselves to the peer review process of the Institute of Chartered Accountants of India and hold a valid certificate issued by the Peer Review Board of the Institute.

[154] Clause (b) of sub-section (1) of section 26 of the Companies Act; rule 4 of the Companies (Prospectus and Allotment of Securities) Rules, 2014; clause (B) of sub-paragraph (IX) of paragraph (2) of Part A of Schedule VIII to the ICDR Regulations.

[155] Sub-clause (9) of clause (B) of sub-paragraph (IX) of paragraph (2) of Part A of Schedule VIII to the ICDR Regulations.

[156] Clause (E) of sub-paragraph (IX) of paragraph (2) of Part A of Schedule VIII to the ICDR Regulations.

or its ability to pay its liabilities within the next 12 months.[157] The MD&A allows the company to explain its financial results to the investors, and provide a perspective beyond the mere numbers contained in the audited report.

Litigations and Government Approvals

The prospectus must state the different types of legal proceedings that the company, its subsidiaries, promoters, directors, and other entities are or have been involved in.[158] Statutory and regulatory approvals in relation to investment in the company and its business activities must also be disclosed in the prospectus.[159]

Other Regulatory and Statutory Information

Other than details of authority for the public issue and compliance with eligibility conditions, this section contains standard disclosures such as disclaimer clauses of regulatory authorities; expenses of the public issue; details of previous public issues; and mechanisms to redress investor grievances.[160]

Offering Information

This section of the prospectus contains information about the terms of the public issue and issue procedure. The former consists of a set of terms on which the company proposes to issue the shares such as issue price; ranking of the equity shares with the existing shares; and rights of the equity shareholders. The company must provide an undertaking that it shall refund the subscription amount with interest (in case of delay) if the

---

[157] Sub-clause (2) of clause (E) of sub-paragraph (IX) of paragraph (2) of Part A of Schedule VIII to the ICDR Regulations.

[158] Clause (A) of sub-paragraph (X) of paragraph (2) of Part A of Schedule VIII to the ICDR Regulations.

[159] Clause (B) of sub-paragraph (X) of paragraph (2) of Part A of Schedule VIII to the ICDR Regulations.

[160] Sub-paragraph (XI) of paragraph (2) of Part A of Schedule VIII to the ICDR Regulations.

required minimum subscription is not received.[161] In the latter section, the company provides customary information on the procedure being followed for the public issue as determined by statutes and regulations. The information relates to areas such as manner of application in the public issue by different categories of investors; restrictions and prohibitions on applying in the public issue on certain investors; mode of making payment; processing of applications; basis of allotment; and refund of application money.[162] Finally, the company must undertake to carry out or refrain from a set of activities prescribed by securities laws, and clearly state the restrictions around utilization of the public issue proceeds.[163]

Description of Equity Shares and Terms of Articles of Association

The prospectus must describe the terms of equity shares and rights associated with it—rights of members regarding voting, dividend, lien on shares, and the process for modification of such rights and forfeiture of shares. Prospectus must also state the main regulations of the articles of association of the company including regulations on the rights of members regarding voting, dividend, lien, and forfeiture of shares.[164]

List of Material Contracts and Documents for Inspection

The prospectus must provide a list of all material contracts and documents (identified in accordance with the ICDR Regulations) and state the time and place at which they can be inspected until the date of closure of the public issue. The company must also disclose any IPO grading report that it may have obtained.[165]

---

[161] Clause (A) of sub-paragraph (XII) of paragraph (2) of Part A of Schedule VIII to the ICDR Regulations.

[162] Clause (B) of sub-paragraph (XII) of paragraph (2) of Part A of Schedule VIII to the ICDR Regulations.

[163] Sub-clauses (30) and (31) of clause (B) of sub-paragraph (XII) of paragraph (2) of Part A of Schedule VIII to the ICDR Regulations.

[164] Sub-paragraph (XIII) of paragraph (2) of Part A of Schedule VIII to the ICDR Regulations.

[165] Clause (A) of sub-paragraph (XVI) of paragraph (2) of Part A of Schedule VIII to the ICDR Regulations.

Declaration

The prospectus must end with a declaration signed by each of the directors of the company, manager (if any), and the chief financial officer (whole-time finance director or any other person heading the finance function and discharging the function).[166] The signatories must declare compliance by the company with the provisions of the Companies Act, and make a statement to the effect that all disclosures made in the prospectus are true and correct and nothing in the prospectus is contrary to the provisions of the Companies Act, the Securities Contracts (Regulation) Act, 1956 (or the SCRA), the SEBI Act, and the rules and regulations made thereunder.[167]

Principal Contents of a Prospectus for Preference Shares and Debentures

The prescribed content of a prospectus for preference shares and debentures is almost uniform. It is significantly shorter than a prospectus for equity shares due to fewer matters being prescribed by SEBI under the Preference Shares Regulations and the Debt Securities Regulations, respectively, for obvious reasons. The disclosure requirements under the Companies Act remain the same. An overview of matters that a prospectus for preference shares and debentures must contain is as follows.

Risk Factors

Risk factors disclosure must also be made in a prospectus for preference shares and debentures.[168] Though the Preference Shares Regulations and the Debt Securities Regulations do not expressly mandate disclosure of risk factors, norms of the ICDR Regulations, customized for fixed income securities, are followed to prepare risk factors disclosure.

---

[166] Clause (B) of sub-paragraph (XVI) of paragraph (2) of Part A of Schedule VIII to the ICDR Regulations.

[167] Clause (c) of sub-section (1) of section 26 of the Companies Act.

[168] Item (A) of sub-clause (xi) of clause (a) of sub-section (1) of section 26 of the Companies Act.

Introductory Information

The prospectus must state the general information about the company, its directors, company secretary, auditor, compliance officer, debenture trustee, and legal adviser; and securities market intermediaries involved in the public issue.[169]

Information about the Company

The prospectus must contain a brief summary of the business of the company and its corporate structure along with information in the prescribed manner about key operational and financial parameters for the last three audited years.[170] Details of the company's share capital; capital structure and changes to it; details of any acquisition or reorganization; and the shareholding pattern must also be provided.[171]

Company's Borrowings

With preference shares and debentures being fixed income securities, the prospectus must contain full and complete details of all forms of the company's borrowings, segregating them into rupee denominated and foreign currency denominated. The types of borrowings must cover secured and unsecured loans; debentures; preference shares; corporate guarantees issued by the company; commercial paper; and such other types. The company must also disclose details of all defaults or delays in payment of interest and principal of any kind of term loans, debt

---

[169] Sub-clause (i) of clause (a) of sub-section (1) of section 26 of the Companies Act; sub-rule (1) of rule 3 of the Companies (Prospectus and Allotment of Securities) Rules, 2014; sub-clause (i) of clause (B) of Part II of Schedule I to the Preference Shares Regulations; sub-clause (a) of clause (A) of paragraph 3 of Schedule I to the Debt Securities Regulations.

[170] Sub-clause (ii) of clause (B) of Part II of Schedule I of the Preference Shares Regulations; sub-clause (b) of clause (A) of paragraph 3 of Schedule I to the Debt Securities Regulations.

[171] Sub-clauses (iii) and (iv) of clause (B) of Part II of Schedule I to the Preference Shares Regulations; sub-clauses (c) and (d) of clause (A) of paragraph 3 of Schedule I to the Debt Securities Regulations.

securities, and other financial indebtedness including corporate guarantee given by the company in the past five years.[172]

Financial Information

Unlike an equity shares prospectus, the principal component of financial information in this case, as prescribed by the Companies Act, is the auditor's report, which is generally prepared on a standalone as well as on a consolidated basis, on the company's profits and losses, assets and liabilities, and other prescribed matters. The report must be made upon profits and losses of the company for each of the five financial years immediately preceding the issue of the prospectus and assets and liabilities on the last date to which the accounts of the business were made up, being a date not more than 180 days before the issue of the prospectus.[173] Neither any adjustment to the financial statement nor a disclosure of MD&A is required. Under the Preference Shares Regulations and Debt Securities Regulations, other than some abridged financial information, the prospectus must disclose any material event or development having implications on the financial condition or credit quality at the time of issue, which may affect the public issue or the investor's decision to invest in the securities.[174]

Litigations

The prospectus must state any legal action taken against the promoter(s) of the company; and details of pending litigation involving the company, its promoter(s), directors, subsidiaries, group companies, or any other

---

[172] Sub-clause (vii) of clause (B) of Part II of Schedule I to the Preference Shares Regulations; sub-clause (g) of clause (A) of paragraph 3 of Schedule I to the Debt Securities Regulations.

[173] Clause (b) of sub-section (1) of section 26 of the Companies Act; rule 4 of the Companies (Prospectus and Allotment of Securities) Rules, 2014.

[174] Sub-clause (xi) of clause (B) of Part II of Schedule I to the Preference Shares Regulations; sub-clause (k) of clause (A) of paragraph 3 of Schedule I to the Debt Securities Regulations.

person, the outcome of which could have a material adverse effect on the position of the company.[175]

Credit Rating and Securities-specific Information

Credit rating being mandatory for the public issue of preference shares and debentures, the prospectus must contain information about it and the rating rationale.[176] Similarly, certain securities-specific information such as the nature of the investment instrument; creation of redemption reserve; and details of the debenture trustee and its consent must be provided.[177]

Issue Details

The prospectus must contain issue details in the form of a summary term sheet covering matters such as the nature of the investment instrument, eligible investors, place of listing, objects of the public issue and details of utilization of the issue proceeds, dividend or interest, date of redemption, put and call options, issue timing, details of security, events of default, and such covenants of fixed income securities.[178]

Declaration

The prospectus must end with a declaration signed by each of the directors of the company. The signatories must declare compliance by the company with the provisions of the Companies Act, and make a statement to the effect that nothing in the prospectus is contrary to the

---

[175] Sub-rule (4) of rule 3 of the Companies (Prospectus and Allotment of Securities) Rules.

[176] Sub-clause (xii) of clause (B) of Part II of Schedule I to the Preference Shares Regulations; sub-clause (m) of clause (A) of paragraph 3 of Schedule I to the Debt Securities Regulations.

[177] Sub-clause (xiv) of clause (B) of Part II of Schedule I to the Preference Shares Regulations; sub-clauses (l), (o), and (q) of clause (A) of paragraph 3 of Schedule I to the Debt Securities Regulations.

[178] Part III of Schedule I to the Preference Shares Regulations; clause (B) of paragraph 3 of Schedule I to the Debt Securities Regulations.

provisions of the Companies Act, the SCRA, the SEBI Act, and the rules and regulations made thereunder.[179]

Limitations on Publicity, Research Reports, and Financial Assistance

Securities laws are designed to ensure that the prospectus forms the basis for the public issue and the company does not induce any member of the public to participate in it through other forms of communication or by means of any incentive or financial assistance. This policy forms the basis for limiting the freedom of the company and associated entities to make and distribute publicity material, issue or provide information for 'research reports', and extend financial assistance for subscribing or purchasing shares.

The Companies Act permits a company to release advertisements or use any media, marketing, or distribution channels to inform the public at large about the public offer.[180] The only condition it imposes is that where an advertisement of any prospectus is published in any manner, it shall be necessary to specify some basic details such as contents of the company's memorandum of association as regards the objects and its capital structure.[181] Unbridled public communication is, however, open to misuse to the detriment of investors and the securities market. For example, the company may release information in the public domain that it is otherwise not permitted to include in the prospectus such as projections and estimates about its financial performance. Alternatively, it may begin conditioning the public mind or arouse public interest in its securities much before it registers and issues the prospectus. Even upon registering the prospectus, the company may release material information about its securities to a selective class of investors who intend to purchase large blocks of its securities. The SEBI regulations, therefore, address these and other problems around the making of publicity. For obvious reasons, the regulation is much more detailed and stringent

---

[179] Clause (c) of sub-section (1) of section 26 of the Companies Act.

[180] The opposite is the case in private placement. See sub-section (8) of section 42 of the Companies Act.

[181] Section 30 of the Companies Act.

for public offerings of equity shares than for preference shares and debentures.

Though SEBI regulations permit and facilitate publicity of the public offer, they limit certain forms of public communications and their timing. These fall into four classes: (a) regulation of public communication to check conditioning of the public mind; (b) prohibition on public communication of information that is extraneous to the contents of the prospectus; (c) prohibition on releasing selective or additional information outside the contents of the prospectus to anyone; and (d) obligation to inform the public about material developments.[182]

To check conditioning of the public mind, the ICDR Regulations mandate that all public communication or publicity material[183] must be consistent with past practices during the period commencing from the date of the meeting of the board of directors of the company in which the public issue is approved till the date of filing the draft prospectus with SEBI. Else, the company must caution the public by displaying or announcing in the said public communication that the company is proposing to make a public issue of equity shares in the near future and is in the process of filing a draft prospectus with SEBI.[184] During the period commencing from the date of filing the draft prospectus with SEBI till the date of allotment of equity shares offered in the issue, all public communications must announce that the company proposes to make a public issue and give information about the places where the draft prospectus or the prospectus is available.[185] The ICDR Regulations also mandate that any public communication by the company must contain only factual information and must not contain projections, estimates, conjectures, or any matter extraneous to the contents of the prospectus.[186] Similarly,

---

[182] Regulation 60 of the ICDR Regulations.

[183] Clause (I) of the Explanation to regulation 60 of the ICDR Regulations defines 'public communication or publicity material' to include 'corporate, product and issue advertisements of the issuer, interviews by its promoters, directors, duly authorized employees or representatives of the issuer, documentaries about the issuer or its promoters, periodical reports and press releases.'

[184] Sub-regulation (2) of regulation 60 of the ICDR Regulations.

[185] Sub-regulation (3) of regulation 60 of the ICDR Regulations.

[186] Sub-regulations (1) and (5) of regulation 60 of the ICDR Regulations.

the company or any member of the public issue management team must not give any selective or additional information or information which is extraneous to the information disclosed to the public through the prospectus or otherwise to any particular section of the investors or to any research analyst in any manner whatsoever.[187] Finally, the company must make prompt, true, and fair disclosure of all material developments between the date of registering the prospectus and the date of allotment of shares relating to its business and securities and also relating to the business and securities of its subsidiaries and group companies which may have a material effect on the company.[188]

Other than these norms, the ICDR Regulations contain several dos and don'ts on public communication or publicity material.[189] In line with these norms, the Preference Shares Regulations and the Debt Securities Regulations too, in small measures, limit the company's freedom to generate publicity. Thus, the company must not issue an advertisement which is misleading in material particulars or which contains any matter which is extraneous to the contents of the prospectus.[190]

Research Reports

Limitations on publicity in the public issue of equity shares also affect the involvement of entities associated with the public issue in the preparation of a research report. Before examining this aspect, some comments are in order on what research reports are. Quite often, investors cannot pay attention to and scrutinize the merits of the many securities being offered in the securities market. Instead, they avail the services of research analysts. Research analysts cover certain companies in the securities market, and perform research and analysis on them in order to evaluate securities and estimate their value as investments. They collect and process information from a variety of sources, both inside and

---

[187] Sub-regulation (13) of regulation 60 of the ICDR Regulations.

[188] Sub-regulation (4) of regulation 60 of the ICDR Regulations.

[189] Sub-regulations (5) to (11) and (14) of regulation 60 of the ICDR Regulations.

[190] Regulation 8 of the Preference Shares Regulations and Debt Securities Regulations.

outside the company.[191] The research analyst then produces a research report—a statement of facts and opinions about the subject company, and a recommendation advising the investor to buy, sell, or continue to hold the securities—and sells it to its clients.[192] Research analysts thus play an important role in the operation of the securities market and investors are known to rely on their recommendations.

In India, historically, research analysts have been free from regulation, but are now regulated under the Securities and Exchange Board of India (Research Analysts) Regulations, 2014. These regulations principally aim at checking conflict of interest among research analysts such that they provide objective and reliable recommendations. Given the role of research analysts, the ICDR Regulations contain special provisions to regulate research activities on companies making public offerings of equity shares. The principal provision is that a research report prepared by the issuer company or an intermediary concerned with the public issue or their associates must not contain any matter extraneous to the contents of the offer document.[193] For a research report being prepared by others, the company or any member of the issue management team must not give selective or additional information.[194] This is to ensure that such entities that are in possession of material information concerning the offering do not discriminate among different classes of investors.

Financial Assistance

Another control on a company's efforts at selling its securities is prohibiting it from financially supporting the acquisition of its shares. The prohibition is that no public company 'shall give, whether directly or indirectly and whether by means of a loan, guarantee, the provision of security, or otherwise, any financial assistance for the purpose of, or in connection with, a purchase or subscription made or to be made, by any

---

[191] Jill E. Fisch and Hillary A. Sale, 'The Securities Analyst as Agent: Rethinking the Regulation of Analysts' (2003) 88 Iowa Law Review 1035, at p. 1040.

[192] Fisch and Sale (n. 191), at p. 1041.

[193] Sub-regulation (1) of regulation 60 of the ICDR Regulations.

[194] Sub-regulation (13) of regulation 60 of the ICDR Regulations.

person of or for any shares in the company or in its holding company'.[195] We examine this prohibition in general under the company law and in particular to the public offering of corporate securities.

In general, this provision was originally part of the capital maintenance rules that we examined in Chapter 1.[196] However, the provision is widely worded and its effect extends far beyond actions that infringe capital maintenance rules. What constitutes financial assistance is illustrated by an indicative list, which list itself is liberally worded. The indicative list is loan, guarantee, the provision of security, or otherwise, whether directly or indirectly. Further the causal connection between the financial assistance and the purchase or subscription of shares is very weak. Financial assistance not just for the purpose of acquisition of shares, but also in connection with the acquisition is prohibited. Lastly, the recipient of the financial assistance need not necessarily be the person who has acquired the shares. As a result, on the face of it, it prohibits actions that are legitimate business transactions and courts have had to clarify and restrict its application on a case-by-case basis. Thus, in *Unity Company Private Limited* v. *Diamond Sugar Mills*,[197] the plaintiff sought to bring a transaction within the prohibition on the ground that the money with which the shares had been purchased had been paid by the defendant company to enable the purchasers to purchase the shares. The court found that the company had made the payment in repayment of legitimate business dues. It, therefore, disregarded the wide phraseology of the prohibition, and held that payment of any sum in repayment of legitimate dues, with whatever intention such payment may be made, cannot be construed to mean rendering of any financial assistance within the meaning of the provision.

In the context of public offerings of shares, this prohibition does serve some useful functions, though it was not enacted with that intent. For example, in a public issue of shares, it is quite possible for companies to, in the absence of the prohibition, secretly finance subscription of shares

---

[195] Sub-section (3) of section 67 of the Companies Act lays down three exceptions to this rule for the benefit of employees of the company, and to exempt banking companies.

[196] See the section 'Capital Requirement of Companies' in Chapter 1 of this volume.

[197] AIR 1971 Cal 18.

during the public issue thereby creating a false or misleading appearance that there is genuine demand for its shares. However, the wide phraseology, especially the weak causal link, once again has the effect of impacting genuine activities. There is therefore a need for the prohibition to be worded with precision to target primary market manipulative activities. To an extent, SEBI has done this under the PFUTP Regulations. This regulation prohibits 'advancing or agreeing to advance any money to any person thereby inducing any other person to offer to buy any security in any issue only with the intention of securing the minimum subscription to such issue'.[198]

---

[198] Clause (c) of sub-regulation (2) of regulation 4 of the PFUTP Regulations.

6. *Public Offering Programme: Public Issue*

We now examine the mechanics of the issue of corporate securities by way of a public offer, for which the preceding chapter has set the foundation. At the outset, we must note that the Securities and Exchange Board of India (Issue and Listing of Debt Securities) Regulations, 2008 (or the Debt Securities Regulations), the Securities and Exchange Board of India (Issue of Capital and Disclosure Requirements) Regulations, 2009 (or the ICDR Regulations), and the Securities and Exchange Board of India (Issue and Listing of Non-Convertible Redeemable Preference Shares) Regulations, 2013 (or the Preference Shares Regulations) largely govern the actual mechanics of undertaking public issue of corporate securities. These, being delegated laws, are often amended by the Securities and Exchange Board of India (SEBI) to address new developments in the securities market. Nonetheless, their core features remain intact and we expect it to be so, given their recent origin. This chapter focuses more on the core features and makes a reference to peripheral matters for adding completeness and coherence. Some of the peripheral matters, such as issue procedure—how to apply in the public issue and how applications are processed—have been simplified for a meaningful analysis.

With this prelude, we divide a public issue of corporate securities into three stages—organizing the prospectus, issue of the prospectus, and allotment and listing of securities. This division will help in understanding the mechanics of the issue of corporate securities by way of a public offer in its proper context. Similar to Chapter 5, this chapter also uses the expression 'equity shares' to mean equity shares and corporate securities convertible into equity shares.

Organizing the Prospectus

The stage of 'organizing the prospectus' may be understood to be the period prior to the issue of the prospectus. It is during this period that the company undertakes the pre-offering matters discussed in the previous chapter, files the prospectus with regulatory authorities for review, and registers the prospectus with the registrar of companies. Exactly when this stage begins is not always clear. It should ideally begin with an act of the organ of the company that has the power to issue securities and thus, set in motion the public issue programme. Generally, such an act is a special resolution passed at the general meeting of the company followed by resolutions passed at the meeting of the board of directors for the public offer of equity shares and preference shares;[1] and a resolution passed at the meeting of the board of directors of the company for the public offer of debentures.[2]

---

[1] Clause (c) of sub-section (1) of section 62 of the Companies Act, and clause (c) of sub-section (3) of section 179 of the Companies Act read with Article 1 of Table F of Schedule I to the Companies Act. However, for the public issue of shares that qualifies to be rights issue, no special resolution passed at the general meeting of the company is required. In such a case, the board of directors has the exclusive power to issue shares.

[2] Clause (c) of sub-section (3) of section 179 of the Companies Act. However, a special resolution passed at the general meeting of the company would also be required if the money to be borrowed by issue of debentures, together with the money already borrowed by the company will exceed the aggregate of its paid-up share capital and free reserves. This rule does not apply

The above is, however, not followed in practice. In practice, one or more of the directors and some of the key managerial personnel of the company commence the public offer programme by appointing the intermediaries and other participants, and prepare the prospectus. The necessary corporate resolutions are passed when the filing of the draft prospectus with regulatory authorities is around the corner. At least for a public issue of equity shares, the purpose of this approach seems to be to circumvent the early application of regulation of the company's public communications, which, as discussed in the previous chapter, is set off from the date of the meeting of the board of directors in which they decide to undertake the public issue.[3] Such an approach works legally as long as the resolution ratifies the acts of the officers done previously.

The first step in the public offering programme is generally the appointment of a merchant banker with whom the company enters into an 'issue agreement' for managing the public issue. The contracting parties determine the terms and conditions of the issue agreement, though for a public issue of equity shares, the ICDR Regulations prescribe certain mandatory clauses on matters such as due diligence, restriction on public communication, and appointment of other intermediaries.[4] In a public issue of debentures, the company must also appoint the debenture trustee and enter into an agreement with it in accordance with the Securities and Exchange Board of India (Debenture Trustees) Regulations, 1993 (or the Debenture Trustees Regulations). In discussion with the merchant banker, the company chooses a trading segment for its securities, determines its eligibility to make the public issue, and assembles the team for preparing the prospectus in the manner discussed in the previous chapter. At the same time, the merchant bankers carry out 'due diligence'—a process that we examined in Chapter 5—the

---

to banking companies, and temporary loans obtained from the company's bankers in the ordinary course of business are excluded from the portion of money already borrowed by the company. Clause (c) of sub-section (1) of section 180 of the Companies Act.

[3] See the section 'Limitations on Publicity, Research Reports, and Financial Assistance' in Chapter 5 of this volume.

[4] Sub-regulation (5) of regulation 5 read with Schedule II to the ICDR Regulations.

result of which is reflected in the document.[5] During this period, the company also addresses the initial considerations referred to in the previous chapter, and appoints the registrar to the issue. If the securities of the company are in physical form, the company enters into an agreement with the share transfer agent and the depository for dematerialization of its securities.

Review of the Draft Prospectus

Once the draft prospectus is ready, it must be presented for review by the regulatory authorities.

For a public issue of equity shares proposed to be listed on the Main Board of the stock exchanges, SEBI and the stock exchanges review the draft prospectus, and the public is invited to provide comments for a period of at least 21 days.[6] Thus, a company is prohibited from making a public issue of equity shares unless it files the draft prospectus with SEBI for review through the lead merchant banker at least 30 days prior to registering the prospectus with the registrar of companies.[7] This 30-day period is misleading and the ICDR Regulations grant SEBI the leeway to keep extending this review period. In practice, therefore, SEBI's review of the prospectus can be a lengthy process spanning into several months. During this period, SEBI reviews the draft prospectus and specifies changes or issues observations through letters to the lead merchant banker to ensure adequate disclosure as per the ICDR Regulations.[8] The letter may specify changes to the disclosure, or contain observations in the form of questions seeking assurance that the draft prospectus makes certain required disclosures. SEBI may want undertakings from the company and the lead merchant banker for certain prospective actions such as form of advertisements and application form, which do not directly relate to prospectus disclosure. The company

[5] See the section 'Merchant Banker' in Chapter 5 of this volume.

[6] Sub-regulation (1) of regulation 9 of the ICDR Regulations.

[7] Sub-regulation (1) of regulation 6 of the ICDR Regulations. Along with the draft prospectus, the lead merchant bankers must also file several other documents such as the due diligence certificate. Sub-regulation (1) of regulation 8 of the ICDR Regulations.

[8] Sub-regulation (2) of regulation 6 of the ICDR Regulations.

and the lead merchant bankers are expected to respond to these letters and specify consequent changes being made to the draft prospectus.[9] Though rare in practice, SEBI may also seek information or clarification from another regulator on disclosures being made in the prospectus.

Filing of a draft prospectus with SEBI does not guarantee observations on improving disclosure and an eventual approval. If SEBI is of the view that the disclosure is not adequate and the quality not satisfactory, or that investors may not be able to assess the risks associated with the public issue, it may reject the draft prospectus. This is despite the fact that the company may otherwise be eligible to access the primary market. SEBI takes such a decision as per the Securities and Exchange Board of India (Framework for Rejection of Draft Offer Documents) Order, 2012. This order contains the standards based on which SEBI may reject the draft offer document such as the capital structure of the company containing circular transactions to build up the capital, and financial statements showing a sudden surge in business just before filing the draft prospectus. Some of the standards such as the business model of the company being exaggerated, complex, or misleading are generalized and entail a highly subjective analysis, thereby conferring immense discretion on the officers of SEBI reviewing the draft prospectus. Expectedly mere triggering of any or few standards does not lead to an automatic rejection of the draft prospectus. SEBI takes a final view on rejection after considering the materiality of the findings and facts and circumstances of each case. Nevertheless, if it does reject the draft prospectus, the consequences are severe such as the company being prohibited from accessing the capital markets for at least one year from the date of such rejection.[10] These processes of draft prospectus review are not complete till the lead merchant bankers resolve SEBI's comments and satisfy it with the disclosure. When all this is done, SEBI permits the lead merchant banker to go ahead with registering the prospectus with the registrar of companies.

Simultaneous to filing the draft prospectus with SEBI, the lead merchant bankers must also file a copy with the recognized stock exchanges

---

[9] Sub-regulation (3) of regulation 6 of the ICDR Regulations.

[10] Clause (4) of the Securities and Exchange Board of India (Framework for Rejection of Draft Offer Documents) Order, 2012.

where the equity shares are proposed to be listed.[11] The stock exchanges check the draft prospectus to ensure that it is in accordance with their listing requirements. Compared to the extent of review and time taken by SEBI, the stock exchanges' review process is minimal. The draft prospectus is hosted on the websites of SEBI, the stock exchanges where the equity shares are proposed to be listed, and the merchant bankers, for comments from the public for a period of at least 21 days.[12] Through advertisement in newspapers, the company is required to inform the public about the filing of the draft prospectus and invite the public to give comments on the draft prospectus to SEBI.[13] After the expiry of the 21-day period, the lead merchant bankers must file with SEBI a statement giving information of the comments received by them or the company on the draft prospectus and the consequent changes, if any, to be made in the draft prospectus.[14]

This multi-pronged review of the draft prospectus is not required for a public issue of equity shares proposed to be listed on the SME Exchanges. In such cases, only stock exchanges review the draft prospectus.[15] Similarly, for public issues of debentures and preference shares, the Debt Securities Regulations and the Preference Shares Regulations mandate a two-pronged review: one by the designated stock exchange and the other by the public through invitation of comments for a period of seven working days.[16]

This varying degree of ex ante enforcement through prospectus review and pre-clearance is based on the fact that the level of risk for both investors and the market varies in the case of equity shares, and debentures and preference shares. However, in each case SEBI seeks to maintain some form of regulatory oversight through the intermediaries. Thus for public issue of any corporate security, merchant bankers are required to submit a due diligence certificate that confirms to SEBI that

[11] Sub-regulation (5) of regulation 6 of the ICDR Regulations.

[12] Sub-regulation (1) of regulation 9 of the ICDR Regulations.

[13] Sub-regulation (3) of regulation 9 of the ICDR Regulations.

[14] Sub-regulation (2) of regulation 9 of the ICDR Regulations.

[15] Proviso to sub-regulation (3) of regulation 106M of the ICDR Regulations.

[16] Regulation 6 of the Debt Securities Regulations and Preference Shares Regulations.

the disclosure being made in the prospectus is true, fair, and adequate to enable the investors to make a well-informed decision.[17] In a public issue of debentures, the debenture trustee too must furnish a due diligence certificate to SEBI prior to the opening of the public issue.[18]

Approval from Stock Exchange for Listing of Securities

We have already discussed the listing requirement in Chapter 3.[19] Every company making a public offer of its securities must, before making such offer, make an application to one or more recognized stock exchange(s) and obtain permission for the securities to be dealt with in such stock exchange(s).[20] This application is made along with the draft prospectus submitted for review. If the stock exchange accepts the application, it provides its permission to the company in the form of an 'in-principle' approval.[21] This approval self-evidently is only an approval in principle and the company is required to file another final application for listing and trading of the securities upon completion of the public issue and allotment of securities.

For wider access to trading in its securities, the company may choose to apply to more than one recognized stock exchange for listing of its securities. In such a case, it must choose one of them as the 'designated stock exchange'.[22] Such a stock exchange performs certain additional regulatory functions in comparison to other stock exchanges. The

[17] Regulation 8 of the ICDR Regulations, sub-regulation (7) of regulation 6 of the Debt Securities Regulations, and sub-regulation (7) of regulation 6 of the Preference Shares Regulations.

[18] Sub-regulation (8) of regulation 6 of the Debt Securities Regulations

[19] See the section 'Listing of Securities and Types of Public Offering' in Chapter 3 of this volume.

[20] Sub-section (1) of section 40 of the Companies Act; clause (d) of sub-regulation (2) of regulation 4 of the ICDR Regulations; clause (a) of sub-regulation (2) of regulation 4 of the Debt Securities Regulations and the Preference Shares Regulations.

[21] Regulation 107 of the ICDR Regulations.

[22] Clause (d) of sub-regulation (2) of regulation 4 of the ICDR Regulations; clause (a) of sub-regulation (2) of regulation 4 of the Debt Securities Regulations and the Preference Shares Regulations.

designated stock exchange ensures that the basis of allotment is deter-mined in a fair and proper manner, and in accordance with the allotment procedure prescribed by SEBI's regulations. Further, for public issues of debentures and preference shares, the company is required to file the draft prospectus for review only with the designated stock exchange.[23]

Registration of the Prospectus

Upon completion of the review of the prospectus by regulatory authorities, and obtaining the in-principle approval for listing from the concerned stock exchanges, the stage is ready for the offer document to be registered as the prospectus (and for a book-built public issue, as the red herring prospectus) with the registrar of companies.[24] The legal basis for this is that no prospectus must be issued by, on behalf of a company, or in relation to an intended company unless on or before the date of its publication, there has been delivered to the registrar of companies a copy of the prospectus for registration. The copy must be dated and signed by every person who is named therein as a director or proposed director of the company or by their duly authorized attor-ney.[25] The date indicated in the prospectus is deemed to be the date of its publication.[26]

The registrar of companies examines the prospectus and registers if everything is in order. The registration process is not as extensive as the review process carried out by SEBI. The registrar of companies certainly does not have the power to refuse registration and reject the prospectus

[23] Sub-regulations (1) of regulations 6 of the Debt Securities Regulations and the Preference Shares Regulations.

[24] However, in case of a public issue of equity shares, if there are changes to the draft prospectus with respect to a few specified matters such as change of promoter or of more than half of the directors, the company is prohibited from registering the offer document as a prospectus with the registrar of com-panies. The cause of the change is irrelevant and the company is required to file a fresh draft prospectus for review by the regulatory authorities, if it wishes to go ahead with the public issue. Sub-regulation (4) of regulation 11 of the ICDR Regulations.

[25] Sub-section (4) of section 26 of the Companies Act.

[26] Explanation to sub-section (3) of section 26 of the Companies Act.

on the grounds on which SEBI does it.[27] The registrar of companies' task is to ensure that the requirements of section 26 of the Companies Act with respect to the registration of the prospectus are complied with and the prospectus is accompanied by the consent in writing of all the persons named in the prospectus.[28] Despite this, the fact that a copy of the prospectus has been delivered for registration to the registrar of companies must not be understood to imply that it will be accepted and registered. In practice, therefore, companies wait for the registrar of companies to provide an endorsement of the registration of the prospectus. Once registered, the prospectus is valid for being issued to the public during a period of 90 days after the date on which a copy thereof was delivered to the registrar of companies for registration.[29] When issued, the prospectus must, on the face of it, state that a copy has been delivered for registration to the registrar of companies.[30]

Prior to registering the prospectus with the registrar of companies, the company appoints a few other intermediaries such as the bankers to the issue and syndicate members whose involvement now becomes necessary. The debenture trust deed is entered into after the issue of the debentures. The details of all such intermediaries are disclosed in the

---

[27] In this regard, observation contained in a 'Report of the Companies Act Amendment Committee' must be noted. Commenting on section 60 of the Companies Act, 1956 (provision corresponding to sub-sections (4) to (8) of section 26 of the Companies Act, 2013), it states:

> It appears that in some cases Registrars have refused to register prospectuses on grounds other than those referred to in section 60(3) (a) and (b). There is no express provision requiring the Registrar to register a prospectus if the requirements of section 60(3) (a) and (b) are complied with, but that is the effect of section 60(3) by implication. In our opinion, it should not be within the province of the Registrar to refuse registration of a prospectus on the ground that the company is directly or indirectly contravening the policy of the Act or that its business is sought to be carried on in a manner contrary to law though it will be in order for him to point out the defects in the documents on scrutiny.

See Ministry of Finance, Government of India, *Report of the Companies Act Amendment Committee* (1957), at p. 36.

[28] Sub-section (7) of section 26 of the Companies Act.

[29] Sub-section (8) of section 26 of the Companies Act.

[30] Sub-section (6) of section 26 of the Companies Act.

prospectus. Thus, each particular in the prospectus registered with the registrar of companies is expected to be complete, except in a red herring prospectus. In a red herring prospectus, the complete particulars of the quantum or price of the securities are included after determination of the issue price. The final prospectus is then filed with the registrar of companies and SEBI.[31]

Gearing up for the Public Issue

After the company has registered the prospectus but before it issues it to the public, the company and merchant bankers attend to the practical matters for making the public issue, key ones being issue materials, arrangement with stock exchanges, and regulatory advertisements.

The company prints copies of the prospectus, abridged prospectus, and application forms (bid-cum-application form for book-built issues) and dispatches them, both in physical and electronic form, to the stock exchanges, syndicate members, underwriters, bankers to the issue, investors' associations, and self certified syndicate banks (SCSBs). The company also enters into relevant agreements with the stock exchanges for providing services such as online book building facility (for book-built public issues) and direct application facility using online interface (for public issue of debt securities).

Lastly, for a public issue of equity shares, the company must make a pre-issue advertisement in one Hindi and one English national daily newspaper with a wide circulation, and one regional language newspaper with a wide circulation at the place where the registered office of the issuer is situated.[32] The ICDR Regulations prescribe the format of this advertisement, wherein certain elementary information about the public issue in more or less a single page must be provided.[33] Another regulatory advertisement is the announcement of the price band or floor price in a public issue of equity shares through the book building method or the alternate method of book building, respectively. Ideally, the company must mention them in the red herring

---

[31] Sub-section (4) of section 32 of the Companies Act.

[32] Sub-regulation (2) of regulation 47 of the ICDR Regulations.

[33] Part A of Schedule XIII to the ICDR Regulations.

prospectus registered with the registrar of companies. However, the ICDR Regulations permit the company to determine it at a later date. In such a situation, the company must determine and announce the price band or floor price at least five working days before the initial public offering (IPO) in all the newspapers in which it has released the pre-issue advertisement.[34]

Issue of the Prospectus

On the date mentioned in the registered prospectus as the date of opening of the issue, the prospectus is issued to the public, meaning thereby that it is circulated among the members of the public and invites offers from the public for the subscription or purchase of the company's securities. The issue opening date must not be more than 90 days after the date on which a copy thereof is delivered to the registrar of companies for registration.[35] For a public issue of equity shares, there are additional conditions. The issue opening date must be within 12 months from the date of issuance of observations by SEBI, or within four months from the date of filing of the draft prospectus with SEBI, if SEBI has not issued any observations.[36] Another factor to be kept in mind is the lapse of information disclosed in the prospectus. The ICDR Regulations mandate that the information contained in the prospectus and the particulars as per audited financial statements in the prospectus are not older than six months from the date of issue opening.[37] For a public issue of equity shares through the book-building method, there must be a gap of at least three working days from the date of registering the red herring prospectus with the registrar of companies and the date of opening of the issue.[38]

---

[34] For a further public offer, the time limit is at least one working day before the offer on account of the fact that the securities of the company are listed on stock exchanges, and are subject to variation on a daily basis. Sub-regulations (1) and (2) of regulation 30 of the ICDR Regulations.

[35] Sub-section (8) of section 26 of the Companies Act.

[36] Sub-regulation (1) of regulation 11 of the ICDR Regulations.

[37] Regulation 68 of the ICDR Regulations.

[38] Sub-regulation (5) of regulation 11 of the ICDR Regulations.

On the date of opening of the public issue, the company and its authorized agents—namely the merchant bankers, syndicate members, stock exchanges, stockbrokers, and SCSBs—issue the prospectus, both in physical and electronic form, to the public. As noted in Chapter 5, in practice the entire copy of the registered prospectus is not issued to the public owing to the size of the document.[39] Instead, what is issued to the public is the application form accompanied with the abridged prospectus. On a request by any person before the closing of the public issue, the company and merchant bankers furnish them with a physical copy of the complete prospectus, and in a public issue of equity shares, also the general information document.[40] Even otherwise, a digital copy of the complete prospectus is available on the website of the company, merchant bankers, stock exchanges, and SEBI.

Anchor Investors

In a public issue of equity shares through the book building method, the company is permitted to open the public issue for one day before the issue opening date for a select class of investors called 'anchor investors'.[41] An anchor investor is a qualified institutional buyer who makes an application for a value of Rs 10 crore or more.[42] For such investors, the company can set aside a sizeable portion of the equity shares on offer.[43] Further, unlike for other investors who are allotted equity shares

---

[39] See the section 'Form and Content of the Prospectus' in Chapter 5 of this volume.

[40] Sub-section (2) of section 33 of the Companies Act, regulation 61 of the ICDR Regulations, regulation 7 of each of the Debt Securities Regulations and the Preference Shares Regulations, and SEBI circular no. CIR/CFD/DIL/12/2013 dated 23 October 2013.

[41] Sub-regulation (3) of regulation 43 of and Schedule XI to the ICDR Regulations.

[42] Clause (c) of sub-regulation (1) of regulation 2 of the ICDR Regulations.

[43] Currently, up to 60 per cent of the portion is available for allocation to qualified institutional buyers, which is around 30 per cent or 45 per cent of the entire offered shares depending on whether the company undertakes book building under sub-regulation (1) or (2) of regulation 26 of the ICDR Regulations. Refer to sub-regulation (3) of regulation 43 of the ICDR Regulations.

on a proportionate basis (this is done when demand exceeds available shares), anchor investors are allotted equity shares on a discretionary basis.[44] Thus, many anchor investors are assured of being allotted equity shares, which benefits them in public issues that sees high demand and is oversubscribed.

Securities laws permit such superior treatment to anchor investors because they perform important functions. Anchor investors are seen as committed investors for merchant bankers who can be relied on to anchor a public issue in all market conditions, adverse or otherwise in return for assured allotment. Significant participation by anchor investors provides an early momentum to the public issue and sends a positive signal to other investors once the public issue opens for all. It is also beneficial for the company as it helps it to select investors that will provide stability and liquidity in the secondary market. In return for the preferential treatment, the ICDR Regulations mandate that equity shares allotted to the anchor investors must be locked-in for a period of 30 days from the date of allotment in a public issue.[45] Further, if the issue price determined after completion of book building is lower than the price at which an anchor investor had applied, he is not entitled to a refund.[46] Obviously, if an anchor investor had applied at a price lower than the issue price, he must bring in the additional application money.

Issue Period

Once the public issue for equity shares opens on the issue opening date, it must be kept open for application for at least three working days but not more than 10 working days.[47] No such period is prescribed for public issues of debentures and preference shares, and these public issues are generally kept open for a month, with the option of early closure or extension.

---

[44] There is some limitation on the process of discretionary allotment. For details, see paragraph 10 of Part A of Schedule XI to the ICDR Regulations.

[45] Clause (j) of paragraph (10) of part A of Schedule XI to the ICDR Regulations.

[46] Clause (h) of paragraph (10) of part A of Schedule XI to the ICDR Regulations.

[47] Regulation 46 of the ICDR Regulations.

During the issue period, which is the period from the issue open-ing date till the issue closing date, investors begin to apply for the issue, depending on its merits, through the application forms (or bid-cum-application forms in book-built public issues). There are detailed rules around using application forms and it is advisable that investors read the prospectus along with the application form and the abridged prospectus. Investors must also read these documents to determine whether they are eligible to make an application in the public issue and, if eligible, the category in which they may apply. Quite often certain classes of non-resident investors are ineligible to participate in the public issue on account of restriction or prohibition by Indian foreign exchange laws on holding of securities by non-residents. Alternatively, even if eligible, they may not be permitted to hold securities in excess of certain limits. Finally, investors must also ensure that they comply with technical crite-ria for applying in the public issue such as being competent to contract; and having an address, bank account, permanent account number, and depository account for receiving the securities.

Applicants are required to submit the application form to the desig-nated entities, which may refuse to accept it on technical grounds. In a public issue of debt securities, investors also have the option of directly applying in the public issue using the online interface with online payment facility provided by the stock exchanges. In a public issue of equity shares through the book building method, the designated entities namely syndi-cate members, stockbrokers, registrars to an issue, share transfer agents, depository participants, and SCSBs register the bids using the online facility of the stock exchanges for 'building the book'. Only bids that are uploaded on the stock exchanges are considered for allotment. This is also done in a public issue of debentures and the designated entities that have accepted the application, register them on stock exchanges using the online facility. Stock exchanges publicly display a graphical representation of the consolidated demand for the securities during the issue period. At the specified time on the issue closing date, the authorized entities stop accepting the application forms and the public issue is closed.

Allotment and Listing of Securities

To understand allotment and listing of securities, we examine equity shares separately from debentures and preference shares.

Public Issue of Equity Shares

After the public issue closes, the company and the public issue team must complete the following tasks:

1. Process the applications
2. Determine the issue price, enter into the underwriting agreement, and file the final prospectus (in book-built issues)
3. Ensure compliance with minimum subscription and minimum number of allottees
4. Finalize the basis of allotment and get it approved by the designated stock exchange
5. Receive the share application money and refund the excess amount
6. Allot the securities and get them credited into the depository account of the allottees
7. Apply for and obtain the final listing and trading approval from the stock exchanges and execute the listing agreement.

At least the first four activities are not undertaken in the given order but take place concurrently. But the entire set of activities must be completed within five working days from the issue closing date, such that trading in the equity shares can commence on the sixth working day.[48] With advancement in technology, SEBI aims at shortening this period to reduce the risk of change in the price of equity shares.

For processing the applications, the registrar to the issue plays a dominant role and coordinates with the stock exchanges that have the application details. The objective is to reject the applications that are not in accordance with the terms and conditions mentioned in the prospectus. Simultaneously, in book-built issues, the issue price is determined and the company enters into an underwriting agreement. With details of the issue price and total capital being raised at hand, the company files the final prospectus with the registrar of companies and SEBI.

At this stage, the company must ascertain whether the public issue complies with two dictates—minimum subscription and minimum number of allottees. The minimum subscription to be received in a

---

[48] SEBI circular no. CIR/CFD/POLICYCELL/11/2015 dated 10 November 2015.

public issue, except for a public issue consisting of an offer for sale, must not be less than 90 per cent of the offer through the prospectus.[49] In the event of non-receipt of the minimum subscription, the public issue is unsuccessful and the company must refund the application money to all the applicants within a specified period.[50] The risk of not meeting the minimum subscription is higher in a book-built public issue under sub-regulation (2) of regulation 26 of the ICDR Regulations. This is because in such book-built issues, 75 per cent of the public issue that the company must compulsorily allot to qualified institutional buyers cannot be allotted through underwriting.[51] Thus, if qualified institutional buyers do not apply for the requisite number of equity shares, the public issue fails and the company must refund the application money. Similarly, the company must ensure that the prospective number of allottees pursuant to the public issue is not less than 1,000.[52]

Once past the hurdle of minimum subscription and minimum number of allottees, the company, merchant bankers, and the registrar to the issue finalize the basis of allotment. This must be done in accordance with the ICDR Regulations that prescribe the manner of allotting equity shares in the event there is under-subscription or oversubscription in any category. The designated stock exchange then approves the basis of allotment, which forms the basis for transfer of the application money to the company or the selling shareholder. Excess application money is refunded or released back to the applicants. Other than for an offer for sale, this transfer of application money to the company is kept in a separate bank account called the public issue account.

Having received the application money, the company proceeds to allot the equity shares or the selling shareholder transfers the equity shares, and the depository credits them into the depository account of the allottees or the transferees. The company then makes the application for the listing and trading of the equity shares to the stock exchanges that had granted the 'in-principle' approval.[53] Stock exchanges, upon ensuring

---

[49]   Sub-section (1) of section 39 of the Companies Act and regulation 14 of the ICDR Regulations.

[50]   Sub-regulation (2) of regulation 14 of the ICDR Regulations.

[51]   Sub-regulation (2) of regulation 13 of the ICDR Regulations.

[52]   Sub-regulation (4) of regulation 26 of the ICDR Regulations.

[53]   Sub-regulation (2) of regulation 108 of the ICDR Regulations.

that the issue and allotment of equity shares was proper, grant listing and trading approval for the equity shares, and the company executes the listing agreement.[54] Primary market activities thus over, equity shares are listed and their trading commences in the secondary market.

Public Issue of Debentures and Preference Shares

For public issues of debentures and preference shares too, the company must complete the tasks outlined for equity shares above. The process is, however, less complex since ordinarily these public issues are priced through the fixed price method and not the book-building method. There is no requirement of a minimum number of allottees. For debentures, the minimum subscription limit is fixed at a lower limit at seventy-five per cent of the issue size.[55]

But there are three tasks specific to a public issue of debentures that must be completed after the issue of debentures, and their listing and trading are complete—execution of the debenture trust deed, creation of security in favour of the debenture trustee, and creation of a debenture redemption reserve account. Having appointed the debenture trustee before the public issue itself, the company must execute the debenture trust deed within three months of the closure of the public issue.[56] The trust deed must contain the clauses prescribed under Schedule IV to the Debenture Trustees Regulations.[57] The trust deed must not contain a clause that has the effect of:

1. limiting or extinguishing the obligations and liabilities of the debenture trustees or the issuer company in relation to any rights or interests of the debenture holders;

[54] Regulation 110 of the ICDR Regulations, and SEBI circular no. CIR/CFD/CMD/6/2015 dated 13 October 2015.

[55] SEBI circular no. CIR/IMD/DF/12/2014 dated 17 June 2014.

[56] Sub-regulation (1) of Regulation 15 of the Debt Securities Regulations. However, in case of the public issue of secured debentures, the time limit for executing the debenture trust deed is not later than 60 days after the allotment of the debentures. Clause (c) of sub-rule (1) of rule 18 of the Companies (Share Capital and Debentures) Rules, 2014.

[57] Sub-regulation (2) of regulation 15 of the Debt Securities Regulations, and regulation 14 of the Debenture Trustees Regulations.

2. limiting or restricting or waiving the provisions of the SEBI Act, Debt Securities Regulations, and circulars or guidelines issued by SEBI;

3. indemnifying the debenture trustees or the issuer company for loss or damage caused by their act of negligence, commission, or omission.[58]

In case of secured debentures, the company must execute, not later than 60 days after the allotment of the debentures, the debenture trust deed and the security documents.[59] Security must be by way of a charge or mortgage created in favour of the debenture trustee on (a) any specific movable property of the company (not being in the nature of pledge); or (b) any specific immovable property wherever situated, or any interest thereon.[60] The value of the property over which security has been created must be sufficient for the due repayment of the amount of the debentures and interest thereon.[61] The company is prohibited from using the proceeds from the issue of debentures until the security documents have been duly executed.[62]

Lastly, the company must create a debenture redemption reserve account out of the profits of the company available for payment of dividend and the amount credited to such account must not be used by the company except for the redemption of debentures.[63]

---

[58] Sub-regulation (3) of regulation 15 of the Debt Securities Regulations.

[59] Clause (c) of sub-rule (1) of rule 18 of the Companies (Share Capital and Debentures) Rules, 2014.

[60] There are some exceptions to these rules on creation of security. For details, see clause (d) of sub-rule (1) of rule 18 of Companies (Share Capital and Debentures) Rules, 2014.

[61] Clause (b) of sub-rule (1) of rule 18 of the Companies (Share Capital and Debentures) Rules, 2014.

[62] Sub-regulation (3) of regulation 17 of the Debt Securities Regulations.

[63] Sub-section (4) of section 71 of the Companies Act, regulation 16 of the Debt Securities Regulations, and sub-rule (7) of rule 18 of the Companies (Share Capital and Debentures) Rules, 2014. No debenture redemption reserve account is required to be created by all India financial institutions regulated by the Reserve Bank of India (RBI) and banking companies. See clause (b) of sub-rule (7) of rule 18 of the Companies (Share Capital and Debentures) Rules, 2014.

Life as a Listed Company

Now that the public offering of corporate securities is over and the securities are listed and traded on the stock exchanges, the company becomes a 'listed company'. It is subject to a far greater number of securities laws on an ongoing basis. It is not within the scope of this book to examine the life of a listed company. Nonetheless, we examine certain matters regarding the public offering programme that have a bearing on the listed company.

Variation in Terms of Contract or Objects in Prospectus

A company must not vary the terms of a contract referred to in the prospectus or objects for which the prospectus was issued, except subject to the approval of, or except subject to an authority given by the company in general meeting by way of special resolution.[64] For the information of shareholders, details of the notice in respect of the resolution must also be published in newspapers (one in English and one in a vernacular language) in the city where the registered office of the company is situated, clearly indicating the justification for the variation.[65] With regards to the limitations on the variation that can be made to the objects for which the prospectus was issued, we examined these in Chapter 5.[66] Deviations in the use of proceeds from the objects stated in the prospectus also attract compliances under the Securities and Exchange Board of India (Listing Obligations and Disclosure Requirements) Regulations, 2015 (or the LODR Regulations). This aspect also was examined in Chapter 5.[67]

The scope of this statutory restriction on variation of terms of contracts or objects in the prospectus appears to be limited to prospectuses

[64] Sub-section (1) of section 27 of the Companies Act and sub-rule (1) of rule 7 of the Companies (Prospectus and Allotment of Securities) Rules, 2014. See also sub-section (8) of section 13 of the Companies Act and rule 32 of the Companies (Incorporation) Rules, 2014.

[65] Sub-section (1) of section 27 of the Companies Act and sub-rule (2) of rule 7 of the Companies (Prospectus and Allotment of Securities) Rules, 2014.

[66] See the section titled 'Principal Contents of a Prospectus for Equity Shares' in Chapter 5 of this volume.

[67] See the section 'Principal Contents of a Prospectus for Equity Shares' in Chapter 5 of this volume.

for the issue of shares, and not of debentures. Thus, at the passing of the resolution, dissenting shareholders, being those shareholders who have not agreed to the proposal to vary the terms of contracts or objects referred to in the prospectus, must be given an exit offer by promoters or controlling shareholders. The exit offer must be at such price, and in such manner and on such conditions as SEBI specifies.[68] Though this is a statutory restriction seemingly limited to a prospectus for the public issue of shares, it is quite conceivable to have these restrictions through contractual terms and conditions for a public issue of debentures also.

Annually Updating the Prospectus

A listed company must disclose certain information on a periodic basis, such as financial information and shareholding pattern, and other information on an as-and-when basis, such as unpublished price-sensitive information—any information which relates directly or indirectly to a company and which if published is likely to materially affect the price of the securities of the company. These obligations arise out of LODR Regulations, Securities and Exchange Board of India (Prohibition of Insider Trading) Regulations, 2015 (or the PIT Regulations), and Securities and Exchange Board of India (Substantial Acquisition of Shares and Takeovers) Regulations, 2011. The listed company must disclose this information to the stock exchanges, which then disseminate it to the public for the benefit of the secondary market investors.

Traditionally, all this information was available in fragments and there was no single document that contained all updates of the company after the public offering programme at one place. SEBI has, therefore, mandated that the disclosure made in the prospectus while making an IPO must be updated on an annual basis by the company and must be made publicly accessible in the manner specified by it.[69]

---

[68] Chapter VI-A of the ICDR Regulations specifies the conditions and manner of providing exit opportunity to dissenting shareholders.

[69] Regulation 51A of the ICDR Regulations.

7. Liabilities and Regulatory Actions

This chapter considers the different forms and bases of liabilities and regulatory actions in respect of the public offering of corporate securities. There is no gainsaying that regulation of the public offering of corporate securities would be ineffective in the absence of a liability regime. No doubt ex ante mechanisms—vetting and registration of a prospectus before its issue to the public, mandatory due diligence by securities market intermediaries, etc., which we examined in the preceding chapters—reduce the scope for violation of securities laws. However, they have their limitations. Given the volume of activities and large number of parties involved in a public offering programme, it would be impractical, time consuming, and very costly to subject every conduct to ex ante review. Some violations, such as whether the prospectus indeed discloses all material information, are also difficult to detect in advance. Resultantly, liabilities and regulatory actions in respect of the public offering of corporate securities exist to enforce securities laws and enable recovery of compensation after a violation has occurred. These liabilities and regulatory actions exist along a continuum of civil action and criminal prosecution—the distinction between the two extremes is well established and understood in our legal system. In between the two lie pecuniary penalty and regulatory action.

The dominant theme of all forms of liabilities and regulatory actions is checking misstatement, particularly fraudulent misstatement. Misstatement (or misrepresentation, under contract law) broadly means a false statement. Fraud may be described 'as the procuring of advantage to oneself, or furthering some purpose of one's own, by causing a person with whom one deals to act upon a false belief'.[1] At the very outset, it must be clarified that both misstatement and fraud do not have a single definition or meaning in the context of liability. As we see later in this chapter, under each form of liability, the elements of what constitutes misstatement and what constitutes fraud somewhat differ.

Checking misstatement is the dominant theme of all forms of liabilities and regulatory actions because the common feature of most activities in a public offering programme is the making of statements—statements by the company to the investors either in the prospectus or outside it, statements by investors to the company in the application form, statements by intermediaries and other participants either to the company or to other persons such as the regulatory authorities, etc. Nothing is therefore, more serious than misstatements in a public offering programme, whatever the cause may be—ignorance, negligence, or outright fraud. All forms of liabilities and regulatory actions are, to an extent, designed to respond to it. Among the different causes of misstatements, the liability regime is quite zealous in responding to misstatements caused by fraud. The reason for this is repeated instances of such acts by directors and promoters to the detriment of investors. On certain occasions, existing liability provisions were found to be wanting in acting as a deterrent to fraud or compensating the injured party. The legislature and the courts, therefore, responded by newer set of norms. At present, we have a large body of liability provisions that deal fraudulent misstatement, which at times are incoherent and confusing.

---

[1] Sir Frederick Pollock, *The Law of Fraud, Misrepresentation and Mistake in British India* (Thacker, Spink & Co. 1894), at p. 17. See also *Dr. Vimla v. Delhi Administration*, AIR 1963 SC 1572.

We now examine the different forms and bases of liabilities, namely civil liability, criminal liability, pecuniary penalty, and regulatory actions in relation to the public offering of corporate securities.

Civil Liability

By being involved in a public offering programme, every participant is exposed to some form of civil wrong, which may be either contractual, tortious, or statutory. The remedy against these wrongs principally consists of (a) rescission of the contract and restitution; and (b) compensation for rescission of contract, for breach of contract, under the tort of fraud and negligent misstatement, and under the Companies Act. For contractual liability, we limit the analysis to the supervening contracts of subscription or sale of securities that the prospectus induces. It is needless to examine liability under other contracts such as underwriting agreements and the issue agreement, since, albeit the core commonality, these contracts are extensively negotiated and their content differs from one transaction to the other. In any event, liabilities ensuing from these contracts would be of types similar to that of the contracts of subscription or sale of securities that the prospectus induces.

To understand contractual liability, we first examine the nature of the contracts of subscription or sale of securities that the prospectus induces. From the perspective of the general law of contract, statements contained in a prospectus are of two types. Statements may be terms of the ensuing contract by virtue of the abridged prospectus that accompanies and forms part of the application form. These terms are in addition to the terms stated in the application form itself. Else, statements may be representations that induce the ensuing contract, but are not its terms.[2]

---

[2] Theoretically, statements may also fall into a third type, namely sales puffs, given that a prospectus, as discussed in the section titled 'Prospectus' in Chapter 3 of this volume, is generally styled as an 'invitation to treat'. Sales puffs are statements made at the pre-contractual stage as part of an invitation. They do not have legal consequences as no reasonable person relies on them to enter into a contract. In practice, however, it is a rarity for statements in a prospectus to fall into this category because securities laws on disclosure restrict the making of such statements, and securities laws as well as the company and investors expect that every statement in the prospectus can be relied upon by the investors for entering into the supervening contract.

Representations are statements or affirmations that the maker asserts as being true and which operate to induce a contract. A term, on the other hand, is the promise or the set of promises that parties to a contract have made and are obligated to fulfil.[3] As we see later in this chapter, majority of the statements in a prospectus are representations, and not terms of the supervening contract.

The distinction between terms and representations is vital as there are different remedies for representations that are found to be false and for non-performance or breach of a term of the contract. The remedy against the former is setting aside the contract (or rescission) and restitution, whereas the remedy against the latter is a suit for specific performance of the contract, injunction, and damages. Essentially, the relief sought in case of misrepresentations is that the contract ought not to be enforced and the parties should be restored to their pre-contractual position, as there is a defect in the formation of the contract. Contrarily, in case of breach of terms, the plaintiff seeks to enforce the contract as per its terms and in the alternative, seeks damages so as to be put in a position had the contract been performed by the parties. The distinction is also somewhat vital due to the 'parol evidence rule' and 'estoppel' contained in sections 91 and 92 of the Indian Evidence Act, 1872. The parol evidence rule means that when the terms of a contract have been reduced to the form of a document, such terms must be proved only by the document itself. When the terms of the contract have been proved accordingly, no evidence of an oral agreement or statement must be admitted, as between the parties to the contract, for the purpose of contradicting, varying, adding to, or subtracting from, the terms.[4] Estoppel is again a rule of evidence and applies to representations. It means that 'When one person has, by his declaration, act or omission,

---

[3] At least in special contracts like a contract for the sale of goods, terms may be further divided into conditions and warranties. A condition is a stipulation essential to the main purpose of the contract, the breach of which gives rise to a right to treat the contract as repudiated. A warranty, on the other hand, is a stipulation collateral to the main purpose of the contract, the breach of which gives rise to a claim for damages but not a right to reject the goods and treat the contract as repudiated. See section 12 of the Sale of Goods Act, 1930.

[4] This is a general statement of the parol evidence rule, and the rule is subject to certain exceptions. For details, see sections 91 and 92 of the Indian Evidence Act, 1872.

intentionally caused or permitted another person to believe a thing to be true and to act upon such belief, neither he nor his representative shall be allowed, in any suit or proceeding between himself and such person or his representative, to deny the truth of that thing.'[5]

There is another aspect of the supervening contracts of subscription or sale of securities that we must take note of. In the past, a contract of subscription of equity shares consisted of reciprocal promises—the applicant paying part of the share application money and promising to pay the unpaid share capital when it is called up, in exchange for the promise by the company to issue the equity shares. The contract was, therefore, an executory contract—a contract which is either wholly unperformed or in which there remains something to be done on both sides.[6] The performance too remained pending for long and sometimes extended up to the commencement of winding up proceedings when the company would call up unpaid share capital.

Now, with the depository system for the issue of securities and the ability of the applicants to pay the full share application money at the stage of the application itself, the constituents of this contract are different. This contract of subscription of equity shares consists of a performance by the applicant in exchange for a promise by the company to issue equity shares. The contract is, therefore, an executed contract—a contract performed wholly on one side.[7] The applicant

[5] Section 115 of the Indian Evidence Act, 1872. See also *Parma Nand* v. *Champa Lal*, AIR 1956 All 225.

[6] Sir William R. Anson, *Principles of the English Law of Contract and of Agency in its Relation to Contract* (Oxford at the Clarendon Press 1923), at p. 21.

[7] As Sir William Anson has explained, in contract law, 'executed' and 'executory' are used in three different senses depending on the substantive with which the adjective is joined. 'Executed contract' means a contract performed wholly on one side, while an 'executory contract' is one which is either wholly unperformed or in which there remains something to be done on both sides. 'Executed consideration' as opposed to 'executory consideration' means present as opposed to future, an act as opposed to a promise. 'Executed contract of sale' means a bargain and sale which has passed the property in the thing sold, while 'executory contract of sale' is a contract as opposed to conveyance, and creates rights *in personam* to a fulfillment of their terms instead of rights *in rem* to an enjoyment of the property passed. See Anson (n. 6), at pp. 21 and 121.

makes an offer by paying the entire subscription amount, and the company, if the offer is acceptable, accepts it. The performance and discharge of this executed contract too does not remain pending for long. The company immediately allots the equity shares and intimates the fact of allotment to the depository, which in turn immediately credits the equity shares to the applicants' depository account. Soon thereafter, the company obtains listing and trading permission for the equity shares and begins trading them on the stock exchanges. Therefore, the time gap between the formation of the contract and its performance by both the parties is very short. Now that the equity shareholder is a member of the company, a new contract between the company and the equity shareholder comes into being by virtue of the articles of association. The same result is reached in a contract of sale of equity shares in an offer for sale by the selling shareholder. Similarly, the contract of subscription of debentures or preference shares too is an executed contract; the applicant in the offer does all that he/she is bound to do under the contract, leaving an outstanding performance on one side only. However, unlike for equity shares, this executed contract remains unperformed by the company until redemption of the debentures and preference shares.

Lastly, before examining the different forms of civil liabilities, it will be useful to have clarity on the legal relationship between the company and the selling shareholder in an offer for sale of shares under section 28 of the Companies Act. In a public offer of securities involving issue of shares, there is a bipartite contract between the company and the

---

See also Sir Frederick Pollock, *The Indian Contract Act, with a Commentary, Critical and Explanatory* (Sweet & Maxwell Limited 1909), at p. 24. Here Sir Frederick Pollock discusses 'consideration' under the Indian Contract Act, 1872 and states:

> A consideration which consists in performance (or so far as it consists in performance) is said to be executed. If and so far as it consists in promise, it is said to be executory.... It is obvious that the consideration cannot be wholly executed on both sides. For where performances, and performances only, are exchanged, of which sale of goods over the counter for ready money is a familiar example, nothing remains to be done by either party, and there is no promise at all and nothing for the law to enforce.

subscriber of the securities. However, in an offer for sale of shares under section 28 of the Companies Act, it is a tripartite contract between the company and the selling shareholder on the one hand, and the purchaser of shares on the other hand. Each of the parties exchange promises—the selling shareholder promises to sell the shares, the purchaser promises to buy, and the company promises to get the shares listed on the stock exchange and carry out the necessary activities in relation to the public offer. There is one more contract in operation in these cases, which is the contract of agency between the selling shareholder and the company. As per sub-section (3) of section 28 of the Companies Act, the selling shareholder authorizes the company to take all actions in respect of the 'offer for sale', for and on the shareholder's behalf. This grant of authority to the company to act for and on behalf of the selling shareholder would make the selling shareholder the principal, the company an agent, and the relationship between the two parties that of an agency.[8]

The nature of this agency is such that the company's agents employed in relation to the public offering of shares would be sub-agents of the selling shareholder.[9] The selling shareholders would in effect be engaging the company to sell the shares on their behalf and to represent the selling shareholders in dealings with the public investors. Given the nature of the transaction, the authorization would undoubtedly be in a documentary form and will thus constitute a power of attorney.[10] This agency terminates upon completion of the public offering programme. Beyond this, it is outside the scope of this book to examine the nature

---

[8] Section 182 of the Indian Contract Act, 1872 defines agent and principal in the following terms. 'An "agent" is a person employed to do any act for another, or to represent another in dealings with third persons. The person for whom such act is done, or who is so represented, is called the "principal".' See *Chairman, Life Insurance Corporation and Ors v. Rajiv Kumar Bhasker*, (2005) 6 SCC 188; *P. Krishna Bhatta and Ors v. Mundila Ganapathi Bhatta and Ors*, AIR 1955 Mad 648; *State of Bihar v. Dukhulal Das and Anr*, Appeal from Original Decree No. 398 of 1957, decided on 1 November 1961 by the High Court of Patna (unreported judgment).

[9] Sections 190 and 191 of the Indian Contract Act, 1872.

[10] Section 1A of the Powers-of-Attorney Act, 1882 defines powers of attorney to 'include any instrument empowering a specified person to act for and in the name of the person executing it'.

of this agency. Nonetheless, one must bear in mind the statutory duty of indemnity that a principal owes towards its agent, which is relevant in a public offering programme. The selling shareholder, as the principal, is bound to indemnify the company against the consequences of all lawful acts done by the company in exercise of the authority conferred upon it.[11] If the company does an act in good faith, the selling shareholder will be liable to indemnify the company against the consequences of that act, though it may cause an injury to the rights of third persons.[12]

Rescission

Some introduction of rescission of contract is necessary for a proper perspective of this remedy in public offering contracts. Rescission is the avoidance of a contract. The parties are then placed back in the position as if there had been no contract, though that may not always be possible. Rescission may take place either by act of parties or by a suit under the Specific Relief Act, 1963. By act of parties, rescission may take place in the following circumstances:

1. An agreement between the parties to rescind the contract, to alter the terms of the contract (which puts an end to the terms of the old contract), or to substitute a new contract for the old contract;[13]

2. An agreement between the original parties to the contract and a third person, by which the third person takes the place of one of the original contracting parties (commonly called novation);[14]

3. An exercise of the right to rescind, which right results to the injured party when the original agreement is a voidable contract. An agreement is a voidable contract when consent to the agreement is caused by coercion, undue influence, fraud, or misrepresentation. In these situations, the agreement is a contract voidable at the option of the party whose consent was so caused;[15]

[11] Section 222 of the Indian Contract Act, 1872.
[12] Section 223 of the Indian Contract Act, 1872.
[13] Section 62 of the Indian Contract Act, 1872.
[14] Section 62 of the Indian Contract Act, 1872.
[15] Sections 19 and 19A of the Indian Contract Act, 1872.

4. An exercise of the right to rescind, which right results to the injured party when the contract becomes a voidable contract. A contract becomes a voidable contract when a contract contains reciprocal promises, and one party to the contract prevents the other from performing the promise. In such a situation, the contract becomes voidable at the option of the party so prevented.[16] A contract also becomes a voidable contract when a party to the contract promises to do a certain thing at or before specified times, and fails to do any such thing at or before the specified time. Then the contract, or so much of it as has not been performed, becomes voidable at the option of the promisee, if the intention of the parties was that time should be of the essence of the contract;[17] and

5. An exercise of the right to rescind, which right results to the injured party when the other party to the contract has refused to perform, or disabled themselves from performing the promise in its entirety. The injured party may then rescind the contract, unless they have signified, by words or conduct, their acquiescence in its continuance.[18]

Obviously, rescission by act of parties may also take place by exercise of a power to rescind reserved by the contract itself in favour of one or both the parties to the contract, or if a special statute confers such a right on a contracting party.[19]

Under the Specific Relief Act, 1963, any person interested in a contract may sue to have it rescinded, and such rescission may be adjudged by the court in the following two cases:

1. where the contract is voidable or terminable by the plaintiff;

2. where the contract is unlawful for causes not apparent on its face and the defendant is more to blame than the plaintiff.[20]

---

[16] Section 53 of the Indian Contract Act, 1872.

[17] Section 55 of the Indian Contract Act, 1872.

[18] Section 39 of the Indian Contract Act, 1872.

[19] Sir Edward Fry, *A Treatise on the Specific Performance of Contracts* (Universal Law Publishing 1921), at p. 477.

[20] Section 26 of the Specific Relief Act. Rescission under the Specific Relief Act is subject to extensive rules that govern under what circumstances the court

With respect to the public offering of corporate securities, the type of rescission that is relevant is rescission of a voidable contract on account of fraud or misrepresentation. Thus, when consent of any party to the agreement of subscription or sale of securities in a public offering is caused by fraud or misrepresentation, the agreement is a contract voidable at the option of the said party and he/she may choose to rescind the contract. The aggrieved party is generally the applicant investor seeking rescission of the contract against the company or the selling shareholder for having committed the fraud or made the misrepresentation in the prospectus. However, it is not inconceivable for the company or the selling shareholder to be the aggrieved party where an applicant made a misrepresentation or fraudulent misstatement in the application form. Given that this remedy is limited to parties to the contract, an action for rescission of the contract will not lie against the directors of the company or the expert whose report has been included in the prospectus.

Before moving on to examine the different aspects of rescission of a contract of subscription or sale of securities in a public offering that is voidable on account of fraud or misrepresentation, we must take note of an inadequacy in this area of law. The circumstances in which rescission may take place under the Indian Contract Act, 1872 and the Specific Relief Act, 1963, outlined in the preceding paragraphs, suggest that rescission means determination of unperformed contractual obligations and is, therefore, limited to executory and executed contracts, but not to contracts that have been performed and discharged.[21] In the case of rescission of voidable contracts, the problem is further compounded by the fact that the expression 'voidable contract' is itself defined as 'an agreement which is enforceable by law at the option of one or more of

---

may refuse to rescind the contract. See sub-section (2) of section 26 of the Specific Relief Act.

[21] Technically though, rescission when applied to the latter kind is the abrogation of what may be called the status of parties effected by the performance of the contract, and is not the rescission of 'the contract' because the contract having been performed, there is no obligation left on which rescission can operate. See, Charles Bruce Morrison, *Rescission of Contracts* (Steven & Haynes 1916), at p. 2.

the parties thereto, but not at the option of the other or others'.[22] There is nothing left to enforce in a contract that has been wholly performed. This creates a peculiar problem in the case of rescission of a contract of subscription or sale of equity shares pursuant to public offers as this contract is performed very soon after its formation. Nothing remains to be done or enforced by either of the parties to the contract and the contract is discharged. Thus, in all likelihood, an applicant would discover that their consent to the agreement for subscription or sale of equity shares was caused by fraud or misrepresentation after the discharge of the contract. Despite this apparent restriction, one could perhaps take the view that rescission can be applied to the above class of discharged contracts. The Indian Contract Act, 1872 does not profess to be a complete code dealing with the law relating to contracts.[23] The common law of England as at the commencement of the Constitution of India did recognize an action of rescission for discharged contracts also.[24] Also, so much of the English common law which was adopted as the law of India before the Constitution of India came into force continues to be Indian law.[25] Though it is not clear from the reported decisions whether this part of English common law was adopted in India, if one were to go by the statutory enactments, the intent seemed to be to, in principle, permit

---

[22] Clause (i) of section 2 of the Indian Contract Act, 1872.

[23] Judgment of the Privy Council in *The Irrawaddy Flotilla Company* v. *Bugwandas*, (1891) 18 Ind App 121.

[24] However, the right appeared to have been limited to cases of fraud only and not to misrepresentation (or an innocent misrepresentation as referred to under English law). See *Kennedy* v. *The Panama, etc., Mail Co.*, LR 2 QB 580 [1867]; *Seddon* v. *North Eastern Salt Co. Ltd.*, [1905] 1 Ch. 326; and Report of the Contracts and Commercial Law Reform Committee (UK), *Misrepresentation and Breach of Contract* (1967). The (UK) Misrepresentation Act, 1967 finally removed the uncertainty, and confirmed the right of rescission of a contract that has been performed but which was otherwise vitiated by fraud or misrepresentation.

[25] Sub-article (1) of Art. 372 of the Constitution of India. See *Superintendent and Legal Remembrancer, State of West Bengal* v. *Corporation of Calcutta*, AIR 1967 SC 997; *Shantilal Ambalal Mehta* v. *M.A. Rangaswamy*, 1977 MhLJ 587.

rescission of discharged contracts that were voidable on account of fraud and misrepresentation.[26]

Elements and Proof of Rescission

A case of rescission of a contract of subscription or sale of securities in a public offering, for fraud or misrepresentation, would involve proof of the following matters. For fraud, the applicant must prove that the other party to the contract (or some other person with his connivance) or his agent

1. made suggestion, as a fact, of that which is not true, or actively concealed a fact;
2. did not believe the fact to be true, or had knowledge or belief of the concealment of the fact; and
3. this was done with the intent to either deceive the applicant or to induce him to enter into a contract.[27]

---

[26] See section 108 (now repealed) of the Indian Contract Act, 1872 and illustration (e) to it, and section 29 of the Sale of Goods Act, 1930. On rescission of contract after a breach has occurred, see Law Commission of India, *13th Report on Contract Act, 1872* (1958), at pp. 34–5.

[27] Section 17 of the Indian Contract Act, 1872. Under this section, there are other acts too that constitute fraud but those are not relevant to a contract of subscription or sale of securities in public offerings. Further, as per the Explanation to Section 17 of the Indian Contract Act, 1872, mere silence as to facts likely to affect the willingness of a person to enter into a contract is not fraud. This rule does not apply in two situations: (a) the circumstances of the case are such that, regard being had to them, it is the duty of the person keeping silence to speak, and (b) the silence is, in itself, equivalent to speech. Though the former exception has traditionally been applied to cases where a fiduciary duty was involved, the language of the statutory provision permits it to be applied to cases of statutory duty also. This qualification to the rule of silence will, therefore, apply to public offering contracts since securities laws impose a duty on the company to disclose all material facts. This approach is also in line with modern developments. The latter exception too, would generally apply to public offering contracts, for omission to state a material fact in a prospectus would make the statement of the rest, though literally true so far as it goes, as misleading as an actual falsehood. This will then become equivalent to speech.

Proof of these matters would, in essence, mean that the company, with a fraudulent intention, made a false statement of fact having knowledge of its falsity. For misrepresentation, the applicant must prove that

1. the company made a positive assertion of that which is not true though it believes it to be true; and
2. the said assertion was not warranted by the information of the company.[28]

This means that the company must have made a false statement without any reasonable ground. Unlike fraud, the applicant need not prove guilty mind or knowledge of the falsity of the statement, though the effect of both fraud and misrepresentation is the same—it renders the contract voidable. It would also be misrepresentation if there were 'any breach of duty which, without an intent to deceive, gains an advantage to the person committing it, or any one claiming under him, by misleading another to his prejudice, or to the prejudice of any one claiming under him'.[29] The latter ground affords a lower standard of proof of misrepresentation since securities laws impose a duty that the prospectus must contain all material disclosures, which are true and adequate to enable the applicant to make an informed investment decision. Therefore, for both fraud and misrepresentation, the common element is false statement or non-disclosure in terms of the foregoing.

Though we have noticed above the constituents of fraud and misrepresentation, we must also note some legal principles on those constituents. At least for fraud, the false statement or non-disclosure is limited to any statement of fact[30] and the same would be the case for misrepresentation as well.[31] Under the general law of contract, this

[28] Section 18 of the Indian Contract Act, 1872. It is also misrepresentation if the company causes, 'however innocently, [the applicant] to make a mistake as to the substance of the thing which is the subject matter of the agreement'. However the likelihood of mistake as to the subject matter of the agreement, namely securities in public offering contracts, is unlikely.

[29] Clause (2) of section 18 of the Indian Contract Act, 1872.

[30] Clause (1) of section 17 of the Indian Contract Act, 1872.

[31] Pollock (n. 7), at p. 97.

proposition is said to exclude a statement of future conduct and intention, statement of belief or opinion, and statement of law.[32]

In the past, this distinction has come to the aid of persons issuing a prospectus. Thus in *Shiromani Sugar Mills Limited* v. *Debi Prasad*,[33] the Allahabad High Court held that the statement in the prospectus that 'the Managing Agents with their friends, promoters and directors have already promised to subscribe share[s] worth Rs. 6,00,000' was not a statement of fact but of future conduct, and absolved the company from the claim of misrepresentation. The court went to the extent of holding that as long as there is no misrepresentation of fact, 'some amount of puffing must be allowed in a prospectus'. Securities laws today clearly do not support this proposition. Further, even the distinction between a statement of fact and other kinds of statements may not be of much aid to issuers of a prospectus today because, on account of securities laws on disclosure in a prospectus, a large part of the prospectus consists of statements of existing facts. Portions of the prospectus that do contain statements of future conduct and intention such as objects of the public issue, and statements of belief or opinion such as the risk factors are substantiated by detailed statements of facts. It will, therefore, not be unreasonable to hold those statements to be statements of facts. As far as a statement of laws is concerned, if the same is expressed in terms of a positive assurance that the law is so and so, it will constitute a statement of fact.[34] Even otherwise, given the circumstances and position of the contracting parties, it may be reasonable for the applicant to treat statements of law in the prospectus as statements of fact and rely on it, instead of verifying the law himself.

It must be noted that even if the false statement or non-disclosure is proved, it is no misrepresentation if the applicant 'had the means of discovering the truth with ordinary diligence'.[35] However, the defendant will find it difficult to apply this defence due to the nature of securities and the information asymmetry between the contracting parties. A possibility of discovering the truth by inquiries involving trouble or expense

---

[32] Pollock (n. 1), at p. 103.
[33] AIR 1950 All 508.
[34] Pollock (n. 7), at p. 97.
[35] Exception to section 19 of the Indian Contract Act, 1872.

out of proportion to the value of the whole subject matter would not be 'means of discovering the truth with ordinary diligence'. Ordinary diligence also does not mean that every statement in the prospectus should be checked and its accuracy investigated.[36] Another limitation to rescission on the ground of fraud or misrepresentation is that a 'fraud or misrepresentation which did not cause the consent to a contract of the party on whom such fraud was practiced, or to whom such misrepresentation was made, does not render a contract voidable'.[37] The principle stated here is obvious. A false representation, whether fraudulent or innocent, is irrelevant if it has not induced the applicant to act upon it and the applicant cannot complain of having been misled by a statement that did not lead him at all.[38] This rule introduces the element of materiality and it will be a defence to say that no reasonable applicant would have been induced to enter into the contract due to the immaterial false statement.[39]

Given these factors, the entire prospectus and any other communication made by the company or its agents to the applicant, to cause the applicant to consent to entering into the contract, is liable to be tested for any fraud or misrepresentation. This would include statements made by the experts in their report included in the prospectus because the company expressly declares that all statements made in the prospectus are true and correct. This would also be the case for the contract between the selling shareholder and the applicant in an offer for sale of shares. This is because misrepresentations made or fraud committed by agents acting in the course of their business for their principals have the same effect on agreements made by such agents as if such misrepresentations or fraud had been made or committed by the principals.[40]

Generally speaking, the effect of the fraud or misrepresentation is limited to the contract of subscription or sale of securities between the company and the applicant. It will not extend to subsequent contracts

[36] *Calcutta Celluloid Works Limited* v. *Labanya Mohan Ghatak*, 47 CWN 421 (1942).

[37] Explanation to section 19 of the Indian Contract Act, 1872.

[38] Pollock (n. 7), at p. 102.

[39] *Bhagwani Bai* v. *Life Insurance Corporation of India*, AIR 1984 MP 126; *Shiromani Sugar Mills Limited* v. *Debi Prasad*, AIR 1950 All 508.

[40] Section 238 of the Indian Contract Act, 1872.

of sale of securities by the applicant. The reason is obvious as the subsequent contracts are separate and independent from the previous contract induced by the prospectus and the prospectus is not addressed to subsequent contracting parties.[41] However, given that the subsequent transaction of the securities in the secondary market will be a sale of goods, special rules under the Sale of Goods Act, 1930 will become applicable, one of which is under section 29 of this act. This section states that when the seller of goods has obtained possession thereof under a contract voidable under section 19 or section 19A of the Indian Contract Act, 1872, but the contract has not been rescinded at the time of the sale, the buyer acquires a good title to the goods, provided he buys them in good faith and without notice of the seller's defect of title.

Modes of Rescission

Earlier we noted the lack of clarity under the Indian Contract Act, 1872 on rescission of a contract that has been performed and discharged. Therefore, we now examine separately the modes of rescission of an executory or executed contract, and rescission of a contract that has been performed and discharged. The consequences of rescission are largely common for both the classes.

If the contract of subscription or sale of securities is still executory or executed but not been fully performed and discharged, the applicant who is defrauded or misrepresented, though having a right to rescind, need not necessarily rescind the contract. He/she may, if they think fit, insist that the contract is performed, and that he/she is put in the position which would have been applicable if the representations had been true.[42] If the applicant elects to rescind the contract, no particular form is necessary. They may rescind it by their act and the rescission may be communicated in the same manner, and subject to the same rules under the Indian Contract Act, 1872 as apply to the communication of a proposal.[43] At

---

[41] *Collins v. Associated Greyhound Racecourses Limited*, [1930] 1 Ch. D. 1. The principles stated in this case would be applicable under the Indian Contract Act, 1872.

[42] Section 19 of the Indian Contract Act, 1872.

[43] Section 66 of the Indian Contract Act, 1872. *Official Receiver, Jhansi v. Jugal Kishore Lachhi Ram*, AIR 1963 All 459.

least under the Indian Contract Act, 1872, rescission by the act of the applicant is available as a matter of right and no court order is necessary for the rescission to take effect.

Another mode of rescission is that the applicant may sue under section 27 of the Specific Relief Act, 1963 to have the contract rescinded.[44] However, this mode of rescission is not available as a matter of right and the court may refuse to rescind the contract:

1. where the applicant has expressly or impliedly ratified the contract; or

2. where, owing to the change of circumstances which has taken place since the making of the contract (not being due to any act of the defendant himself), the parties cannot be substantially restored to the position in which they stood when the contract was made; or

3. where third parties have, during the subsistence of the contract, acquired rights in good faith without notice and for value; or

4. where only a part of the contract is sought to be rescinded and such part is not severable from the rest of the contract.[45]

If the contract has been performed and discharged, the mode of rescission is unclear as the Indian Contract Act, 1872 and the Specific Relief Act, 1963 do not contemplate such rescissions. Clearly, the rescission is not possible by the unilateral act of the applicant as the contract has been discharged. Nonetheless, as discussed earlier, given that a case can be made out for such rescissions, the mode of rescission would have to be a suit before a civil court. Though the Specific Relief Act, 1963 would not be expressly applicable to such suits, it is quite likely that the court would be guided by the legal principles codified under the Specific

---

[44] Section 27 of the Specific Relief Act. See also *Raja Rajeswara Dorai v. Arunachellam Chettiar*, (1915) ILR 38 Mad 321. An applicant may also set up rescission as a defence in a suit for specific performance by the company or the selling shareholder. However, now the likelihood of such a remedy is remote given the very short period within which the contract of subscription or sale of securities is formed and performed by both the parties leaving nothing to be enforced thereafter.

[45] Section 27 of the Specific Relief Act.

Relief Act, 1963 outlined earlier, on which rescission may be refused to a party.

Consequences of Rescission and Time Limit

Before examining the consequences of rescission, we examine the time within which to rescind the contract. If rescission is by an act of the party and of the contract of subscription of equity shares, it must be done promptly, that is, within reasonable time of the applicant becoming aware of the fraud or misrepresentation giving them the right to rescind. Else, an adverse inference may be drawn that the applicant has affirmed the contract in terms of section 19 of the Indian Contract Act, 1872. Another reason is that the register of shareholders is generally the creditors' guarantee, showing them to whom and to what they have to trust. A shareholder knowing that he/she was induced by fraud or misrepresentation to subscribe to the shares cannot rest, let his/her name remain in the register, and let third parties enter into contracts with the company on the faith of the register.[46] Though the latter reason cannot be applied for rescission of sale of equity shares, or subscription of preference shares and debentures, the former reason will and the same rule will apply as the law disfavours an unreasonable delay in exercising a claim.

If rescission of the contract of subscription or sale of securities is by filing a suit, the same foregoing principles apply as delay in filing the suit may lead to an adverse conclusion that the plaintiff has ratified the contract.[47] However, because of an express provision in the Limitation Act, 1963 that the limitation period of suits for rescission is three years from the date when the applicant first had knowledge of the facts entitling him to rescind the contract, courts have treated the matter somewhat differently.[48] Thus, in *Calcutta Celluloid Works Limited v. Labanya Mohan Ghatak*,[49] the Calcutta High Court held that a delay of around 22 months did not prevent the allottee of shares from rescinding the

---

[46] *Shiromani Sugar Mills Limited v. Debi Prasad*, AIR 1950 All 508.

[47] *Pusarala Sanyasi v. The Guntur Cotton, Jute and Paper Mills Company Limited*, 26 Ind Cases 349 (1917).

[48] Clause (j) of section 2 and section 3 read with Article 59 of the Schedule to the Limitation Act, 1963.

[49] 47 CWN 421 (1942).

contract on account of fraudulent statement and misrepresentation in the prospectus.[50] The applicant may also lose the right to rescind the contract if winding up proceedings of the company are commenced. The reason for this is in such cases the company ceases to be a going concern and the shareholder becomes a contributory, who can then be compelled to pay the unpaid capital without any defence of rescission as that would prejudice the interests of the creditors of the company.[51]

As regards the consequences, upon rescission by an act of the applicant under the Indian Contract Act, 1872, the company need not perform the contract of subscription or sale of securities.[52] The contract becomes void *ab initio* and the company will have to return to the applicant the application money or any other benefit received from the applicant (or make compensation for it).[53] The applicant is further entitled to compensation for any damage which he has sustained through the non-fulfilment of the contract of subscription or sale of securities.[54] If rescission is adjudged under the Specific Relief Act, 1963, the court may require parties rescinding to do equity, meaning that 'the court proceeds on the principle that, as the transaction ought to have never taken place, the parties are to be placed, as far as possible, in the situation in which they would have stood if there had never been any such transaction'.[55]

---

[50] Sir Frederick Pollock too has taken this view. See Pollock (n. 1), at p. 36.

[51] *Hirji Khetsey v. The Indian Specie Bank Limited*, 1914 (17) BomLR 65 relying on the decision of the House of Lords in *Richard Oakes v. William Turquand*, (1867) LR 2 HL 325; *In Re: Jagannath Prasad*, AIR 1938 All 193; *Shiromani Sugar Mills Limited*, AIR 1950 All 508; *Chunnilal Onkarmal v. Vikram Sugar Mills Limited*, AIR 1959 MP 316; *Blanche Fonseca v. Jupiter Airways Limited*, AIR 1953 Bom 417; *Mansukhlal Dhanji Vora v. Jupiter Airways Limited*, AIR 1953 Bom 112.

[52] Section 64 of the Indian Contract Act, 1872.

[53] Section 65 of the Indian Contract Act, 1872.

[54] Section 75 of the Indian Contract Act, 1872.

[55] Satish Chandra Banerji, *The Law of Specific Relief in British India* (2nd edn, R. Cambray & Co. 1917), at p. 470. Section 30 of the Specific Relief Act, 1963 on 'Court may require parties rescinding to do equity' states the rule in the following manner: 'On adjudging the rescission of a contract, the court may require the party to whom such relief is granted to restore, so far as may be, any benefit which he may have received from the other party and to make any compensation to him which justice may require.'

In a case of a successful rescission of a contract that has been performed and discharged, the court should grant the same relief as above, which is restitution and compensation.

Constructive Trust

The company or the selling shareholder upon receiving notice from the applicant of rescission of the contract of subscription or sale of securities must hold the application money in trust for the benefit of the applicant. This constructive trust arises by virtue of section 86 of the Indian Trusts Act, 1882 and protects the applicant against the risk that the application money becomes part of the pool of assets of the company or the selling shareholder if they become insolvent prior to restitution upon rescission being completed.[56]

Summing Up the Section

In the past, rescission of the contract of subscription or sale of securities pursuant to the public offer was generally set up as a defence in a suit for specific performance of the contract by the company to obtain the called-up capital. Thus, in *Bansidhar Durgadatt v. The Tata Power Company Limited*,[57] the company filed a suit to recover the amount in respect of the called-up capital and the subscribers, by way of a counter claim, sought for a declaration that the contract of subscription of shares was not binding on them and ought to be rescinded. Rescission was pleaded on the ground that they had applied for the shares on the faith of

---

[56] *Official Receiver, Jhansi*, AIR 1963 All 459. Section 86 of the Indian Trusts Act, on 'Transfer Pursuant to Rescindable Contract' that falls under Chapter IX of the Act on 'Of Certain Obligations in the Nature of Trusts' states that 'Where property is transferred in pursuance of a contract which is liable to rescission or induced by fraud or mistake the transferee must, on receiving notice to that effect hold the property for the benefit of the transferor, subject to repayment by the latter of the consideration actually paid.'

[57] 1924 (23) BomLR 330. See also *Anandji Visram v. The Nariad Spinning and Weaving Company Limited*, (1877) ILR 1 Bom 320; *In Re: Jagannath Prasad*, AIR 1938 All 193; *Shiromani Sugar Mills Limited*, AIR 1950 All 508; *Pusarala Sanyasi*, 26 Ind Cases 349 (1917).

certain representations in the prospectus which representations turned out to be false. The Bombay High Court dismissed the counter claim of the defendants on the ground that they were not induced to apply for the shares by what was represented in the prospectus. Such suits are unlikely now given that nothing remains to be enforced against the applicants. On the other hand, suits by applicants to have the contracts rescinded and to restore advantage or obtain compensation from the company may be difficult given the conditions under which the court generally refuses to rescind the contract. In practice, this remedy may, therefore, not be very useful and an applicant wronged by fraudulent misstatement or misrepresentation is most likely to invoke statutory remedies under the Companies Act. We examine this remedy in the later part of this chapter.

Specific Performance of the Contract

So long as the contract of subscription or sale of securities remains unperformed, the company and the applicant can file a suit for performance of the obligations by the other party. This is called a suit for specific performance and the plaintiff will essentially ask the court to order the defendant to do the very act, which the defendant is under a contractual obligation to do. In all likelihood, these would be obligations of the company or the selling shareholder as per the application form and the prospectus, such as issue or transfer of securities at the agreed price, refund of excess application money, listing of the securities on the stock exchanges within the agreed time, and payment of interest or dividend and redemption. This suit for specific performance of the contract is part of a distinct branch of civil law called specific relief and is principally governed by the Specific Relief Act, 1963.[58]

Owing to historical reasons, the law of specific relief is fraught with several peculiarities.[59] First, it leans in favour of granting compensation

[58] Though the Specific Relief Act contains most of the specific reliefs that courts grant like specific performance, injunction, rescission, rectification, and declaration, a few specific reliefs can also be found under other statutes. For instance, the Transfer of Property Act, 1882 provides for the remedy of foreclosure and redemption of the mortgaged property in a mortgage contract.

[59] The Indian law on specific relief is entirely Anglo-Indian in origin. In England, the oldest form of actions at common law was for specific relief and

instead of specific performance. Second, directing specific performance is a matter of discretion for the court. Discretion does not mean that it is open to a court to do just what it pleases in an individual case.[60] It means that mere existence of a legal right is not sufficient to attract the remedy. In addition to the facts, events, and relations that give rise to the certain and absolute legal right, there may be other facts, circumstances, and incidents that modify the remedy, or, perhaps, entirely prevent its exercise.[61] For example, the plaintiff's own conduct may have been unconscionable. The Specific Relief Act, 1963 itself states the many principles that guide the court in the exercise of its discretion.[62]

Nevertheless, the general requirements for obtaining specific performance of the contract of subscription or sale of securities are as follows. First, the contract must be enforceable, for the defendant may plead by way of defence any ground which is available to them under

---

damages. In later days, the common law courts seemed to have confined their jurisdiction to actions for damages only, which made the common law too rigid. Though theoretically it was possible for the legislature to change the rules of the common law courts to enable them to do complete justice, it did not happen. Instead, a separate court of equity came into being under the aegis of the chancellor that would grant specific relief to people to prevent or stop unconscionable conduct. Two branches of the judiciary began to operate, namely the common law courts and courts of equity, and specific relief fell within the jurisdiction of the latter. Finally, through legislation in 1873 and 1875, both the courts were fused and both branches of English law began to be administered by the same courts. In India, this division in the administration of justice never existed. However, owing to the Anglo-Indian origin of our laws, rules and traditions of the courts of equity made their way into the law of specific relief, and the Specific Relief Act, 1877 came to be enacted. The Specific Relief Act, 1963 subsequently replaced this Act. See Banerji (n. 55), at p. 20; Edmund Snell, *The Principles of Equity* (Stevens & Haynes 1898), at p. 2; and Eva Micheler, *Property in Securities: A Comparative Study* (Cambridge University Press 2007), at pp. 26–7.

[60] Banerji (n. 55), at p. 31.

[61] Banerji (n. 55), at p. 32.

[62] See sections 16 and 20 of the Specific Relief Act, 1963.

the Indian Contract Act, 1872.[63] Second, specific performance can be had only 'when there exists no standard for ascertaining the actual damage caused by the non-performance of the act agreed to be done'; or 'when the act agreed to be done is such that compensation in money for its non-performance would not afford adequate relief'.[64] For obligations that are non-monetary in nature, such as issue or transfer of securities, or obtaining listing of securities on the stock exchange, it is quite likely that the latter condition would be satisfied owing to the unique nature of the transaction.[65] Third, specific performance of part of the contract is subject to some additional rules under section 12 of the Specific Relief Act, 1963. Once these are established, the court will exercise its discretion and may specifically enforce the obligations that remain unperformed under the contract of subscription or sale of securities.

Constructive Trust

An important implication of specific performance of a contract of sale of securities is that an obligation in the nature of trust is created, where a person acquires the securities with notice that another person has entered into an existing contract affecting the securities of which specific performance could be enforced. In this case, the former person is under a legal obligation to hold the securities for the benefit of the latter to the extent necessary to give effect to the contract.[66]

---

[63] Section 9 of the Specific Relief Act, 1963.

[64] Sections 10 and 14 of the Specific Relief Act, 1963.

[65] If specific performance is being sought for transfer of securities pursuant to an offer for sale, the court will not grant specific performance except where the securities are 'not an ordinary article of commerce, or [are] of special value or interest to the plaintiff, or consists of goods which are not easily obtainable in the market'. See Explanation (ii) to section 10 of the Specific Relief Act, 1963. Although the Specific Relief Act, 1963 lays down these rules for contract to transfer movable property (and hence in strict terms, these rules would not be applicable to a contract of subscription of securities), in principle, these rules should also be applicable to a contract of subscription of securities.

[66] Section 91 of the Indian Trusts Act, 1882.

Damages for Breach of Contract

In the early part of this chapter, we noted that the statements contained in a prospectus may be either representations that induce the supervening contract, or the terms itself of the supervening contract for subscription or sale of securities.[67] If the company or the selling shareholder breach the terms of the contract, the applicant investor has a right to claim contractual damages. Breach of contract is actionable per se and unlike damages for the tort of misstatement that we examine subsequently, the cause of action for breach of contract does not require any damage to have been suffered.[68] The rule for ascertaining damages is:

> when a contract has been broken, the party who suffers by such breach is entitled to receive from the party who has broken the contract, compensation for any loss or damage caused to him thereby, which naturally arose in the usual course of things from such breach, or which parties knew, when they made the contract, to be likely to result from the breach of it.[69]

This compensation is not recoverable 'for any remote and indirect loss or damage sustained by reason of the breach'.[70] In addition to these general principles, special provisions under the Sale of Goods Act, 1930 are also applicable in case of breach of a contract of sale of securities under an offer for sale. Though the provisions of the Sale of Goods Act, 1930 on breach of contract have largely been enacted keeping in view tangible goods, there is one rule that is relevant in the context of securities. Thus, in a suit for breach of a contract of sale of securities, the court may, if it thinks fit, on the application of the plaintiff investor, by its decree direct that the contract would be performed specifically, without giving the defendant the option of retaining the goods on payment of the damages.[71]

---

[67] See the section 'Civil liability' of this chapter.

[68] Adam Kramer, *The Law of Contract Damages* (Hart Publishing 2014), at p. 4.

[69] Section 73 of the Indian Contract Act, 1872.

[70] Section 73 of the Indian Contract Act, 1872.

[71] Section 58 of the Sale of Goods Act, 1930.

Damages for Tortious Misstatement

Under rescission, we examined the effect of fraud only so far as the consent of a party to a contract is procured by it. Fraud is also a tort, called deceit, if the investor suffers any damage. There is no obstacle in claiming the remedy of tort over the contractual remedy, though the investor cannot obtain compensation both under tort and contract. The law of tort or civil wrongs is, however, fraught with a peculiarity—it is Anglo-Indian in origin and remains uncodified. It is Anglo-Indian law meaning it is the common law of England as received in British India and applied, with suitable variations, as rules of justice, equity, and good conscience, in the first instance exclusively by the English courts of the presidency towns, and afterwards more generally.[72] So much of this law of tort as existing immediately before the commencement of the Constitution of India became part of Indian law and continues to remain in force.[73] After the commencement of the Constitution, the common law of England ceased to be in force in India.[74] This prelude will serve in understanding the scope of the law of damages for tortious misstatement since the English common law on fraud or deceit was developed much prior to the commencement of the Constitution and applied by the courts of British India. However, the English common law on liability for negligent or careless misstatement causing financial loss developed only in the year 1963.

Deceit

The decision of the House of Lords in July 1889 in *William Derry and Ors v. Sir Henry William Peek*[75] (commonly referred as *Derry v. Peek*) set the boundaries of the tort of deceit, which has since then been accepted

---

[72] Pollock (n. 1), at p. 12; M.C. Setalvad, *The Common Law in India* (Stevens & Sons Limited 1960), at p. 110.

[73] Article 372 of the Constitution of India.

[74] See the case of *Superintendent and Legal Remembrancer, State of West Bengal v. Corporation of Calcutta*, AIR 1967 SC 997. However, Indian courts continue to rely heavily on the English common law of tort to develop the Indian law of tort.

[75] (1889) 14 App Cas 337.

and applied as a civil wrong by the courts in India.[76] In this case, a special legislation incorporating a tramway company provided that the carriages might be moved by animal power, and, with the consent of the concerned authority, by steam power. The directors of the tramway company issued a prospectus containing a statement that by the special legislation, the company had the right to use steam power instead of horses. The plaintiff took shares on the faith of this statement. The concerned authority afterwards refused their consent to the use of steam power and the company was wound up. The plaintiff then brought an action of deceit against the directors. The trial judge dismissed the action on the ground that the directors honestly believed in the truth of the statement.

The Court of Appeal reversed the decision of the trial judge. It held that it is deceit if someone makes a representation, though believing it to be true, with the view of it being acted upon if he did not have reasonable grounds for his belief. The House of Lords rejected the formulation of the Court of Appeal. It held:

> First, in order to sustain an action of deceit, there must be proof of fraud, and nothing short of that will suffice. Secondly, fraud is proved when it is shown that a false representation has been made (1) knowingly, or (2) without belief in its truth, or (3) recklessly, [without caring] whether it be true or false.... Thirdly, if fraud be proved, the motive of the person guilty of it is immaterial.[77]

The absence of reasonable grounds for the defendant's belief and his carelessness in making the statement are evidence, but not necessarily conclusive evidence, of the absence of any real belief of the truth of the statement and the consequent presence of fraud.[78] *Derry v. Peek* thus

---

[76] See *Abdullah Khan v. Abdur Rahman Beg*, (1896) ILR 18 All 322; *United Motor Finance Co. v. Romer Dan and Company*, AIR 1937 Mad 897; *United Motor Finance Company v. Addison and Company Limited*, 1937 (39) BomLR 706; *Trojan & Co. Limited v. N.N. Nagappa Chettiar*, AIR 1953 SC 235; *Hariprasad Jaiswal v. Union of India*, AIR 1959 MP 389; *S. Chatterjee v. Dr. K.L. Bhave and Ors*, AIR 1960 MP 323; *Al Mustaneer Establishment for Trade v. Varuna Overseas Private Limited*, 72 (1998) DLT 186.

[77] *Derry v. Peek*, (1889) 14 App Cas 337, at p. 374.

[78] *Derry v. Peek*, (1889) 14 App Cas 337, at p. 369. See also Sir Nathaniel Lindley, *Supplement to a Treatise on the Law of Companies* (Sweet & Maxwell Limited 1891), at pp. 1–2.

laid down the essence of an action for deceit, though did not exhaustively deal with all its ingredients.[79]

From *Derry v. Peek*, the ingredients of the tort of deceit have been shaped by subsequent judgments, and are as follows:

1. there must be a representation of fact. The phrase will include a case where the defendant has manifestly approved and adopted a representation made by some third person;
2. the representation is false;
3. the representation was made with the requisite knowledge of its falsehood;
4. the representation was made with the intention that it should be acted upon by the plaintiff, or by a class of persons which will include the plaintiff. This must be distinguished from motive or intention to cheat. The motive of the defendant or the fact that he had no intention to cheat or injure the person to whom the statement was made is immaterial; and
5. the plaintiff has acted upon the false representation and has sustained damage by so doing.[80]

The law on statement of fact as distinguished from statement of future conduct and intention, statement of belief or opinion, and statement of law, as discussed earlier under rescission, is equally applicable to the first two ingredients of the tort of deceit. Under the general law of tort of deceit, a mere omission to state a material fact is not fraud.[81] But given the obligations on statements in a prospectus that we examined in the previous chapters, this general rule may not be applicable in the securities law context. There is clear authority for the proposition that statements are deemed to be false if they are misleading in the form and context in which they are included, which means that if an omission presents a misleading picture, it will constitute a false statement.[82]

[79] Peter Macdonald Eggers, *Deceit The Lie of the Law* (Informa 2009), at p. 19.

[80] *Bradford Third Equitable Benefit Building Society v. Borders*, [1941] 2 All ER 205, 211; *United Motor Finance Company*.

[81] *Sorabshah Pestonji v. The Secretary of State for India*, AIR 1928 Bom 17.

[82] *S. Chatterjee v. Dr. KL Bhave and Ors*, AIR 1960 MP 323.

The above proposition can be illustrated by the decision of the high court of Madhya Pradesh in *S. Chatterjee v. Dr. K.L. Bhave and Ors.*[83] Here the directors and an agent of National Nutriments Limited published a booklet containing testimonials from eminent persons, statements regarding dividends and other matters conveying an impression to the reader that the company was in a very flourishing and prosperous condition. Armed with the booklet, the agent set out to sell to the public the shares of the company and met the plaintiffs. The agent made several promising statements about the affairs of the company and relied on the booklet to substantiate them. The plaintiffs, believing the statements to be true, were induced into purchasing the shares. Subsequently, the plaintiffs discovered that the statements of the agent and those contained in the booklet were false to the knowledge of the agent and the directors of the company. The plaintiffs, therefore, filed a suit against the directors and the agent for refund of the original amount along with interest and costs. The trial court decreed the suit in favour of the plaintiffs holding that deceit had been proved and the plaintiffs were entitled to receive by way of damages the original amount along with interest at six per cent per annum. On appeal, the high court of Madhya Pradesh noticed that the suit was not for rescission of the contract but for the tort of deceit.[84] Upon examining the booklet, the high court found that it might be possible to demonstrate that every particular statement in the booklet was factually true, but it certainly gave a very misleading picture of the financial condition of the company. The high court held that a particular statement may be verbally accurate but in effect might be a false statement. If by a number of statements one intentionally gives a false impression and induces a person to act upon it, it is not the less false, although if one takes each statement by itself there may be a difficulty in showing that any specific statement is untrue.[85]

An action of deceit will lie against persons who made the false representation with the requisite knowledge of falsehood with the intention that it should be acted upon by the plaintiff. In the case of false statements in a prospectus, provided the fraudulent state of mind can be

[83] *S. Chatterjee* case, AIR 1960 MP 323.

[84] *S. Chatterjee* case, AIR 1960 MP 323, at p. 329.

[85] *S. Chatterjee* case, AIR 1960 MP 323, at p. 327.

proved, this will certainly make the company and the directors of the company liable: these persons approve and adopt every statement made in a prospectus including that of the expert and the selling shareholder, and vouch for the accuracy of the statements in the prospectus. If the false statement is attributable to the expert and the selling shareholder, they too shall be liable, provided the other ingredients are satisfied. The selling shareholder's liability for the deceit committed by the company through the prospectus issued in an offer for sale will be determined as per rules of agency and vicarious liability. Of course, if the selling shareholder himself, with fraudulent intention, authorized the company to make the false statement, the selling shareholder will be primarily liable for the tort of deceit. Other than these persons, it may be difficult to proceed against other persons such as the promoter unless those persons assumed responsibility for the statements in the prospectus.

The person who can institute the action will be the applicant who participated in the public issue and acted upon the false statement, thereby subscribing or purchasing the securities. Here the common law rule in *William Peek v. J.H. Gurney and Ors*[86] must be noted. This case held that prospectus liability for deceit does not follow the shares on their transfer from the allottee to the vendee. Thus an investor who had purchased the shares in the secondary market on the faith of the prospectus did not have a right of action in deceit since the prospectus was only intended to induce subscriptions of shares from the company and not subsequent purchases in the secondary market. In order to maintain an action, the subsequent purchaser must show some direct connection between himself and the defendants in the communication of the prospectus and its influence upon his conduct in becoming a purchaser of the shares.

Once deceit is proved, the remedy consists principally of compensatory damages in respect of the loss sustained by the claimant by reason of the deceit. The measure of damages will be as per the general rule of compensatory damages under tort law—the claimant is entitled to an award which would put him or her in the same position which he/she would have been had the tort not been committed.[87] The application of this rule

---

[86] (1873) LR 6 HL 377.
[87] Peter Macdonald Eggers (n. 79), at p. 197.

to fraudulent subscription or purchase of securities can create challenges. The courts have, therefore, provided some guidance on the measure of damages in such cases like the *S. Chatterjee v. Dr. K.L. Bhave and Ors* case.

In this case, the high court of Madhya Pradesh held that ordinarily the measure of damages is the difference between the price paid by the plaintiffs and the actual market value of the securities purchased by them. This approach may not be feasible because there can be no market value of the same security minus the defect; market value if any would itself be the result of the fraudulent misrepresentation complained of. The court must, therefore, determine the intrinsic value of the securities. But then again, determination of the intrinsic value is only possible by an appraisal of the company's assets by an independent audit, which in most cases would entail prohibitory costs, and in any case, would only be speculative as regards their value on the date when the transaction occurred or when the fraud was discovered. On the issue of time in relation to which the loss should be measured, the court, in *S. Chatterjee*, gave a conclusive view. It held that the plaintiffs who admittedly had bought the shares for investment are not expected to dispose of them before they actually discover the fraud. If any independent forces operated in the intermediate period, the loss must yet fall on the wrongdoer.[88] Applying the law to the facts, the court held that the company had stopped paying dividends and mortgaged its assets for a paltry sum of Rs 15,000 when the plaintiffs purchased the shares. The company's condition had become much worse when the fraud was discovered, and when the plaintiffs filed the suit, the company had already gone into liquidation. It was thus apparent that the shares were worthless from the time they were fraudulently sold to the plaintiffs because of the inherent defect in the project itself. The measure of damages would, therefore, be the price the plaintiffs were induced to give for such worthless shares by the fraud of the defendants.[89] The court thus dismissed the appeal of the defendants.

Negligent Misrepresentation

The effect of *Derry v. Peek* was that tort law imposed liability only if there was fraud; no liability ensued for negligent or careless statements,

---

[88] *S. Chatterjee* case, AIR 1960 MP 323, at p. 330.
[89] *S. Chatterjee* case, AIR 1960 MP 323, at p. 330.

which had caused the plaintiff to suffer financial loss.[90] This changed at least in the English law of tort with the decision of the House of Lords in May 1963 in *Hedley Byrne & Co. Ltd. v. Heller & Partners Limited*.[91] In this case, the plaintiff was an advertising agent and had provided a substantial amount of advertising on credit for a third party. If this third party failed to pay, the plaintiff would have been responsible for the credit. The plaintiff was concerned that the third party would not be in a financial position to pay the debt and sought assurances, through its own bank, from the third party's bank (the defendant) that that party was in a position to pay for the credit. The defendant gave a favourable report of the third party's financial position, but stipulated that the report was given without responsibility. On the strength of the report given by the respondent, the plaintiff placed additional orders on behalf of the third party, which eventually resulted in a loss. The plaintiff then brought an action against the respondent for damages under the tort of negligence. The House of Lords held that a negligent, although honest, misrepresentation, might give rise to an action for damages for financial loss even if there was no contract between the advisor and the advisee and no fiduciary relationship. The law will imply a duty of care when the advisee seeks information from an adviser who has special skill and where the advisee trusts the adviser to exercise due care, and that the adviser knew or ought to have known that his skill and judgement was being relied upon. However, in the present case,[92] there was an express disclaimer of responsibility and there was, therefore, no liability. This case established the tort of negligent misrepresentation.

There are, however, difficulties in applying this tort to representations made to induce subscription or purchase of securities in public issues. Under the English common law, there is considerable doubt whether such

---

[90] However, in cases where there was a fiduciary relationship between the parties, the law of tort did impose liability for negligent or careless misstatements on which the claimant relied and suffered damage. See *Nocton v. Lord Ashburton*, [1914] AC 932. This rule is not relevant in the present context as no fiduciary relationship is stated to exist between the company or the selling shareholder and the applicants for the securities.

[91] [1964] AC 465.

[92] [1964] AC 465.

a duty of care exists in respect of prospectuses.[93] Even otherwise, this tort of negligent misrepresentation originated and became part of English common law in May 1963, which is after the commencement of the Constitution of India. This tort, therefore, despite being part of English common law, is not the law in force in India and will not be so until an Indian court recognizes it as a substantive ground for action in tort.

Summing Up the Section

The law of civil wrongs, being uncodified, relies heavily on tort litigation for its development. At least in England, this branch of law has engaged itself with the changing times. In *Possfund Custodian Trustee Limited and Anr v. Diamond and Ors*,[94] the court of Chancery Division recognized that persons responsible for the issue of a modern prospectus could owe a duty of care to purchasers of securities in the secondary market. To establish this duty of care, the plaintiff must prove either express communication to him of the intention of the defendant to assume such a duty or that the plaintiff reasonably relied on the material representation and believed that the representor intended him to act upon it.[95] In India, however, tortious liability for misstatement continues to be the English common law as on the date of the commencement of the Constitution of India.

Compensation under the Companies Act for Misstatements in a Prospectus

The *Derry v. Peek* decision discussed earlier, though based on sound principles, did not sufficiently address investor protection concerns in the public issue of corporate securities. As could be understood from this case, nothing short of fraud would make the persons issuing a prospectus liable. The British Parliament, therefore, immediately responded by enacting the Directors' Liability Act, 1890. The main object of this

[93] See Robert R. Pennington, *Company Law* (Oxford University Press 2001), at p. 328.
[94] [1996] 1 WLR 1351.
[95] [1996] 1 WLR 1351, at p. 1364.

enactment was to provide a statutory remedy for misstatement in the prospectus by codifying the English common law on deceit with variations as to burden of proof. It did so by relieving the plaintiff of the onus of proving fraud in the first instance, and allowed the defendant to raise a defence that he had reasonable grounds to believe that the statement was true.[96] The provisions of this Act on civil liability found their way into the then Anglo-Indian company law. Section 100 of the Indian Companies Act, 1913 on 'Liability for Statements in Prospectus' provided, to the extent it is relevant, that:

(1) Where a prospectus invites persons to subscribe for shares in or debentures of a company every person who is…shall be liable to pay compensation to all persons who subscribe for any shares or debentures on the faith of the prospectus for all loss or damage they may have sustained by reason of any misleading or untrue statement therein…unless it is proved –

(a) …that he had reasonable ground to believe and did up to the time of the allotment of the shares or debentures, as the case may be, believe that the statement fairly represented the facts or was true;

Despite repeal of the Indian Companies Act, 1913 and enactment of the Companies Act, 1956, the conceptual basis of this statutory liability remained the same. Section 62 of the Companies Act, 1956 on 'Civil Liability for Mis-statements in Prospectus' provided, to the extent it is relevant, that:

(1) Subject to the provisions of this section, where a prospectus invites persons to subscribe for shares in or debentures of a company, the following persons shall be liable to pay compensation to every person who subscribes for any shares or debentures on the faith of the prospectus for any loss or damage he may have sustained by reason of any untrue statement included therein, that is to say, –

(a) every person…
(2) No person shall be liable under sub-section (1), if he proves –
…
(d) that –

[96] George Spencer Bower, *The Law of Actionable Misrepresentation* (Butterworths & Co. 1911), at p. 307.

(i) ...he had reasonable ground to believe, and did up to the time of the allotment of the shares or debentures, as the case may be, believe, that the statement was true;

This statutory civil liability for misstatements in a prospectus is now purportedly contained in section 35 of the Companies Act. This provision on 'Civil Liability for Misstatements in Prospectus' states:[97]

(1) Where a person has subscribed for securities of a company acting on any statement included, or the inclusion or omission of any matter, in the prospectus which is misleading and has sustained any loss or damage as a consequence thereof, the company and every person who—

    (a) is a director of the company at the time of the issue of the prospectus;

    (b) has authorised himself to be named and is named in the prospectus as a director of the company, or has agreed to become such director, either immediately or after an interval of time;

    (c) is a promoter of the company;

    (d) has authorised the issue of the prospectus; and

    (e) is an expert referred to in sub-section (5) of section 26,

shall, without prejudice to any punishment to which any person may be liable under section 36, be liable to pay compensation to every person who has sustained such loss or damage.

(2) No person shall be liable under sub-section (1), if he proves—

    (a) that, having consented to become a director of the company, he withdrew his consent before the issue of the prospectus, and that it was issued without his authority or consent; or

    (b) that the prospectus was issued without his knowledge or consent, and that on becoming aware of its issue, he forthwith gave a reasonable public notice that it was issued without his knowledge or consent.

(3) Notwithstanding anything contained in this section, where it is proved that a prospectus has been issued with intent to defraud the

---

[97] Companies (Amendment) Bill, 2016, introduced in the lower house of the Parliament on 16 March 2016, has proposed insertion of a new clause (c) after clause (b) of sub-section (2) of section 35 of the Companies Act. This new clause seeks to provide an additional defence to the defendants. We analyse this proposed amendment in the later part of this section.

applicants for the securities of a company or any other person or for any fraudulent purpose, every person referred to in sub-section (1) shall be personally responsible, without any limitation of liability, for all or any of the losses or damages that may have been incurred by any person who subscribed to the securities on the basis of such prospectus.

Before we examine the constituent elements of this section, we must note at the very outset that the conceptual basis of this section has changed. Now there are two separate types of liabilities—one described under sub-sections (1) and (2), and the other under sub-section (3). Under sub-sections (1) and (2), the conceptual basis has changed from a fault-based liability to a liability without fault, or strict liability. The earlier defence that the defendant had 'reasonable ground to believe, and did up to the time of the allotment of the shares or debentures, as the case may be, believe, that the statement was true'[98] is no longer available. This defence is now only available to escape criminal liability under section 34 of the Companies Act. Thus a misstatement in the prospectus need not be fraudulent (or even negligent); it is actionable per se if the plaintiff has acted on the misstatement, subscribed for the securities, and sustained any loss or damage. For few of the defendants, the only defence, as we examine later in detail, is that the defendant is not responsible for the misstatement, and hence did not make the misstatement. It is unclear what precipitated this change from a fault-based liability to strict liability, as strict liability is reserved for cases where the defendant undertakes hazardous activities.[99] Even in such cases, courts are generally reluctant to apply the rule of strict liability and have carved several exceptions to the rule.[100]

Given the foregoing, we first examine the strict liability under sub-sections (1) and (2), and the fault-based liability under sub-section (3) of section 35.

---

[98] See sub-clause (i) of clause (d) of sub-section (2), and clause (c) of sub-section (3) of section 62 of the Companies Act, 1956.

[99] See *Jay Laxmi Salt Works (P) Limited v. State of Gujarat*, (1994) 4 SCC 1. See generally, Ken Oliphant, 'The Nature of Tortious Liability' Andrew Grubb (ed), *The Law of Tort* (LexisNexis 2007), at p. 27.

[100] See *State of Punjab v. Modern Cultivators, Ladwa*, AIR 1965 SC 17.

Misstatements

Sub-section (1) of section 35 imposes civil liability for misstatements in a prospectus. Civil liability under the tort of deceit pertains to representations—a well understood legal term, but here, the reference is to statements. This difference is more a semantic one and not a conceptual one. What constitutes misstatement has, however, not been defined adequately and with precision. Nonetheless, it is a misstatement if any statement or any matter included in the prospectus is misleading, or omission of any matter from the prospectus is misleading.[101] It is not clear whether a plain false statement would amount to misstatement because a false statement may not be a misleading statement. It would, however, be absurd to exclude those statements from the scope of section 35. Apart from the obvious absurdity of such a construction, it must be noted that section 34 imposes criminal liability for untrue or false statements in a prospectus.

As to what constitutes a misleading statement, reference can be made to the earlier discussion under the tort of deceit with two qualifications. First, misleading statement does not mean that there must be an intention to mislead or deceive or commit fraud. The history of civil liability for misstatement in a prospectus under the company statute supports this interpretation. The burden on the claimant will be simply to plead the meaning of the statements on which he/she claims to have relied— the meaning which has now been found to be false due to hidden meanings, half-truths, etc. Second, the general distinction under the tort of deceit between a statement of fact on the one hand, and a statement of future conduct and intention, statement of belief or opinion, and statement of law may not be applicable for civil liability under sub-section (1) of section 35 as its plain interpretation does not warrant such a distinction. Perhaps, this is an expression of the legislative intent that in prospectuses all such statements would inevitably constitute statements of fact. Neither will it be relevant that the misstatement was not material, though, as we shall see later, materiality of the misstatement would become relevant for proving loss or damage.

---

[101] Sub-section (1) of section 35 of the Companies Act.

Persons Entitled to be Compensated

For compensation under sub-section (1) of section 35, a person must prove that he/she:

1. subscribed for securities of a company;
2. did so by acting on any misstatement in the prospectus; and
3. as a consequence thereof, has sustained any loss or damage.

These requirements are largely a codification of the ingredients of the tort of deceit relating to reliance and causation. In the first requirement, 'subscribed' indicates that only persons who have in fact subscribed for securities directly from the company under the prospectus are eligible for relief.[102] Due to the statutory fiction that sections 25 and 28 of the Companies Act create, purchasers of securities in terms of those sections too, can maintain a claim.[103] No other person would be entitled to compensation including those who may have purchased securities in the secondary market. The second requirement embodies the concept of reliance. The claimant must prove misstatement in the prospectus, and the fact that he acted on the misstatement to subscribe for securities. Lastly, the claimant must prove loss or damage and a causal nexus between that loss or damage and a reliance on the misstatement.[104] It is quite possible that courts will introduce the concept of materiality under reliance or causation as it is unlikely that a person who has used the prospectus to base his investment decision would have relied on immaterial statements to subscribe for the securities. Similarly, it may be difficult to prove loss or damage due to immaterial statements, which turned out to be untrue or misleading. The test of materiality will be those considerations that are likely to materially affect the mind of a reasonable investor.

---

[102] *Kimsuk Krishna Sinha v. Securities and Exchange Board of India*, [2010] 155 Comp Cas 295 (Del).

[103] This is due to the statutory provisions themselves. See the section 'Proponents of Public Offer and Offer for Sale' in Chapter 3 of this volume.

[104] *Bhupinder Kaur Singh v. Registrar of Companies*, [2010] 159 Comp Cas 92 (Del).

Persons Liable to Compensate

The liability to compensate the claimant lies with the company and persons belonging to five classes. There is a burden on the claimant to prove that the defendant belongs to any of these classes. The first class represents every person who is 'a director of the company at the time of the issue of the prospectus'.[105] This is an easily identifiable class and the prospectus contains the details of directors appointed to the board of directors of the company at the time of issue of the prospectus.

In the second class is every person who has 'authorised himself to be named and is named in the prospectus as a director of the company, or has agreed to become such director, either immediately or after an interval of time'.[106] In the former part of this class would fall persons who make the offer of securities for sale to the public in terms of section 25 of the Companies Act, and in the latter part of the class would fall persons agreeing to become directors of an intended company that would be formed subsequent to the public offering of securities. This class is a remnant of the Directors' Liability Act, 1890 and has little utility now, for, as we examined in Chapter 3, in practice the likelihood of public offerings in relation to an intended company is remote.[107]

The third class consists of every person who 'is a promoter of the company'.[108] Companies Act defines a 'promoter' to mean a person: '(a) who has been named as such in a prospectus or is identified by the company in the annual return referred to in section 92 [of the Companies Act]; or (b) who has control over the affairs of the company, directly or indirectly whether as a shareholder, director, or otherwise; or (c) in accordance with whose advice, directions or instructions the Board of Directors of the company is accustomed to act'.[109] The last category, (c), does not apply to a person who is acting merely in a professional capacity.[110]

There are considerable flaws in section 35 of the Companies Act with respect to liability of 'a promoter of the company' both from a definitional

---

[105] Clause (a) of sub-section (1) of section 35 of the Companies Act.
[106] Clause (b) of sub-section (1) of section 35 of the Companies Act.
[107] Sub-section (1) of section 3 of the Directors' Liability Act, 1890.
[108] Clause (c) of sub-section (1) of section 35 of the Companies Act.
[109] Clause (69) of section 2 of the Companies Act.
[110] Clause (69) of section 2 of the Companies Act.

and conceptual perspective. On definition, company law for the first time has a legislative definition of promoter. But this definition does not take into account persons who are promoters prior to the formation of the company. Recall the discussion on promoters in Chapter 3 where we observed that the expression has been defined judicially and that it means a person 'who undertakes to form a company with reference to a given project and to set it going, and who takes the necessary steps to accomplish this purpose'.[111] Thus in a case where the prospectus is issued prior to the formation of the company, a person who is otherwise a promoter as per the judicial definition may not qualify to be a promoter as per the legislative definition unless the person voluntarily names himself as the promoter in the prospectus.[112] This is not a minor anomaly as the Companies Act now imposes statutory liability on persons including the promoter for other wrongful acts prior to the incorporation of the company.[113] As regards persons who will qualify to be promoters after the formation of the company, the definition is too wide and is unsuited for prospectus liability. Under the company law which is based on a division of ownership and management, there is no reason why a controlling shareholder (who will now qualify to be a promoter) should be saddled with liability and that too, with the same level of liability as directors who have the real control over and responsibility for the preparation and issue of a prospectus. Clearly a person by virtue of being merely a controlling shareholder has no role in the preparation and issue of a prospectus.

This brings us to the conceptual flaws in section 35 of the Companies Act on promoters' liability. In the past, there was strong justification for imposing statutory liability on promoters for they were engaged in the

[111] See the section 'Proponents of Public Offer and Offer for Sale' in Chapter 3 of this volume. See also *D.R. Patel v. A.S. Dimellow*, AIR 1961 MP 4; and *Probir Kumar Mishra v. Ramani Ramaswamy*, [2010] 154 Comp Cas 658 (Mad).

[112] If the prospectus is for the issue of equity shares, such a situation may not arise because the judicial definition of promoter is contained in the definition of promoter under regulation 2(1)(za) of the Securities and Exchange Board of India (Issue of Capital and Disclosure Requirements) Regulations, 2009 (or the ICDR Regulations).

[113] See sub-section (6) of section 7 of the Companies Act.

formation of the company and authorized the issue of the prospectus of the intended company. Also, as discussed in the preceding section, the tort of deceit was unsuited to redress the wrongs of prospectus mis-statement. But even then, the statute did not impose liability on every promoter, but only on the 'promoter who was a party to the preparation of the prospectus or of the portion thereof containing the untrue statement.'[114] As examined in Chapter 3, the common practice is for companies to issue the prospectus subsequent to their formation and not for the promoters prior to their formation.[115] After a company is formed and commences its business and operations, promoters are generally the principal shareholders of the company, and thus are not engaged in the management of the company. In cases where they happen to be a director on the board of the company, the statutory liability arises by virtue of their role as the director who is involved in the management of the company and authorizes the issue of the prospectus. Therefore, though the basis for imposing statutory liability to pay compensation for misstatements in a prospectus has weakened, the legislature has acted in the reverse direction. Even though the promoter does not authorize the issue of a prospectus and may not be a party to the preparation of the prospectus, he is saddled with potential civil liability. Given that the basis of liability under section 35 of the Companies Act is tortious liability, this goes against the fundamental principles of liability in tort law. In tort law, no one can be held liable for a wrong unless the wrong is caused by their own act or the act of another person for which they are responsible. Clearly, a promoter is not vicariously liable for the acts of the company, the directors, and others who authorize the issue of the prospectus, for such persons are not the employees or partners or agents of the promoter.

There is also an element of arbitrariness in clause (c) of sub-section (1) of section 35 of the Companies Act. Unlike the first class where liability is imposed on directors of the company 'at the time of issue of

---

[114] See clause (a) of sub-section (6) of section 62 of the Companies Act, 1956, and clause (a) of sub-section (5) of section 100 of the Indian Companies Act, 1913.

[115] See the section 'Proponents of Public Offer and Offer for Sale' in Chapter 3 of the volume.

the prospectus', the legislature has not narrowed down the class of pro-moters to a reasonable class of persons on whom to impose liability. This arbitrariness did not arise in the Companies Act, 1956, as it defined a promoter to mean 'a promoter who was party to the preparation of the prospectus or of the portion thereof containing the untrue statement'.[116] The open-ended nature of clause (c) of sub-section (1) of section 35 of the Companies Act will, therefore, cause uncertainty about which promoters can become liable to pay compensation, for there can be dif-ferent promoters at different crucial stages—at the stage of formation of the company, preparation and registration of the prospectus, issue of the prospectus, and finally at the stage of institution of a claim for compen-sation under section 35 of the Companies Act.

The fourth class consists of experts referred to in sub-section (5) of section 26 of the Companies Act, that is, experts who have given their written consent to the issue of the prospectus and have not with-drawn such consent before the delivery of a copy of the prospectus to the registrar of companies for registration. Though experts as a class were potential defendants under the Companies Act, 1956 also, the Companies Act, 2013 has substantially increased their extent of liabil-ity. Under the Companies Act, 1956, the liability of the expert was only 'in respect of an untrue statement, if any, purporting to be made by him as an expert'.[117] Evidently, this is not the case now, and liability of the expert is for misstatements in the entire prospectus—coterminous with that of the directors—even though an expert has no control over state-ments in the prospectus that are not part of the expert's report. This is once again contrary to the fundamental principles of liability stated earlier and is purportedly an arbitrary provision as it treats unequals equally.

Lastly, the fifth class consists of every person who 'has authorised the issue of the prospectus'.[118] This class is most suited for civil liability because they make the statements and must be held responsible for the misstatements. The Indian Companies Act, 1913 and Companies Act, 1956 imposed civil liability for misstatements, subject to necessary

---

[116] Clause (a) of sub-section (6) of section 62 of the Companies Act, 1956.

[117] Proviso to sub-section (1) of section 62 of the Companies Act, 1956.

[118] Clause (d) of sub-section (1) of section 35 of the Companies Act.

qualifications, on directors, promoters, and experts expressly because there was a statutory presumption that they authorized the issue of the prospectus. The plaintiff was, therefore, not required to prove that they in fact authorized the issue of the prospectus. Though sound in principle, determining the defendants falling in this class is a challenge due to the indeterminacy of this clause. In the past, this was not so since inviting offers from the public for subscription through issue of a prospectus was less complex. Fewer people were responsible for preparing and issuing the prospectus with very few legal compliances. The preceding chapters make it clear that this is not the case today. This phrase is, therefore, bound to create confusion, and this is compounded by the fact that unlike the Companies Act, 1956, the Companies Act, 2013 provides no guidance on who may or may not fall within this residual category.[119] The indeterminacy will also cause hardship because, as we see later, the only statutory plea applicable to this class is in reality futile because there is a contradiction in saying that the defendant 'has authorized the issue of the prospectus' but the 'prospectus was issued without his knowledge or consent'.

To begin with, 'authorised' has a range of possible meanings starting with 'to give legal authority or to empower' to something as simple as 'formally approve or to sanction'.[120] This meaning casts the net too wide and imposes civil liability for compensation on innocent persons such as regulatory authorities who approve and register the prospectus thereby permitting its issuance, and shareholders of the company who decide on

---

[119] Section 62 of the Companies Act, 1956, on 'Civil Liability for Misstatements in Prospectus' clarified that where 'the consent of a person named in a prospectus such as auditor, legal adviser, attorney and broker of the company is required and he has given that consent, he shall not, by reason of having given such consent, be liable under this sub-section as a person who has authorised the issue of the prospectus except in respect of an untrue statement, if any, purporting to be made by him as an expert'. An exception to this rule was the liability of a person named as an expert in the prospectus and which expert had given his consent to the issue of the prospectus. The expert was liable as a person who has authorized the issue of the prospectus, but only in respect of misstatement, if any, purporting to be made by him as an expert.

[120] Bryan A. Garner (ed.), *Black's Law Dictionary* (9th edn, West 2009), at p. 153.

further issue of shares and authorize the board of directors to prepare and issue the prospectus. It could also cover legal advisors because without their positive opinion, the company does not issue the prospectus. These are difficult enquiries and much will depend on the facts of the particular case.

Nonetheless, in addition to the persons expressly mentioned in section 35 of the Companies Act that we discussed earlier, persons belonging to two classes may be said to have authorized the issue of the prospectus. These are selling shareholders and merchant bankers. The Companies Act impliedly prohibits a selling shareholder from using any document to invite offers from the public for purchase of his shares without the document being a prospectus in compliance with the Act. The company issues this prospectus in relation to the offer for sale of shares and the selling shareholder authorizes the company to take all actions in respect of the offer for sale.[121] Even otherwise, in the absence of a statutory requirement of the company issuing the prospectus, the selling shareholder would have to issue the document inviting offers from the public and would be liable for misstatements under the tort of deceit. In fact, in an offer for sale of shares, selling shareholders confirm the accuracy of the statements and assume responsibility for them, though practice varies on the extent of responsibility. It is, therefore, reasonable for selling shareholders to fall under the ambit of section 35 since this provision is essentially a codification of the tort of deceit.

Conceptually, it is difficult to call a merchant banker a person who has authorized the issue of the prospectus. They are intermediaries providing services and are not party to the contract of subscription or sale of securities, and hence have no authority to issue the prospectus to induce this contract. This approach, however, oversimplifies the method of public issue of corporate securities in the present times. The preceding chapters have indicated that merchant bankers exercise significant power and control in the preparation and issue of the prospectus. In the absence of their due diligence certificates to the Securities and Exchange Board of India (SEBI) and other activities at

---

[121] Sub-section (3) of section 28 of the Companies Act. See the section 'Proponents of Public Offer and Offer for Sale' in Chapter 3 of this volume, and the section 'Civil Liability' of this chapter.

several stages of the public issue programme, it is not possible for the company to issue the prospectus.

A decision of the Supreme Court of New South Wales, Australia in *NRMA Limited v. Morgan*[122] is relevant here. The court was put to interpret sub-section (1) of section 996 of the [Australian] Corporations Act, 1989, which, insofar that it is relevant, stated: 'A person must not authorise or cause the issue of a prospectus in relation to securities of a corporation if…either: (i) material statement in the prospectus is false or misleading; or (ii) there is a material omission from the prospectus.' Interpreting the expression 'authorise or cause the issue of a prospectus', the court held:

> [T]hose words postulate a specific event, the issue of a prospectus. The event will normally follow a conscious and relatively formal decision that the prospectus should issue. The statement of the alternatives 'authorise' and 'cause' gives colour to what each means, causation being a more direct connection with the happening of the event and authorisation being less direct, but the authorisation in my view must still be part of the decision-making process. The directors of the relevant company no doubt authorise (and cause) the issue of a prospectus, because they make the decision but an adviser whose advice is taken into account by the decision-makers is not relevantly part of the decision-making process. His advice may affect the decision, but the decision is not his, and that remains the case even if, had the adviser given advice which if accepted would have meant a negative decision, the adviser did not so advise. Conceivably someone such as an underwriter may be regarded as part of the decision-making process, because he is able to impose his will on the issuer to ensure the accuracy of disclosure, but someone such as a solicitor will normally not have that control or even be concerned with the content of much of the prospectus. Unless there are unusual circumstances, a solicitor acting as adviser will not authorise the issue of the prospectus.[123]

Undoubtedly, a merchant banker does not merely advise the company, but is able to 'impose his will on the issuer to ensure accuracy of disclosure'.

---

122   [1999] NSWSC 407.
123   *NRMA Limited v Morgan*, [1999] NSWSC 407, at paragraphs 1472–3.

Defences

On defence, section 35 of the Companies Act, 2013, departs significantly from section 62, the corresponding provision, of the Companies Act, 1956, and tortious liability on deceit. Once the claimant has proved that the defendant is any of the above persons, he/she need not prove that the defendant made the misstatement. Neither is this a defence to the civil liability. Thus an expert like an auditor cannot take the defence that the misstatement does not form part of the statements contained in the report made by them and included in the prospectus. Similarly, as discussed earlier in this section, the defence available under section 62 of the Companies Act, 1956, that the defendant has reasonable grounds to believe, and did up to the time of allotment of securities believe, that the statement was true is now not available.

Nevertheless, some defence is available to the defendant. Defence to civil liability under section 35 of the Companies Act for all categories of defendants is that 'the prospectus was issued without his knowledge or consent'.[124] Clearly, the defendant must prove each of the elements of the defence and it will not be sufficient for him to simply give a notice to

---

[124] Clause (b) of sub-section (2) of section 35 of the Companies Act. The Companies (Amendment) Bill, 2016, introduced in the lower house of the Parliament on 16 March 2016, has proposed insertion of a new clause (c) after clause (b) of sub-section (2) of section 35 of the Companies Act. This new clause seeks to provide an additional defence to the defendants:

> (c) that, as regards every misleading statement purported to be made by an expert or contained in what purports to be a copy of or an extract from a report or valuation of an expert, it was a correct and fair representation of the statement, or a correct copy of, or a correct and fair extract from, the report or valuation; and he had reasonable ground to believe and did up to the time of the issue of the prospectus believe, that the person making the statement was competent to make it and that the said person had given the consent required by sub-section (5) of section 26 to the issue of the prospectus and had not withdrawn that consent before delivery of a copy of the prospectus for registration or, to the defendant's knowledge, before allotment thereunder.

Given the wording and nature of this defence, it cannot be availed of by the expert himself. It is ideally suited for defendants who are directors and defendants who have authorized the issue of the prospectus.

the company or the public severing his association with the prospectus. However, it is difficult to see how this statutory plea can aid a defendant who 'has authorized the issue of the prospectus', because there is a contradiction in saying that the defendant 'has authorized the issue of the prospectus' but the 'prospectus was issued without his knowledge or consent'.

Persons falling under the second part of clause (b) of sub-section (1) of section 35 of the Companies Act, namely 'a person who has agreed to become the director of the company, either immediately or after an interval of time', are entitled to an additional defence: 'having consented to become a director of the company, he withdrew his consent before the issue of the prospectus, and that it was issued without his authority or consent'.

Extent of Liability

The extent of liability is compensation for any loss or damage as a consequence of the wrongful act.[125] As regards measure of damages, it may be difficult to apply the principles of the tort of deceit as sub-sections (1) and (2) of section 35 of the Companies Act have deviated significantly from this tort. Nonetheless, given that the foundation of this liability rests in tort law, one may take the aid of the general principles of the measure of damages under tort law.

Fraudulent Prospectus

Civil liability under sub-section (1) of section 35 of the Companies Act is incurred for misstatements in a prospectus—whether innocent, negligent, or fraudulent. But if the prospectus is fraudulent, sub-section (3) of section 35 of the Companies Act lays down a different standard of liability. In such a case, the claimant needs to prove that:

1. a prospectus has been issued with intent to defraud the applicants for the securities of a company; or a prospectus has been issued with intent to defraud any other person; or a prospectus has been issued for any fraudulent purpose;

---

[125] Sub-section (1) of section 35 of the Companies Act.

2. the claimant subscribed to the securities on the basis of such prospectus;
3. the claimant incurred loss or damage; and
4. the defendant is a person belonging to any of the classes referred to in sub-section (1) of section 35 of the Companies Act.

Given that the prospectus has been issued to commit fraud, the standard of reliance and causation for imposing liability is lower. Unlike sub-section (1) of section 35 of the Companies Act, the claimant need not prove that he/she acted on the fraudulent misstatements and, as a consequence thereof, suffered the loss or damage. They only need to prove that they acted on the prospectus and subscribed on the basis of such prospectus and have incurred loss or damage. Once this is proved, the defendants are 'personally responsible, without any limitation of liability, for all or any of the losses or damages that may have been incurred by [the claimant]'.[126] No defence is permitted to absolve or reduce liability.

What is meant by 'intent to defraud' and 'fraudulent purpose', as per sub-section (3) of section 35 of the Companies Act, is not clear. It is also not clear whether it relates to fraudulent misstatement in the prospectus or an act of fraud through the prospectus. This distinction may not be relevant in most cases but it is not inconceivable for a prospectus to be free from fraudulent misstatements, yet be used to commit fraud. In the absence of an express definition, it may not be unreasonable to rely on the definition of fraud under section 447 of the Companies Act, which has been explained subsequently. Though section 447 of the Companies Act deals with criminal liability, it broadly codifies the concept of fraud under civil as well as criminal law.

Joint and Several Liability, and Indemnity and Contribution

A claimant's right of compensation under sub-section (1) as well as under sub-section (3) of Section 35 of the Companies Act is for a single set of losses or damages and the claim lies against several defendants. In general, these several defendants act in concert and incur a common liability whose supposed basis is that they have all authorized the issue

---

[126] Sub-section (3) of section 35 of the Companies Act.

of the prospectus which contains a misstatement. Therefore, these several defendants will be considered as joint wrongdoers and the liability of joint wrongdoers will be joint and several. The claimant in such a situation can bring an action against all or any one of the defendants and each defendant will be liable for the full amount of loss or damage.[127]

In cases of civil liability for misstatement in a prospectus, the Companies Act, 1956 provided a statutory right of indemnity and contribution among the defendants in specified circumstances.[128] These are absent under section 35 of the Companies Act, 2013. Therefore, right of indemnity and contribution among the defendants will be determined on the basis of the contract among them in this regard. Such contracts must stand the test of enforceability under contract law, in particular section 23 of the Indian Contract Act, 1872 which renders an agreement void whose object 'is of such a nature that, if permitted, it would defeat the provisions of any law', or the court regards it as 'opposed to public policy'.

Prospectus Issued by a Promoter

So far we have examined the different types of civil liability in the context of a dispute between the company or the selling shareholder and the applicant investors. We did so because it is the company that issues, or is authorized by the selling shareholder to issue, the prospectus inviting subscription or purchase of securities from the applicant investors. However, though rare in practice, it is not inconceivable that the promoter, who is engaged in the formation of a company, issues the prospectus of the anticipated capital base of the intended company.[129] If the public offering is successful, the promoter would form the company, which would then issue and allot the securities. This fact situation will not affect our discussion on civil liability in tort and the Companies Act.

---

[127] Vivienne Harpwood and Ken Oliphant, 'Joint and Several Liability in Tort' in Andrew Grubb (ed.), *The Law of Tort* (LexisNexis 2007), at p. 166. See also rule 3 of Order I of the Code of Civil Procedure, 1908.

[128] See sub-sections (4) and (5) of section 62 of the Companies Act, 1956.

[129] See the section 'Proponents of Public Offer and Offer for Sale' in Chapter 3 of this volume.

But it does affect our discussion on liability in contract like rescission, specific performance, and damages for breach of contract. With respect to these contractual liabilities, the company will be responsible if, though the prospectus is issued by the promoter, the board of directors of the company upon its incorporation ratify and adopt the prospectus as the basis of the contract for the shares. Hence, if the company allots the shares knowing that they have been subscribed on a particular prospectus, the company is responsible.[130]

Jurisdiction

Ordinary civil courts have the jurisdiction to try civil suits under the Code of Civil Procedure, 1908 for rescission, specific performance of the contract, damages for tortious misstatement, and damages for breach of contract. Similarly, compensation under section 35 of the Companies Act too, can be recovered by way of a civil suit.[131] Any person, group of persons, or association of persons affected by any misstatements in a prospectus may file this suit.[132]

Criminal Liability

Criminal liability is initiated by the state when a person commits an offence, meaning an act of omission or commission which is punishable by any law for the time being in force.[133] In relation to the public offering of corporate securities, there are five principal types of offences: (a) offence of misstatement or false statement in prospectus; (b) offence of fraudulently inducing persons to invest money; (c) offence of personation for acquisition, etc., of securities; (d) offence of fraud;

---

[130] Sir Francis B. Palmer, *Company Law* (Stevens and Sons 1902), at p. 285.

[131] *Dharmendra Kumar Lila v. Registrar of Companies*, [2011] 161 Comp Cas 301 (Del); *Rajeev Shukla v. Registrar of Companies*, 135 (2006) DLT 599; *Manju Yadav v. Registrar of Companies*, 2007 (98) DRJ 312.

[132] Section 37 of the Companies Act.

[133] Section 3 of the General Clauses Act, 1897; clause (n) of section 2 of the Code of Criminal Procedure, 1973; *S.A. Venkataraman v. Union of India*, AIR 1954 SC 375; *Securities and Exchange Board of India v. Ajay Agarwal*, AIR 2010 SC 3466.

and (e) offence for contravening the securities laws. These are offences under securities laws and not the general penal code of India, namely the Indian Penal Code, 1860 (or IPC). Certain acts or omissions in relation to the public offering of corporate securities may also constitute an offence under IPC[134]—the discussion of these is outside the scope of this book. Suffice to say that where an act or omission constitutes an offence under two or more enactments, the offender is liable to be prosecuted and punished under either or any of those enactments but is not liable to be punished twice for the same offence.[135] Thus, no person shall be prosecuted and punished for the same offence more than once.[136] This rule is limited to criminal liability and will not affect civil liability arising out of the same act or omission.[137]

Offence of Misstatement or False Statement in Prospectus

On lines similar to section 35, section 34 of the Companies Act imposes 'Criminal Liability for Misstatements in Prospectus' in the following terms:

> Where a prospectus, issued, circulated or distributed under this Chapter, includes any statement which is untrue or misleading in form or context in which it is included or where any inclusion or omission of any matter is likely to mislead, every person who authorises the issue of such prospectus shall be liable under section 447:
>
> Provided that nothing in this section shall apply to a person if he proves that such statement or omission was immaterial or that he had reasonable grounds to believe, and did up to the time of issue of the

---

[134] See *Iridium India Telecom Limited v. Motorola Incorporated*, AIR 2011 SC 20.

[135] Section 26 of the General Clauses Act, 1897. See also section 300 of the Code of Criminal Procedure, 1973.

[136] Clause (2) of Article 20 of the Constitution of India. But for this protection to operate, the ingredients, which constitute the two offences, must be identical. *State of Bombay v. S.L. Apte*, AIR 1961 SC 578; *State of Bihar v. Murad Ali Khan*, AIR 1989 SC 1.

[137] *N. Devindrappa v. State of Karnataka*, (2007) 5 SCC 228; *Indian Oil Corporation v. NEPC India Limited*, (2006) 6 SCC 736.

prospectus believe, that the statement was true or the inclusion or omission was necessary.

The principal ingredient of the offence under section 34 of the Companies Act is an issued or circulated or distributed prospectus which includes 'any statement which is untrue or misleading in form or context in which it is included or where any inclusion or omission of any matter is likely to mislead'. Chapter 3 of this volume examined what constitutes issue of a prospectus;[138] this is not needed to be repeated here. Though usage of the words 'circulated or distributed' appears to make this provision wider in effect, this is not really the case. A prospectus, if circulated or distributed, would mean that it is 'issued'.

The issued prospectus must either include an untrue statement, meaning a false statement, or a misleading statement. For the meaning of 'misleading statement', readers may refer to its analysis under the section 'Civil Liability' of this chapter. If any of these elements are present, it will constitute an offence for the purposes of section 34 of the Companies Act. It is irrelevant whether the accused is the maker of the statement or whether persons subscribed for securities acting on the untrue or misleading statement. Contrary to the ordinary principles of criminal law, the prosecution also need not prove any guilty mind. Once the prosecution establishes the existence of an untrue or misleading statement in the prospectus, onus then shifts on the accused to prove the defence provided in the proviso to escape liability.

Persons guilty of the offence are 'every person who authorises [sic][139] the issue of such prospectus'. For the scope and meaning of this expression, we must refer to the analysis under the section 'Civil Liability'. As analysed thereunder, this expression is indeterminate and is bound to create uncertainty for imposing criminal liability on persons other than directors, the company, and the expert. Courts may be inclined to interpret its scope narrowly due to the ensuing criminal liability. The accused may plead any of the defences provided in the proviso to section 34. The defences are that such statement or omission was immaterial; or

---

[138] See the section 'Principal Legal Requirements for a Prospectus'.

[139] Section 34 of the Companies Act uses the word 'authorises', which is a drafting error; instead, it should be 'authorised' because authorisation for issuing the prospectus precedes the issue of the prospectus.

that the defendant had reasonable grounds to believe, and did up to the time of issue of the prospectus believe that the statement was true or the inclusion or omission was necessary. The latter defence is based on an objective standard of 'reasonable grounds' and not on the subjective state of the mind of the accused. The punishment for the offence is the liability under section 447 of the Act.

Criminal liability for misstatement in the prospectus may also be applicable under section 448 of the Companies Act that prescribes 'Punishment for False Statement'.

> Save as otherwise provided in this Act, if in any return, report, certificate, financial statement, prospectus, statement or other document required by, or for, the purposes of any of the provisions of this Act or the rules made thereunder, any person makes a statement,—
>
> (a) which is false in any material particulars, knowing it to be false; or
> (b) which omits any material fact, knowing it to be material, he shall be liable under section 447.

Though the subject matter of this offence is similar to the offence under section 34, it differs from it in one material manner. For an offence under section 448, the prosecution must prove both the misconduct (making a statement in a prospectus which is false in any material particulars, or making a statement in a prospectus which omits any material fact) and the guilty mind (knowledge of the misconduct) of the accused.

Offence of Fraudulently Inducing Persons to Invest Money

Section 36 of the Companies Act makes it an offence to fraudulently induce persons to invest money, and is expected to complement section 34 of the Companies Act. Together these two provisions act as the principal deterrent to persons against making untrue or misleading statements in relation to the public offering of corporate securities. Section 36 of the Companies Act on 'Punishment for Fraudulently Inducing Persons to Invest Money' provides as follows:

> Any person who, either knowingly or recklessly makes any statement, promise or forecast which is false, deceptive or misleading, or deliberately

conceals any material facts, to induce another person to enter into, or to offer to enter into,—

(a) any agreement for, or with a view to, acquiring, disposing of, subscribing for, or underwriting securities; or
(b) any agreement, the purpose or the pretended purpose of which is to secure a profit to any of the parties from the yield of securities or by reference to fluctuations in the value of securities; or
(c) any agreement for, or with a view to obtaining credit facilities from any bank or financial institution,

shall be liable for action under section 447.

This is an investment-related offence that involves one of the following to induce another person to enter into, or to offer to enter into the agreement specified in clause (a) above:

1. making a statement, promise, or forecast which is false, deceptive, or misleading, and knowing it to be so; or
2. recklessly making any statement, promise, or forecast which is false, deceptive, or misleading; or
3. deliberately concealing material facts. It implies an element of dishonesty and innocent or inadvertent withholding of material facts would not be sufficient.

These ingredients are essentially that of fraud, and the scope of the section is neither confined to misstatements in a prospectus nor to communications in writing. The punishment for the offence is the liability under section 447 of the Act.

Offence of Personation for Acquisition, etc., of Securities

Unlike other offences where the accused is generally a person issuing the prospectus and inviting investment from applicants, sub-section (1) of section 38 of the Companies Act imposes criminal liability on undesirable applicants. It prescribes 'Punishment for Personation for Acquisition etc. of Securities' in the following terms:

(1) Any person who—

(a) makes or abets making of an application in a fictitious name to a company for acquiring, or subscribing for, its securities; or
(b) makes or abets making of multiple applications to a company in different names or in different combinations of his name or surname for acquiring or subscribing for its securities; or
(c) otherwise induces directly or indirectly a company to allot, or register any transfer of, securities to him, or to any other person in a fictitious name,

shall be liable for action under section 447.

(2) The provisions of sub-section (1) shall be prominently reproduced in every prospectus issued by a company and in every form of application for securities.
(3) Where a person has been convicted under this section, the Court may also order disgorgement of gain, if any, made by, and seizure and disposal of the securities in possession of, such person.
(4) The amount received through disgorgement or disposal of securities under sub-section (3) shall be credited to the Investor Education and Protection Fund.

The utility of this provision can be understood by an example. In 2005, SEBI unearthed irregularities in 21 initial public offerings (IPOs) undertaken during the period 2003–5. Investigations revealed that many persons had cornered shares reserved for retail individual investors by making fictitious applications in the retail category through thousands of fictitious depository accounts and bank accounts. Each application was for a small value so as to be eligible for allotment under the retail category. All these allotments were later pooled together and sold on the first day of listing of the shares, thereby realizing significant gains resulting from the difference between the issue price and the market price. This wrongful act deprived genuine investors whose applications were either unsuccessful or procured them very few shares due to the excess demand in the retail category. The offenders were, therefore, charged and prosecuted for the offence of personation for acquisition of securities.[140]

[140] Securities and Exchange Board of India, *Report of the Committee on Reallocation of Shares in the Matter of IPO Irregularities* (2008).

Offence of Fraud

Section 447 of the Companies Act makes fraud in relation to the affairs of a company or any body corporate an offence in the following terms:[141]

Without prejudice to any liability including repayment of any debt under this Act or any other law for the time being in force, any person who is found to be guilty of fraud, shall be punishable with imprisonment for a term which shall not be less than six months but which may extend to ten years and shall also be liable to fine which shall not be less than the amount involved in the fraud, but which may extend to three times the amount involved in the fraud:

Provided that where the fraud in question involves public interest, the term of imprisonment shall not be less than three years.

Explanation.—For the purposes of this section—

(i) 'fraud' in relation to affairs of a company or any body corporate, includes any act, omission, concealment of any fact or abuse of position committed by any person or any other person with the connivance in any manner, with intent to deceive, to gain undue advantage from, or to injure the interests of, the company or its shareholders or its creditors or any other person, whether or not there is any wrongful gain or wrongful loss;

(ii) 'wrongful gain' means the gain by unlawful means of property to which the person gaining is not legally entitled;

(iii) 'wrongful loss' means the loss by unlawful means of property to which the person losing is legally entitled.

Fraud under section 447 of the Companies Act is not an offence in itself but is considered as an offence when done in relation to the affairs of a company or any body corporate.[142] Public offering of corporate securities

---

[141] Companies (Amendment) Bill, 2016, introduced in the lower house of the Parliament on 16 March 2016, has proposed a lesser punishment for persons found to be guilty of fraud where the fraud involves an amount less than ten lakh rupees or one per cent of the turnover of the company, whichever is lower.

[142] This approach is similar to offences under the Indian Penal Code, 1860 wherein to do something fraudulently is not by itself made an offence but various acts when done fraudulently are made offences. These include

undoubtedly relates to the affairs of a company. Therefore, if the constituent elements of fraud, as defines above, can be established in the public offering, the offence of fraud will get attracted. It must be noted that the concept of fraud under section 447 is similar to how fraud is understood under criminal law except for the fact that it is irrelevant whether injury is caused to the person deceived or the deceiver gains benefit.[143]

Offences for Contravening Securities Laws

In the preceding chapters, we observed that a company and other persons involved in a public offering programme must comply with several statutes, and rules and regulations framed thereunder. Each of those statutes, namely the Companies Act, 2013; Securities and Exchange Board of India Act, 1992 (SEBI Act), Securities Contracts (Regulation) Act, 1956 (SCRA); and the Depositories Act, 1996 (or the Depositories Act) have made the contravention of the statutory provisions, and the rules and regulations framed thereunder an offence. In this regard, the Companies Act follows a twofold approach. Two of the principal statutory provisions on public offer contain a specific punishment clause for their contravention. In addition, there is a default provision prescribing punishment for contraventions for which no penalty or punishment is provided elsewhere in the Companies Act. These offences can be summarized as follows:

1. If a prospectus is issued in contravention of section 26 of the Companies Act (which prescribes the matters to be stated in a prospectus and its registration with the registrar of companies), the company is punishable with fine. The fine would not be less than Rs 50,000 but may extend to Rs 300,000. Further, every person who is knowingly a party to the issue of such prospectus

---

fraudulent removal or concealment of property, fraudulent possession or delivery of counterfeit coin, forgery making or executing a false document, cheating and fraudulently going through marriage ceremony. See, *Md. Ibrahim v. State of Bihar*, (2009) 8 SCC 751.

[143] See *Dr. Vimla*, AIR 1963 SC 1572; *Dr. S. Dutt v. State of Uttar Pradesh*, AIR 1966 SC 523.

is punishable with imprisonment for a term which may extend to three years or with fine which shall not be less than Rs 50,000 but which may extend to Rs 300,000, or with both.[144]

2. If a default is made in complying with the provisions of section 40 of the Companies Act (which mandates securities to be dealt with in stock exchanges), the company is punishable with a fine which shall not be less than Rs 500,000 but which may extend to Rs 5,000,000. Further, every officer of the company who is in default[145] is punishable with imprisonment for a term which may extend to one year or with fine which shall not be less than Rs 50,000 but which may extend to Rs 300,000, or with both.[146]

3. Section 450 of the Companies Act is a default provision prescribing punishment for contraventions for which no penalty or punishment is provided elsewhere in the Companies Act. Thus,

> if a company or any officer of a company or any other person contravenes any of the provisions of this Act or the rules made thereunder, for which no penalty or punishment is provided elsewhere in the Companies Act, the company and every officer of the company who is in default or such other person shall be punishable with fine which may extend to ten thousand rupees.[147]

If the contravention is a continuing one, the offence is punishable with a further fine which may extend to Rs 1,000 for every day after the first during which the contravention continues.

4. If any person contravenes or attempts to contravene or abets the contravention of the provisions of the SEBI Act or of any rules or regulations made thereunder, he is punishable with imprisonment for a term which may extend to 10 years, or with fine, which may extend to Rs 25 crore or with both.[148]

---

[144] Sub-section (9) of section 26 of the Companies Act.

[145] Officer of the company who is in default means the officers referred to by clause (60) of section 2 of the Companies Act. See also *Raymond Synthetics Limited v. Union of India*, AIR 1992 SC 847.

[146] Sub-section (5) of section 40 of the Companies Act.

[147] Section 450 of the Companies Act.

[148] Section 24 of the SEBI Act.

5. If any person contravenes or attempts to contravene or abets the contravention of the provisions of the SCRA or of any rules or regulations or by-laws made thereunder, for which no punishment is provided elsewhere in the Act, he is punishable with imprisonment for a term which may extend to 10 years, or with fine, which may extend to Rs 25 crore or with both.[149]

6. If any person contravenes or attempts to contravene or abets the contravention of the provisions of the Depositories Act or of any rules or regulations or by-laws made thereunder, he is punishable with imprisonment for a term which may extend to 10 years, or with fine, which may extend to Rs 25 crore or with both.[150]

With regard to the general offence of contravening provisions of a statute, or rules and regulations made thereunder, courts often examine whether the provision is directory or mandatory; the offence is made applicable only with respect to the latter category of provisions.[151] To assess such nature, there are several tests such as the purpose for which the statutory provision has been made, the relation of the particular provision to other provisions dealing with the same subject, and the language of the provision. Given the investor protection nature of securities laws, and their negative and prohibitory language to do or refrain from doing certain things, the provisions on the public offering of corporate securities will, in all likelihood, be held to be mandatory and their contravention an offence.

Jurisdiction and Procedure

Code of Criminal Procedure, 1973, the general law on jurisdiction and criminal procedure, is largely applicable for the trial of these offences. Its application is however, subject to some special rules.[152] Thus no court is empowered to take cognizance of any offence committed under

---

[149] Section 23M of the SCRA.

[150] Section 20 of the Depositories Act.

[151] *Mannalal Khetan v. Kedar Nath Khetan*, AIR 1977 SC 536; *Fenner (India) Limited v. Additional Registrar of Companies*, [1994] 80 Comp Cas 1 (Mad); *A.V. Kasargod v. Registrar of Companies*, 2002 (2) Kar LJ 270.

[152] See Chapter XXVIII of the Companies Act.

the Companies Act which is alleged to have been committed by any company or any officer thereof, except on the complaint in writing of certain specified persons like the registrar of companies, a shareholder of the company, or a person authorized by the central government in that behalf.[153] If the offence relates to the issue and transfer of securities, and non-payment of dividend, a person authorized by SEBI too, is empowered to make the complaint.[154] For the offence covered under section 447, the person is the Director, Serious Fraud Investigation Office or any officer of the central government authorized, by a general or special order in writing in this behalf, by the concerned government.[155] Similar rules regarding taking of cognizance also exist with respect to offences under the SEBI Act, the SCRA, and the Depositories Act.[156]

Pecuniary Penalty

Liability arising out of a civil action and criminal prosecution is well understood in our legal system, both in concept and practice. The former seeks to compensate for a wrong and the latter is designed to punish a crime. In between the two is the liability of pecuniary penalty. As a form of liability, it has been in existence for quite some time.[157] But its conceptual basis is far from clear and is still the subject matter of disagreement.[158] Its description too is unsatisfactory—it has been described as liability arising out of breach of 'civil obligation' or 'statutory obligation' or 'statutory civil obligation', though the meaning of each of these expressions is different.[159] Nevertheless, for our present

---

[153] Section 439 of the Companies Act. The Companies (Amendment) Bill, 2016, introduced in the lower house of the Parliament on 16 March 2016, has proposed to include 'a member' also as one of the complainants.

[154] Section 439 of the Companies Act. This rule is subject to certain exceptions like prosecution by a company of any of its officers.

[155] Sub-section (6) of section 212 of the Companies Act.

[156] See section 26 of the SEBI Act; section 26 of the SCRA; and section 22 of the Depositories Act.

[157] See *Maqbool Hussain v. State of Bombay*, AIR 1953 SC 325; *Thomas Dana v. State of Punjab*, AIR 1959 SC 375.

[158] See *Radheshyam Kejriwal v. State of West Bengal*, (2011) 3 SCC 581.

[159] *Commissioner of Sales Tax v. Sanjiv Fabrics*, (2010) 9 SCC 630; *The Chairman, Securities and Exchange Board of India v. Shriram Mutual Fund*, AIR

purposes, pecuniary penalty may be understood to mean monetary penalties imposed through non-criminal processes by statutory authorities, instead of courts or tribunals, for statutory violation, and collected by the government. Until a few decades ago, the unstated legislative policy appeared to be that pecuniary penalties would be imposed for violation of statutes that involved taxation or management of foreign exchange so as to prevent economic loss.[160] Now there is no clear legislative policy behind the imposition of pecuniary penalties and they are a feature of company law and securities laws as well.[161] To discuss this form of liability, this chapter uses the expression 'pecuniary penalty', though the statutes themselves refer to it as 'penalty'. The reason for the deviation is to avoid confusion, since till today the Constitution of India and many statutes refer to penalty as a form of punishment for an offence and imposed through criminal law processes.[162] At times, the usage is contradictory and the term 'penalty' is used within the same statute to mean punishment for an offence as well as pecuniary penalty.[163]

Imposition of Pecuniary Penalty

The Companies Act imposes pecuniary penalty under several provisions for default in complying with the requirements of those provisions. Some of these pertain to the public offering of corporate securities. Thus, if a company makes any default in complying with the provisions of section

---

2006 SC 2278; *Director of Enforcement v. MCTM Corporation Private Limited*, AIR 1996 SC 1100; *Hindustan Steel Limited v. State of Orissa*, AIR 1970 SC 253; *Securities and Exchange Board of India v. Cabot International Capital Corporation*, (2004) 2 Comp LJ 363 (Bom); *Commissioner of Income Tax v. Patram Dass Raja Ram Beri*, AIR 1982 P&H 1.

[160] See *Radheshyam Kejriwal. v. State of West Bengal*, (2011) 3 SCC 581.

[161] The Companies Act, 1956 did have provisions for the imposition of penalty. But in it penalty was imposed as a criminal liability and was used interchangeably with 'fines'.

[162] See Art. 20 of the Constitution of India; section 27 of the Consumer Protection Act, 1986; section 15 of the Environment Protection Act, 1986; Chapter VI of the Air (Prevention and Control of Pollution) Act, 1981; sections 67 and 68 of the Copyright Act, 1957; Chapter VII of the Chartered Accountants Act, 1949; and section 6 of General Clauses Act.

[163] See sections 23–23H of the SCRA.

33 of the Companies Act on 'Issue of Application Forms for Securities', it is liable to a penalty of Rs 50,000 for each default. In case of any default under sub-section (3) or sub-section (4) of section 39 of the Companies Act on minimum subscription and return of allotment, respectively, the company and its officer who is in default are liable to a penalty, for each default, of Rs 1,000 for each day during which such default continues or Rs 100,000, whichever is less. Lastly, if a company makes an offer or accepts monies in contravention of section 42 of the Companies Act on 'Private Placement', the company, its promoters, and directors are liable for a penalty which may extend to the amount involved in the offer or invitation or Rs 2 crore, whichever is higher. The company must also refund all monies to subscribers within a period of 30 days of the order imposing the penalty.

The SEBI Act, the SCRA, and the Depositories Act rely more heavily on pecuniary penalty to secure compliance with the Act.[164] While most of the provisions that impose pecuniary penalty are for specific misconducts not directly related to the public offering of corporate securities, some of the pecuniary penalty provisions do have a bearing on it. Section 15HA of the SEBI Act on 'Penalty for Fraudulent and Unfair Trade Practices' states:

> If any person indulges in fraudulent and unfair trade practices relating to securities, he shall be liable to a penalty which shall not be less than five lakh rupees but which may extend to twenty-five crore rupees or three times the amount of profits made out of such practices, whichever is higher.

The meaning of 'fraudulent and unfair trade practices relating to securities' would be examined later. Suffice to say that it includes activities in relation to the public offering of corporate securities.

Other than the above, the SEBI Act, the SCRA, and the Depositories Act, each has a default provision for imposition of 'Penalty for Contravention where no Separate Penalty has been Provided'. Thus, section 15HB of the SEBI Act states:

> Whoever fails to comply with any provision of this Act, the rules or the regulations made or directions issued by the Board thereunder for which no

---

[164] See Chapter VIA of the SEBI Act; sections 23A–23H of the SCRA; and sections 19A–19G of the Depositories Act.

separate penalty has been provided, shall be liable to a penalty which shall not be less than one lakh rupees but which may extend to one crore rupees.

Section 23H of the SCRA states:

Whoever fails to comply with any provision of this Act, the rules or articles or bye-laws or the regulations of the recognised stock exchange or directions issued by the Securities and Exchange Board of India for which no separate penalty has been provided, shall be liable to a penalty which shall not be less than one lakh rupees but which may extend to one crore rupees.

Section 19G of the Depositories Act states:

Whoever fails to comply with any provision of this Act, the rules or the regulations or bye-laws made or directions issued by the Board thereunder for which no separate penalty has been provided, shall be liable to a penalty which shall not be less than one lakh rupees but which may extend to one crore rupees.

In the preceding chapters, we examined statutory provisions of these Acts and the rules and regulations framed thereunder that companies and other participants must comply with while undertaking a public offering of corporate securities. Upon failure to comply with those provisions, these default penalty provisions will lead to liability of pecuniary penalty.

Procedure for Imposing Pecuniary Penalty

In general, pecuniary penalty as a form of liability lies somewhere between civil remedy and punishment for a criminal offence. The pecuniary penalty provisions under the securities laws make it clear that it is closer to criminal liability. These are intended to have a deterrent effect and their impact is punitive for they involve a very substantial monetary amount.[165] But it does not have the procedural safeguards of a criminal

[165] *The Chairman, Securities and Exchange Board of India v. Shriram Mutual Fund*, AIR 2006 SC 2278; *Securities and Exchange Board of India v. Cabot International Capital Corporation*, (2004) 2 Comp LJ 363 (Bom); *Securities and Exchange Board of India v. Sangeeta Jayesh Valia*, (2004) 2 CompLJ 347 (Bom).

trial. Neither do the rules of civil procedure and evidence law apply, though liability is established on a civil standard of proof and penalty is attracted as soon as the contravention of the statutory obligation is established.[166] Nonetheless, a limited safeguard exists in the form of an adjudication procedure for imposing the pecuniary penalty. For the imposition of pecuniary penalties under the Companies Act, the central government has the power to appoint its own officers, not below the rank of registrar of companies, as adjudicating officers for adjudging penalty in the prescribed manner including giving a right of hearing, and method for quantification of pecuniary penalty.[167] A similar mechanism exists under the SEBI Act, the SCRA, and the Depositories Act.[168]

The payment of pecuniary penalty is enforced by making its non-payment an offence.[169] Additionally, other than for a pecuniary penalty under the Companies Act, the statutory authority may also enforce payment by directly recovering the monetary amount from the offender by any one or more of the following modes, namely:

1. attachment and sale of the person's movable property;
2. attachment of the person's bank accounts;
3. attachment and sale of the person's immovable property;
4. arrest of the person and his detention in prison;
5. appointing a receiver for the management of the person's movable and immovable properties.[170]

---

[166] *The Chairman, Securities and Exchange Board of India* v. *Shriram Mutual Fund*, AIR 2006 SC 2278.

[167] See section 454 of the Companies Act and the Companies (Adjudication of Penalties) Rules, 2014.

[168] Sections 15-I and 15J of the SEBI Act and the Securities and Exchange Board of India (Procedure for Holding Inquiry and Imposing Penalties by Adjudicating Officer) Rules, 1995; sections 23-I and 23J of the SCRA; and sections 19H and 19-I of the Depositories Act and the Depositories (Procedure for Holding Inquiry and Imposing Penalties by Adjudicating Officer) Rules, 1995.

[169] Sub-section (8) of section 454 of the Companies Act; sub-section (2) of section 24 of the SEBI Act; sub-section (2) of section 23M of the SCRA; and sub-section (2) of section 20 of the Depositories Act.

[170] Section 28A of the SEBI Act; section 23JB of the SCRA; and section 19-IB of the Depositories Act.

Settlement of Pecuniary Penalty Proceedings

Securities laws permit settlement of pecuniary penalty proceedings initiated or to be initiated for the alleged defaults under the SEBI Act, the SCRA, and the Depositories Act.[171] The objective is to impose appropriate sanctions and deterrence without SEBI being required to resort to adversarial proceedings, which can be dilatory. It also saves time and effort which can then be used for pursuing more serious violations.[172] Thus, a person against whom any of the above pecuniary penalty proceedings have been initiated, or may be initiated, may make an application to SEBI. SEBI may, after taking into consideration the nature, gravity, and impact of defaults, agree to the proposal for settlement, on payment of a sum by the defaulter or such other terms as may be determined by SEBI. Settlement takes place in accordance with the Securities and Exchange Board of India (Settlement of Administrative and Civil Proceedings) Regulations, 2014.

Regulatory Actions

Chapter 4 examined the legal design in which SEBI functions. A facet of this legal design is to respond to non-compliance of securities laws through regulatory actions. Regulatory actions are the range of measures and directions that SEBI can employ to ensure compliance with a wide set of activities in relation to investors and the securities market.[173] The precise content of the measures and directions has largely been left to the discretion of SEBI, though, in some cases the SEBI Act, does specify what the measures and directions could be. All that the SEBI Act expects is that the regulatory actions must be in the interest of investors in securities or the securities market. In addition to the SEBI Act, the legal basis for the regulatory actions also exists under the SCRA and the Depositories Act.[174]

[171] See section 15JB of the SEBI Act, 23JA of the SCRA, and 19-IA of the Depositories Act, 1996.

[172] *Shilpa Stock Broker Pvt. Ltd. v. Securities and Exchange Board of India*, (2012) 170 Comp Cas 1.

[173] See sections 11, 11A, 11B, 11D and sub-section (3) of section 12 of the SEBI Act for the legal basis of the regulatory actions.

[174] See section 12A of the SCRA and section 19 of the Depositories Act, 1996.

In the context of the public offering of corporate securities, the regulatory actions that SEBI can take are to restrain persons from accessing the securities market and prohibit any person associated with the securities market to buy, sell, or deal in securities.[175] SEBI may also, by general or special orders, prohibit any company from issuing a prospectus, any offer document, or advertisement soliciting money from the public for the issue of securities.[176]Another regulatory action that SEBI may take is 'cease and desist proceedings'. Thus, if SEBI finds, after causing an inquiry to be made, that any person has violated, or is likely to violate, any provisions of the SEBI Act, or any rules or regulations made thereunder, it may pass an order requiring such person to cease and desist from committing or causing such violation.[177] Other than these specific actions, SEBI may exercise its general power under section 11B of the SEBI Act and take any other regulatory action. This provision on 'Power to Issue Directions' is as follows:

Save as otherwise provided in section 11, if after making or causing to be made an enquiry, the Board is satisfied that it is necessary,—

(i)   in the interest of investors, or orderly development of securities market; or

(ii) to prevent the affairs of any intermediary or other persons referred to in section 12 being conducted in a manner detrimental to the interest of investors or securities market; or

(iii) to secure the proper management of any such intermediary or person,

it may issue such directions,—

---

[175] Clause (b) of sub-section (4) of section 11 of the SEBI Act.

[176] Sub-clause (i) of clause (b) of sub-section (1) of section 11A of the SEBI Act.

[177] This power of SEBI is subject to the limitation that SEBI 'shall not pass such order in respect of any listed public company or a public company (other than the intermediaries specified under section 12) which intends to get its securities listed on any recognised stock exchange unless the Board has reasonable grounds to believe that such company has indulged in insider trading or market manipulation.' Section 11D of the SEBI Act.

(a) to any person or class of persons referred to in section 12, or associated with the securities market; or

(b) to any company in respect of matters specified in section 11A, as
may be appropriate in the interests of investors in securities and the
securities market.

Explanation.—For the removal of doubts, it is hereby declared that the
power to issue directions under this section shall include and always be
deemed to have been included the power to direct any person, who made
profit or averted loss by indulging in any transaction or activity in contravention of the provisions of this Act or regulations made thereunder, to
disgorge an amount equivalent to the wrongful gain made or loss averted
by such contravention.

Prohibition of Fraudulent and Unfair Trade Practices

As noted earlier, the only objective that the SEBI Act has set for issuing regulatory actions is to protect the interest of investors in securities
or the securities market. There is, however, a more specific objective
for which SEBI acts and which has a bearing on the public offering of
corporate securities. This specific objective is to check and act against
fraudulent and unfair trade practices relating to the securities market
under the Securities and Exchange Board of India (Prohibition of
Fraudulent and Unfair Trade Practices Relating to Securities Market)
Regulations, 2003 (or the PFUTP Regulations). This regulation first
sets the substantive norms on what constitutes fraudulent and unfair
trade practices relating to the securities market, and then empowers
SEBI to take enforcement actions. The substantive norms, under regulation 3 of the PFUTP Regulations, in relation to the primary market are
the following:

No person shall directly or indirectly—

(a) buy, sell or otherwise deal in securities in a fraudulent manner;
(b) use or employ, in connection with issue, purchase or sale of any security listed or proposed to be listed in a recognized stock exchange, any
manipulative or deceptive device or contrivance in contravention of the
provisions of the Act or the rules or the regulations made there under;

(c) employ any device, scheme or artifice to defraud in connection with dealing in or issue of securities which are listed or proposed to be listed on a recognized stock exchange;

(d) engage in any act, practice, course of business which operates or would operate as fraud or deceit upon any person in connection with any dealing in or issue of securities which are listed or proposed to be listed on a recognized stock exchange in contravention of the provisions of the Act or the rules and the regulations made there under.

The PFUTP Regulations define 'dealing in securities' and 'fraud' as follows:

'dealing in securities' includes an act of buying, selling or subscribing pursuant to any issue of any security or agreeing to buy, sell or subscribe to any issue of any security or otherwise transacting in any way in any security by any person as principal, agent or intermediary referred to in section 12 of the Act.[178]

'fraud' includes any act, expression, omission or concealment committed whether in a deceitful manner or not by a person or by any other person with his connivance or by his agent while dealing in securities in order to induce another person or his agent to deal in securities, whether or not there is any wrongful gain or avoidance of any loss, and shall also include—

(1) a knowing misrepresentation of the truth or concealment of material fact in order that another person may act to his detriment;

(2) a suggestion as to a fact which is not true by one who does not believe it to be true;

(3) an active concealment of a fact by a person having knowledge or belief of the fact;

(4) a promise made without any intention of performing it;

(5) a representation made in a reckless and careless manner whether it be true or false;

(6) any such act or omission as any other law specifically declares to be fraudulent,

---

[178] Clause (b) of sub-regulation (1) of regulation 2 of the PFUTP Regulations.

(7)   deceptive behaviour by a person depriving another of informed consent or full participation,

(8)   a false statement made without reasonable ground for believing it to be true.

(9)   the act of an issuer of securities giving out misinformation that affects the market price of the security, resulting in investors being effectively misled even though they did not rely on the statement itself or anything derived from it other than the market price.

And 'fraudulent' shall be construed accordingly;

Nothing contained in this clause shall apply to any general comments made in good faith in regard to—

(a) the economic policy of the government;
(b) the economic situation of the country;
(c) trends in the securities market;
(d) any other matter of a like nature;

whether such comments are made in public or in private.[179]

Evidently, the meaning of 'fraud' and 'fraudulent' under the PFUTP Regulations is wider that the common law meaning of fraud. This reflects the zealous outlook of SEBI to prevent securities market manipulation at the cost of imposing moral blameworthiness on several actions that may otherwise be negligent.

Other than regulation 3, the other substantive norm that the PFUTP Regulations set is 'Prohibition of Manipulative, Fraudulent and Unfair Trade Practices' (regulation 4). To the extent relevant to the public offering of corporate securities, this regulation is as follows:

(1)   Without prejudice to the provisions of regulation 3, no person shall indulge in a fraudulent or an unfair trade practice in securities.

(2)   Dealing in securities shall be deemed to be a fraudulent or an unfair trade practice if it involves fraud and may include all or any of the following, namely:—

---

[179] Clause (c) of sub-regulation (1) of regulation 2 of the PFUTP Regulations.

...

(c) advancing or agreeing to advance any money to any person thereby inducing any other person to offer to buy any security in any issue only with the intention of securing the minimum subscription to such issue;

(d) paying, offering or agreeing to pay or offer, directly or indirectly, to any person any money or money's worth for inducing such person for dealing in any security with the object of inflating, depressing, maintaining or causing fluctuation in the price of such security;

...

(f) publishing or causing to publish or reporting or causing to report by a person dealing in securities any information which is not true or which he does not believe to be true prior to or in the course of dealing in securities;

...

(k) an advertisement that is misleading or that contains information in a distorted manner and which may influence the decision of the investors;

...

(r) planting false or misleading news which may induce sale or purchase of securities.

...

Explanation.– For the purposes of this sub-regulation, for the removal of doubts, it is clarified that the acts or omissions listed in this sub-regulation are not exhaustive and that an act or omission is prohibited if it falls within the purview of regulation 3, notwithstanding that it is not included in this sub-regulation or is described as being committed only by a certain category of persons in this sub-regulation.

The procedure for taking regulatory actions under the PFUTP Regulations is that SEBI sets up an investigating authority to investigate possible violation of these substantive norms.[180] Based on the report of the investigating authority, SEBI may take regulatory actions like restrain persons from accessing the securities market and prohibit any person associated with the securities market to buy, sell, or deal in securities; and impound and retain the proceeds or securities in respect of any

---

[180] Regulation 5 of the PFUTP Regulations.

transaction which is in violation or *prima facie* in violation of the regula-tions.[181] If an intermediary is the wrongdoer, SEBI may issue a warning or censure, or suspend or cancel the registration of the intermediary.[182]

Prohibition on Insider Trading

Recall our discussion in Chapters 1, 3, and 5 on the nature, value and pricing of corporate securities.[183] Corporate securities are intangible property—shares are constituted by a bundle of rights *in* and *against* the company, and debentures are constituted by rights *against* the company. The value and pricing of corporate securities (and their trade) is therefore dependent on the information relating to the company, such as financial results, proposal to pay dividend, securing large orders from customers, any major expansion plans or execution of new projects, expected default in payment of interest or dividend in fixed income securities, imminent class action suit etc.

This creates a peculiar problem in companies since they are based on the principle of separation of ownership from management. In com-panies, the corporate 'insiders', such as directors (acting for themselves or for the benefit of the controlling shareholders) and key management personnel generally get to know first the information that affects the price and trading of the securities in relation to the company. The corpo-rate 'outsiders', such as minority shareholders, prospective investors, and creditors, must wait for the information to be made public to ascertain the true value of the securities. Resultantly, there is a real possibility that the insiders may act opportunistically and use the information for a gain before the information becomes public. For example, the chief financial officer of a listed company is generally part of meetings to discuss finan-cial results and declaration of interim dividend. On attending a meeting where the board of directors adopts the improved financial results and decides to declare interim dividend, the chief financial officer may, being the insider, before the said decision is made public through press release,

---

[181]   Regulation 11 of the PFUTP Regulations.
[182]   Regulation 12 of the PFUTP Regulations.
[183]   See the sections 'Concept of securities' in Chapter 1, 'Functions of pro-spectus' in Chapter 3, and 'Initial considerations' in Chapter 5.

purchase, either directly or through his relatives, large number of equity shares of the company from the secondary market. After the information becomes public, the price of the equity shares would increase on account of better financial results and interim dividend. The insider would then sell the equity shares and make a profit.[184] This trade in the securities of the company by the insider is commonly referred to as 'insider trading'. All major jurisdictions consider insider trading to be wrongful, and to the detriment of the interest of the investors and development of the securities market, and therefore prohibit it. Companies are obligated to make public all unpublished price-sensitive information, that is, unpublished information relating to the company that is likely to materially affect the price of its securities.

In India, prohibition of insider trading emerged with the enactment of the SEBI Act, which empowered SEBI to take measures for 'prohibiting insider trading in securities', though the act did not define 'insider trading'.[185] Consequently, SEBI framed the Securities and Exchange Board of India (Prohibition of Insider Trading) Regulations, 1992 (or the PIT Regulations, 1992).[186] Prohibition of insider trading under these regulations was in relation to dealings in 'securities of a company listed on any stock exchange'.[187] Therefore, the regulation was not applicable to dealings in securities of an unlisted company and did not affect companies undertaking an IPO (since such companies became listed companies only after the completion of the IPO). The Companies Act, 1956 too did not concern itself with prohibiting insider trading. This approach was justifiable on the grounds that in India unlisted companies—whether private companies or public companies—are family owned and have a small shareholders base. Therefore, the agency problem on account of the separation of management from ownership discussed in the preceding paragraphs is either weak or non-existent. Further, unlisted companies do not have a ready market for trading in

[184] See *Rajeev B. Gandhi and Ors v. SEBI*, SAT order dated 9 May 2008.

[185] Clause (g) of sub-section (2) of section 11 of the SEBI Act.

[186] Later by way of an amendment to the SEBI Act with effect from 29 October 2002, the act too prohibited any person from engaging in insider trading. See clause (d) of section 12A of the SEBI Act.

[187] Regulation 3 of the PIT Regulations, 1992.

their securities unlike the listed companies. The likelihood of trading by using unpublished information is very little.

However, the position changed with the enactment of the Companies Act, 2013. Section 195 of the Companies Act prohibits insider trading of securities of all companies, whether private or unlisted or listed companies. It is not known as to what caused the change in policy. During this period, SEBI reviewed the extant regulation on insider trading and framed the new Securities and Exchange Board of India (Prohibition of Insider Trading) Regulations, 2015 (or the PIT Regulations). The PIT Regulations expanded the scope of prohibition of insider trading to also cover securities proposed to be listed on a stock exchange.[188]

The principal prohibition under regulation 4 of the PIT Regulations is that 'No insider shall trade in securities that are listed or proposed to be listed on a stock exchange when in possession of unpublished price sensitive information.'[189] The PIT Regulations do not explain at what stage can it be said that the securities of a company are proposed to be listed on a stock exchange. This lacuna is bound to create confusion. At least for public issue of equity shares, it could mean the date of the meeting of the board of directors of the company in which the public

---

[188] This appears to have been done primarily on account of provisions of the Companies Act. These are: section 195 of the Companies Act which, as noticed earlier, prohibits insider trading of securities of all companies, and section 458 of the Companies Act that delegates to SEBI the power to enforce the provisions of section 195. However, the Companies (Amendment) Bill, 2016, introduced in the lower house of the Parliament on 16 March 2016, has proposed to omit section 195 of the Companies Act. This would remove the conceptual basis for expanding the scope of the PIT Regulations. See Securities and Exchange Board of India, *Report of the High Level Committee to Review the SEBI (Prohibition of Insider Trading) Regulations, 1992* (December 2013). A case of inconsistency in securities laws is apparent here. Though the PIT Regulations have expanded the scope of the regulations to also cover 'securities proposed to be listed', clause (i) of section 15G that imposes pecuniary penalty for insider trading still refers to insider trading in relation to 'securities of a body corporate listed on any stock exchange'.

[189] The PIT Regulations lay down several other obligations to check insider trading. See regulations 3 to 9 of the PIT Regulations.

issue is approved, which is prior to the date when the draft prospectus is submitted to the regulatory authorities for review.[190] Nevertheless, companies undertaking an IPO of securities and proposing to list their securities on the stock exchange would attract the applicability of the PIT Regulations. The PIT Regulations lay down in detail the ingredients of what constitutes insider trading and the defences available. These are self-explanatory and it is needless to describe them in this book. Reference may be made to the provisions of the PIT Regulations itself.

The PIT Regulations do not lay down any specific mechanism for regulatory actions by SEBI to check violations of its provisions. Instead, any contravention of the PIT Regulations is to be dealt with by SEBI in accordance with the SEBI Act.[191] This means that SEBI may direct an investigating authority to investigate the contravention.[192] Based on the report of the investigating authority, SEBI may pass an order requiring the delinquent to cease and desist from committing the violation[193] or take any other regulatory direction under its general power to issue directions under section 11B of the SEBI Act. Pending investigation or on completion of the investigation, SEBI may also take other measures like restrain the delinquent from accessing the securities market and prohibit him from buying, selling, or dealing in securities; or impound or retain the proceeds or securities in respect of any transaction which is under investigation.[194]

Settlement of Regulatory Actions

We examined the settlement of pecuniary penalty proceedings in the previous section of this chapter. On the same lines, regulatory actions initiated or to be initiated for alleged defaults can also be settled in

---

[190] See regulation 60 of the ICDR Regulations and its analysis in the section titled 'Limitations on Publicity, Research Reports and Financial Assistance' in Chapter 5 of this volume.

[191] Regulation 10 of the PIT Regulations.

[192] Section 11C of the SEBI Act.

[193] Section 11D of the SEBI Act.

[194] Sub-section (4) of section 11 of the SEBI Act.

accordance with the Securities and Exchange Board of India (Settlement of Administrative and Civil Proceedings) Regulations, 2014.[195]

***

Despite a wide range of liability provisions, the enforcement of primary market securities laws (including granting refunds to investors who have been defrauded) occurs largely though regulatory actions. Regulatory actions, on the other hand, have their own limitations. SEBI regulates the entire securities market and public offering of corporate securities is one among the many other components of the securities market. It is also difficult for SEBI to detect violations like misstatements in the prospectus. In fact, investors are better placed to do so for it is they who read and rely on the prospectus to make investment. Administrative inertia can also cause weaker enforcement. One would therefore expect that companies and investors, and other persons, make greater use of the liability provisions to redress the wrongs in relation to public offering of corporate securities. This would complement the regulatory actions and cause an orderly development of the Indian securities market.

---

[195] Section 15JB of the SEBI Act, 23JA of the SCRA, and 19-IA of the Depositories Act, 1996, and regulation 3 of the Securities and Exchange Board of India (Settlement of Administrative and Civil Proceedings) Regulations, 2014.

Index

About the Authors

Raghvendra K. Singh is an advocate practicing adversarial and transactional law in Delhi with specialization in taxation, securities, and commercial laws. In the past, he practiced capital markets and securities law for several years at one of the leading law firms in India. Raghvendra completed BA LLB (Hons) from National Law School of India University, Bangalore, India, where he received the gold medal in taxation law.

Shailendera K. Singh is an advocate practicing adversarial and transactional law with a focus on corporate, securities, and commercial laws. He is an associate at S&R Associates, one of the leading law firms of India, and has previously worked with the counsel for the Securities and Exchange Board of India. Shailendera completed BA LLB (Hons) from Chanakya National Law University, Patna, India.